FAITH

AND

FORTUNE

ALSO BY MARC GUNTHER

THE HOUSE THAT ROONE BUILT
The Inside Story of ABC News

BASEPATHS
From the Minor Leagues to the Majors and Beyond

MONDAY NIGHT MAYHEM
The Inside Story of ABC's Monday Night Football
(with Bill Carter)

HOW

COMPASSIONATE CAPITALISM

IS TRANSFORMING

AMERICAN BUSINESS

 THREE RIVERS PRESS • NEW YORK

FAITH
AND
FORTUNE

MARC GUNTHER

Published in the United States by Three Rivers Press, an imprint of the
Crown Publishing Group, a division of Random House, Inc., New York.
www.crownpublishing.com

Three Rivers Press and the Tugboat design are registered trademarks of
Random House, Inc.

Originally published in hardcover in the United States by
Crown Business, an imprint of the Crown Publishing Group,
a division of Random House, Inc., New York, in 2004.

Library of Congress Cataloging-in-Publication Data
Gunther, Marc, 1951–
Faith and fortune : how compassionate capitalism is transforming
American business / Marc Gunther.
1. Social responsibility of business—United States. 2. Business ethics—
United States. 3. Business—Religious aspects. I. Title.
HD60.5.U5G86   2004
174'.4—dc22   2003028106

ISBN-13: 978-1-4000-4894-6
ISBN-10: 1-4000-4894-X

Printed in the United States of America

DESIGN BY BARBARA STURMAN

10 9 8 7 6 5 4 3 2 1

First Paperback Edition

To Sarah and Rebecca

CONTENTS

FAITH

AND

FORTUNE

INTRODUCTION

Never doubt that a small group of thoughtful, committed citizens can change the world. Indeed it is the only thing that ever has. —MARGARET MEAD

Despite most of what you've read about business lately, corporate America is changing for the better. This is a book about the people who are leading the way, and the companies where they work. Why call it *Faith and Fortune*? Because faith provides the fuel that energizes these people as they strive to do business better. Some have faith in God. Others do not. But all of them have faith in the goodness of people, faith in the possibility of change and, perhaps most surprising, faith that corporations can become a powerful force for good in the world. The people you are about to meet believe that we can take care of business and take care of each other, all at the same time.

Their faith is grounded in practical experience. These business leaders work at a wide variety of companies, from a neighborhood bakery to a global transportation giant that operates in nearly every country in the world. Some make things—toothpaste, furniture, boots, computers, lattes—while others work in service businesses that take the idea of service to heart. Some started their own businesses, while others joined big companies with well-known brands that have been around for decades. These people are all successful in conventional terms. They are leading profitable companies that provide good jobs, good value to their customers and good returns for their shareholders. Some have, in fact, made fortunes. But what drives them is less money than the determination to reshape the way business is done in America so that corporations serve people and not the other way around.

To some people, the idea that business can change the world for the better will seem far-fetched. (When I told an acquaintance that I was writing a book about exemplary corporations, he replied, "Must be a short book.") Certainly you don't need to look hard to find evidence that much of corporate America needs fixing. Hypocrisy abounds in business. Top executives, for example, give lip service to the idea that "people are our most important asset," but few behave as if that were true. If they did, we'd hear a lot less about companies that lay people off while their CEOs enjoy outsized pay and perks, or about employees who are so stressed out that they can barely drag themselves into work on Mondays. Businesses like to say that "the customer is always right" and that "your call is important to us," but they don't act that way. When you call a company because you can't decipher your cell phone bill, get payment for an insurance claim or figure out how to erase a virus from your computer, it's hard to get a satisfactory response—and harder still to get a human on the line. Even the belief that companies are run for the benefit of their shareholders has been undermined by the corporate crime wave of recent years. Shareholders watched in horror as insider dealings and corrupt accounting practices destroyed billions of dollars of stock market value at Enron, as Dennis Kozlowski, the CEO of Tyco, was put on trial for looting his company of $600 million and as massive accounting fraud forced WorldCom into bankruptcy. They were victimized, too, by tainted research on Wall Street, by the market-timing scandals at mutual funds and by the wrongdoing, misdeeds and excesses that afflicted such companies as Adelphia, Global Crossing, Xerox, Sprint, Qwest, Kmart, Lucent, Rite-Aid, Health South and ImClone. In most of these cases, the senior executives were primarily to blame. But we've learned as the scandals unspool that no one—not the boards of directors, not the accountants, not the regulators, not the institutional shareholders and not the press—did their job very well.

It's no wonder that many Americans regard business with a jaundiced eye. Nor is it surprising that many who work in business are deeply alienated from the work they do. Our economic system generates vast material wealth, which is no small accomplishment. We own more stuff than our parents or grandparents did and, as measured by the gross national product or median income, we live better. But we do not seem to feel better. This is because, at least for the moment, American capitalism is fundamentally about money, not meaning. Very few of us can get excited about going to the office to generate shareholder value. Too often, we are unable to connect our deepest values to the work we do. And so we find it difficult to approach our jobs with genuine enthusiasm or to take more than a momentary pride in our accomplishments. According to the Gallup Organization's extensive workplace surveys, fewer than one in three Americans describe themselves as engaged by their work. About 55 percent say they are not engaged, and another 15 percent say they are "actively disengaged." This is more than a big problem for business. It's a terrible waste of human potential.

So what is to be done? How we can find more meaning in our work in business? Can we persuade corporate leaders to care about their employees in a heartfelt way? Can we get them to serve their customers and work on behalf of their shareholders? Can they help solve the world's problems? What would it mean for people in business to treat one another—colleagues, supervisors, employees, customers, suppliers and competitors—the way they would like to be treated?

Put another way, what would corporate America look like if it were guided by what I have decided to call spiritual values? By spiritual values, I mean a set of beliefs that are shared by the world's great religious traditions—the belief that people should be treated with dignity and valued for who they are, the belief that we are all interconnected, and the belief that our purpose on earth is to serve others and to promote the common good. Many religious people are guided by those values, as are others who do not believe in God. People use many words—*faith, spirituality, religion, God, soul, heart, values, ethics, meaning* and *purpose*—when they talk about bringing their whole selves to work and making business more humane. Whatever language we use, our common goal is to find ways to connect our highest and best values to our work—to integrate who we are with what we do. Like it or not, the work we do, and how we do it, matters. The philosopher Alfred North Whitehead put it simply: "Every act leaves the world with a deeper or fainter impress of God." How, then, can we reshape our jobs and our companies so that we leave the world with a deeper impress of God?

That is the question we'll explore in the pages ahead. First, though, meet Kenny Moore, an affable fifty-five-year-old New Yorker who knows something about both faith and fortune.* Moore used to be a Catholic priest. He now works as an executive in the human resources department of KeySpan Corp., a Brooklyn, New York–based utility company with thirteen thousand employees that had revenues of $6.9 billion in 2002. As a latecomer to the world of business, Moore had some catching up to do, so he dutifully plowed through piles of how-to books about corporate America written by management gurus and famous CEOs. But he always got stuck at the part that said something like "Bring everyone together, tell them the plan and get them to believe in and implement it fully." What Moore wanted to know was how. How do you get people to believe in their work? How do you win their trust? How do you inspire them? Because Moore's work at KeySpan revolves around such

---

*All ages in this book are as of January 1, 2004.

questions—he describes his job as "awakening joy, meaning and commitment in the workplace"—he launched an unorthodox experiment in employee motivation a while ago. As it happens, Moore was inspired by a book, although not one that sits on many executives' shelves.

Somebody Loves You, Mr. Hatch, by Eileen Spinelli, is a children's book about a reclusive workingman who has neither family nor friends. "Mr. Hatch was tall and thin and he did not smile" it begins. He takes his meals alone and follows a monotonous routine until the day the postman brings him a heart-shaped box of chocolates accompanied by a note that says simply, "Somebody loves you." It's Valentine's Day, he remembers. Puzzled, Mr. Hatch decides that he has a secret admirer. He laughs—something he'd stopped doing— and, hoping to solve the mystery, gets all dressed up, reaches out to his neighbors, shares candy with his coworkers, makes new friends and even plays an old harmonica he'd put away long ago.

When the postman returns to say that he'd delivered the candy to the wrong house, Mr. Hatch is crestfallen. He begins to withdraw again. This time, though—well, I don't want to reveal the ending, but his new friends won't allow him to resume his solitary ways. When Kenny Moore read *Somebody Loves You, Mr. Hatch* to his son, the story got him thinking. "What would happen if Mr. Hatch worked in corporate America?" he wondered. "What havoc might be wrought by small gifts, anonymously given to an ordinary worker, possibly even the wrong person?" He decided to find out.

Moore came up with the idea of sending a $40 floral arrangement to two KeySpan employees every Monday morning. He called it a "Mr. Hatch award." Some recipients would be selected for their commitment, but others would be chosen at random. With the flowers would come a note saying: "Don't ever think your good efforts go unnoticed." It would be signed: "From someone who cares." Moore had been around business long enough to know that you are supposed to do a pilot program before launching a new project, so he decided to test his idea on his boss, a senior vice president for human resources. "While I personally hate anyone in authority," Moore said—he's kidding, I think—"I notice that no one ever says 'thank you' to executives." He sent a second arrangement to a woman in marketing he barely knew. The only hitch came when Moore visited the corporate florist and saw how few flowers his $40 would buy. The florist also seemed uncomfortable when he asked to send the flowers anonymously and pay in cash. Perhaps she feared becoming party to some harassment scheme.

The day the flowers were delivered, Moore stopped by to see the woman in marketing. "Hey, nice flowers," he remarked. "Is it your birthday?" Her coworkers crowded around; by then, they'd learned that the senior VP had received flowers, too. They seemed both giddy and mystified as they tried to figure out what the woman had in common with the executive and who might have sent them flowers. One had even called the florist to investigate.

Several days later, Moore found himself in the senior VP's office. Before Moore could tell him about the pilot program, his boss brought up the flowers. He had no idea who'd sent them, but he said the gift had inspired him to try to spend more time focusing on individual employees and their needs. "I know it's impractical," he said, "but I'd like to give it a try." Now Moore felt he could not share his secret, for fear of derailing his boss from his newfound good intentions.

Without further testing, Moore launched his project. He'd learned a few things from the pilot. He would run the operation without corporate approval, digging into his own budget for the money. He would preserve the secrecy since that added to the fun. And he would ditch the corporate florist. He found a bodega where $40 bought an impressive array of tulips, roses, baby's breath and birds of paradise. The owner had no problem with either anonymity or cash payments.

Moore still sends flowers every week. He does not claim to have boosted productivity or changed KeySpan's corporate culture. But he counts a few small victories, not the least of which are that he looks forward to going to work on Monday mornings and that a couple of employees go home every Monday night with smiles on their faces. His boss did spend more time meeting one-on-one with people. And Moore made a new friend at the bodega who's happy to see him each week. KeySpan and its world are a little better off than they used to be.

Small stuff, to be sure, but that's why I decided to begin this book with Kenny Moore. His Mr. Hatch project is a simple example of how one person can bring his spirituality to work. Far more, of course, will be needed to reform corporate America and to make work in business more meaningful. But we have to start somewhere. Giving flowers anonymously is, at heart, an act of faith. Moore describes it as "a faith statement in favor of the greatness of our employees—in advance of them actually demonstrating it," a way to tell people that they are valued for who they are, not just for what they've done lately for KeySpan. (In this sense, it is the opposite of a conventional performance evaluation.) The Mr. Hatch awards also are a reminder that you need not be a CEO or a senior executive or even a middle manager to bring your spirituality to work and see it touch others. The way you approach your job and treat those around you reflects your values and who you are. It makes ripples, too. This is what Whitehead meant when he said that every act leaves the world with a deeper or fainter impress of God, and it's what Moore means when he says, "How I respond to coworkers and conduct my menial business tasks makes a difference. A rather powerful one."

Of course, Kenny Moore is not your typical executive. Before joining KeySpan in 1983—it was then called Brooklyn Union Gas—he spent fifteen years with the Salesian monastic order, as a student, teacher and ordained priest. Soon after joining the company, he was diagnosed with what was said to be an incurable form of Hodgkin's disease that required a year of intense, experimental treatments. Surviving cancer left him with a sense of urgency about the rest of his life. Quoting Oliver Wendell Holmes, who once said, "Most of us go to our graves with our music still inside us," Moore says that he wants to play his music before it's too late. He doesn't worry about rocking the boat at KeySpan. "One of the advantages of surviving a near-death experience is you don't give a shit," he says. This approach served him so well that he became a trusted counselor to Bob Catell, KeySpan's chief executive. Recently, they wrote a book called *The CEO and the Monk*.

When we met, Moore told me that his job in human resources is not all that different from his work as a Catholic priest and educator. Both are about helping people to become fully engaged in what they do, whether that's going to church, going to school or going to work. "How do you get people to change?" he asked. "There's a sense of mystery there." Work has changed in the last generation or so, he said. People can no longer be compelled to work harder or smarter, if indeed they ever could. Instead, they must be inspired or persuaded to give of themselves. "We're learning it's more of an invitation than a command," Moore said. "How do you get people to support you when you can't control them? You have to offer them something to believe in that's beyond money." People want to trust their leaders. They want to believe in what they do. They want to feel as if the company cares about them.

"Trust, belief and caring," Moore said. "Those are spiritual issues. Maybe corporate America has a spiritual problem. So it's not a bad idea to have a priest working there."

I DIDN'T find Kenny Moore. He found me. Kenny was one of more than three hundred people who called or sent letters or e-mails—they kept coming for months—after I wrote a story called "God and Business: The Surprising Quest for Spiritual Renewal in the American Workplace" that was published in *Fortune* magazine on July 9, 2001. Since joining *Fortune* as a senior writer in 1996, I've written more than sixty feature stories. No other article generated that kind of response. None came close. The issue was a hit on the newsstands, too.

I can't say that I was surprised that the story had struck a chord.

At thirteen pages, it was one of the longest we'd run all year. The cover art was striking: the words *God* and *business* appeared in incandescent white letters against a deep blue sky, as if illuminated by a higher power. And the idea itself ran against the grain. As my boss, managing editor Rik Kirkland, wrote in the magazine: "God and business? Did you ever expect to see those two words on the cover of this magazine? Me neither. At *Fortune,* our articles of faith are limited to belief in free trade, unfettered competition and the proposition that capitalism works best when companies stick to creating value for shareholders. Our normal beat: mammon." So the story was bound to attract notice.

But there was more to the story's appeal than its novelty. Hundreds of business people responded to "God and Business" because they care deeply about their faith and their work and want very much to reconcile the two. Readers told me about their own religious beliefs and how they struggle to live them at work, even though they were breaching what *Fortune* called "the last taboo in corporate America." These business people firmly reject the conventional wisdom, held by corporate executives and clerics alike, that God and business don't mix. They are unwilling to check their values at the office door and live with what has been called the Sunday-Monday gap. Instead, they are determined to bring their whole selves to work, knowing that their own values may sometimes bump up against marketplace pressures.

"Why would we want to look for God in our work?" asks Gregory F. A. Pierce, an author, publishing executive and Catholic layman who is active in the spirituality-at-work movement. "The simple answer is that most of us spend so much time working that it would be a shame if we couldn't find God there. A more complex answer is that there is a creative energy in work that is somehow tied to God's creative energy. If we can understand that connection, perhaps we can use it to transform the workplace into something quite remarkable." Pierce publishes an Internet newsletter about faith and work, and he helped start a group called Business Executives for Economic Justice (BEEJ) in Chicago, one of dozens of faith-based organizations that see spirituality as a powerful force that can make business better.

Soon after *Fortune* published my story, I began work on this book. My plan was to focus on spirituality and business by writing about people like Greg Pierce and his colleagues at BEEJ and their efforts to live their faith in corporate America. They represented the best hope we have for changing business, I thought. Then something unexpected happened. As I dug deeper, I discovered a bigger and better story. The spirituality-at-work movement, as interesting and potentially important as it is, turned out to be a part—a relatively small part, in truth—of a much broader drive to reform corporate America. This campaign is mostly ad hoc. It is unfolding not in the political arena but in the marketplace. Indeed, most of the people who are doing the hard work that's required to change business for the better don't see themselves as part of a campaign at all. They go to work every day, try to do the right thing, talk quietly about values and lead by their example. A few have managed to build great companies, like the ones in this book. Others—idealists in their thirties and forties—are just now starting their own firms, which are designed to marry profit and purpose. Most are toiling anonymously in the middle ranks of corporate America. For the most part, these people don't use the language of spirituality to describe their work; instead they talk about corporate social responsibility or sustainability or business ethics. In the last decade or so, they have formed organizations like Net Impact, a group of business students and newly minted MBAs who want to do business better, and Business for Social Responsibility, a corporate association whose members include Hewlett-Packard, Ford, McDonald's, BP, Shell and Unilever. These business leaders are at the forefront of a quiet revolution that is reshaping corporate America, which I'll describe in more detail in Chapter 1.

Whether spiritual or secular, these business leaders share common goals. They want corporations to feel a broad sense of responsibility for the well-being of all their stakeholders: not just their owners, but their workers, their customers, their business partners, the communities where they operate and the natural world. More than that, though, they want to rethink the very purpose of business. The purpose of business, they argue, is not to generate profit. The purpose of a business is to better the lives of the people that it touches—and to serve the common good. Profits are essential, but they are no more than the fuel to sustain a business, just as food, water and oxygen sustain us so that we can serve a higher purpose.

This is not quite as lofty as it may sound. Few companies, after all, can sustain themselves over time if they do not make a contribution to people's lives. Yet the idea that the fundamental purpose of business is to serve others has radical implications. "This is about going beyond obligation to being motivated by love of neighbor," says David Miller, who left a successful career in investment banking in the mid-1990s to become an ordained Presbyterian minister. Miller, who is executive director of the Center for Faith and Culture at Yale University and an advisor to businesspeople of faith, says businesspeople who seek to serve others must do more than act honestly and ethically: "Let's say you're in banking. What are you proactively doing to get involved in inner city lending? How do we treat the migrant worker, the single mom, the illegal alien? These are the modern-day equivalents of the biblical poor. . . . God did not intend for faith to be locked away in weekend worship or stuck inside stained glass windows, but to be lived in all of our daily life. Business people shouldn't leave their soul in the parking lot every day." Like Miller, the businesspeople you're about to meet want nothing less than to make the workplace into a profoundly humane arena, one where believers and nonbelievers alike can find fulfillment.

I share that goal. That's one reason why I wrote the "God and Business" story. But I am also skeptical about some attempts to mix faith and business. I'm bothered, for example, by what's known as the prosperity gospel—the claim that God will reward true believers with material wealth. Faith does not lead to fortune, nor should it. Nor does religion per se belong in the workplace. Even devout executives say they don't want to impose their own beliefs or practices on diverse workforces. "We can't and shouldn't and don't want to drive people to a particular religious belief," says Bill Pollard, the chairman of ServiceMaster, a Fortune 500 company that is explicitly committed to serving God. "But we do want people to ask fundamental questions. What's driving them? What is this life all about?"

Despite my skepticism about religion's role in business, I feel bound to disclose that I am a believer, and to explain how I came to write this book. Like most people, religious or not, I have always wanted to live my deepest values at work. That's why I got into journalism thirty years ago. It seemed like a way to make the world a better place—although religion played no role in my life back then.

In truth, Judaism—the religion of my birth—meant little to me until recently. Both my parents grew up in observant households in Europe, but both left their Jewish roots behind when they immigrated to the United States. I grew up in the 1960s in Croton-on-Hudson, a suburb of New York, and became a bar mitzvah at a Reform synagogue. Judaism played only a minor role in our family life. If anything, my father, who had lost close family members in the Holocaust, played down our Jewishness and provided his three sons with the WASPy trappings—Brooks Brothers suits, sailing camp on Cape Cod, and Ivy League diplomas—that he felt would help us to succeed in business, as he had.

But business had no appeal to me. With my privileged upbringing, I felt none of the financial insecurities that my parents had. As an antiwar protestor at Yale, I saw the military-industrial complex and big business as the enemy. When I graduated in 1973, I worked briefly for an environmental group and then became a newspaper reporter. This was the Watergate era—Robert Redford and Dustin Hoffman would play Woodward and Bernstein in *All the President's Men*—and journalism struck me as a noble and glamorous way to earn a living. I intended to "afflict the comfortable and comfort the afflicted," and I covered government and politics before becoming a TV columnist at newspapers in Hartford and Detroit. My column gave me a platform to express my opinions, and I tried not to forget why I'd gone into journalism in the first place.

Twenty years later, I found myself working for *Fortune*. (At least it wasn't *Forbes*, the business magazine whose motto is "Capitalist tool." Even so, my comrades from the 1960s would have been appalled.) I had grown disenchanted with newspapers; under pressure to grow their earnings, most papers were no longer committed to serious journalism or public service. I'd also found it hard to connect my own values to my writing; as a news reporter, I'd felt shackled by the limits of "objective" journalism, and as a TV columnist, I spent too much time reviewing sitcoms and chatting up Hollywood stars. More than any of that, though, conventional ambition had gradually subsumed my youthful ideals. Like my father, like most of my Yale classmates and like many of us in business, I had come to define myself by my job, my title and my resume. I worked too hard. And while I tried to give my wife and two daughters the love and attention they deserved, I did not set aside time for religious or spiritual pursuits, for social or political activism or even to give back to the communities where we lived.

My return to Judaism took time. When our family moved to Bethesda, Maryland, in 1991, my wife and I joined a synagogue, but we rarely attended services or practiced at home. Nevertheless, our older daughter, Sarah, threw herself with passion into a Jewish youth group. Her bat mitzvah ceremony was a watershed moment for me. To my surprise, I was overcome by emotion as I watched her lead the service in Hebrew. Something was missing from my life, I felt, but I wasn't sure Judaism was the answer.

I began to read spiritual books and became intrigued by Buddhism. Buddhist thinking made sense to me, with its emphasis on living in the present moment, avoiding attachments, learning to absorb life's inevitable setbacks and striving to serve others. I attended Buddhist lectures and tried meditating. But it never stuck. I gained insights from the Buddhists and began to live my life with more awareness and purpose. I slowed down some, too. But I could not get comfortable with the rituals of Buddhism.

Right about this time, I realized that something was missing from my work as well. (The fact that I was approaching fifty surely helped prompt all of this self-examination.) *Fortune* had turned out to be a fine employer. The pay was good, as were the perks, and my editors were smart and supportive. I covered a glamorous beat—the entertainment industry—and met colorful people. Working out of my home, I enjoyed a lifestyle that my friends envied. And I took pride in my craft. But it was not enough. I hungered for a sense that my work mattered, that it was making a contribution, however small, to the greater good. To my dismay, I realized that when I wrote about the media conglomerates and their CEOs, men like Michael Eisner and Rupert Murdoch and Sumner Redstone, I judged their success only by the standard measures: how much money they made for their shareholders and for themselves. When *Fortune*'s parent company, Time Warner, announced its merger with America Online in January 2000, I found myself working for the world's most powerful media company. So much for afflicting the comfortable.

Then, for whatever reason—my religious friends would see a higher power at work, although I do not—some exciting things happened. I found the spiritual home I'd been seeking—a Reconstructionist synagogue in Bethesda called Adat Shalom with two wonderful rabbis, a welcoming congregation and services that offered both intellectual stimulation and spiritual succor. Reconstructionism is a small, twentieth-century American branch of Judaism that, to my mind, retains the best of Judaism's traditions and rituals while "reconstructing" those ideas and practices that seem problematic in the modern world. Reconstructionists, for example, tend to reject the view of God as a supernatural being who punishes evil and rewards good; instead, we see the Divinity as a spiritual and ethical force in the universe, perhaps as the potential for goodness that exists in us all.

As I became involved in Adat Shalom, my editors at *Fortune,* who knew about my interest in religion, assigned me to look into the growth of spirituality in the workplace. They had been approached by Keith Ferazzi, a Harvard MBA and former chief marketing officer for the Starwood hotel group, who told them that interest in spirituality and business was exploding, particularly among baby boomers. As I worked on the story that became "God and Business," I began to rethink my entertainment industry coverage as well.

To begin with, I questioned whether the narrow focus on short-term shareholder value that drove both business decision making and financial journalism in the 1990s was a healthy way to think about building companies for the long run. More importantly, I realized that I was under no obligation to frame business "success" solely in financial terms, and that it might be useful to explore the connections among values, character, social responsibility and the bottom line. So when I next wrote about Disney, I argued that Michael Eisner's leadership style—which seemed to me to be arrogant and self-aggrandizing—damaged the company, its employees and its shareholders. In a story about Murdoch and Fox, I raised questions about the effect the network's tawdrier programs had on the broader culture. Venturing outside the world of media, I wrote about an executive training program called the Corporate Athlete that helps businesspeople manage their energy by developing connections between values and what they do. I wrote about shareholder activism and corporate social responsibility, too. Now, I felt, I could bring purpose and significance to my stories.

Still, some big questions loomed over my efforts to take a more spacious view of how business works: What does it mean for a company to be guided by spiritual values? Can people who live their faith at work succeed in business? Can companies do good and do well? Better yet, can companies do well by doing good—that is, can they find a way to profitably solve social problems? I'd raised these questions in Fortune, but they were complicated and the anecdotal evidence was all over the lot.

The conventional view remains that businesses should keep a laserlike focus on the bottom line. As Fortune's Rik Kirkland wrote in his note accompanying my "God and Business" story: "Capitalism works best when companies stick to creating value for shareholders." Certainly the two most celebrated CEOs of our time, Jack Welch of General Electric and Bill Gates of Microsoft, are not known for their sensitivity to spiritual or ethical concerns inside their companies. (Gates' philanthropy is a different matter.) They are tough customers with sharp elbows, as are so many executives who outsmart, outwork and outlast their rivals to survive in the corporate jungle. "I've seen a lot of not very good human beings succeed in business," said the legendary investor Warren Buffett when I asked him about spirituality and business. "I wish it were otherwise."

What's more, as the economic boom of the 1990s gave way to a recession, several companies known for their commitment to spiritual or human values ran into trouble. Sales plummeted at the Body Shop, the global chain of health and beauty stores that pioneered the idea of large-scale "retailing with a conscience." Textile manufacturer Malden Mills, whose CEO, Aaron Feuerstein, became a folk hero when he kept paying thirty-one hundred idled workers after a factory burned down in 1995, filed for bankruptcy. When Levi Strauss, an icon of corporate social responsibility, lost market share to hipper jeans makers, laid off thousands of people and closed all of its plants in North America, critics blamed the family-owned firm's touchy-feely style.

And yet there's a strong argument to be made that companies driven by strong values will endure and prevail. Surely a dose of spiritual values would have saved firms like Enron and WorldCom, which were brought down by a toxic mix of arrogance, greed and corruption. Several core spiritual principles—particularly the idea that people should be treated with dignity and that we are all interconnected—dovetail neatly with contemporary management thinking about what drives great companies, especially in a knowledge-based economy. Great companies don't buy a worker's physical labor for eight hours a day; they rely on fully engaged people with emotional intelligence and a strong sense of purpose. Great companies are about "we," not "me"; they deploy teams of people who collaborate well, and promote learning and listening up and down the ranks.

Great companies also have a mission that transcends the bottom line, a reason for being that inspires their people to give their all. "Spirituality is in convergence with all the cutting-edge thinking in management and organizational behavior," says Hamilton Beazley, an author and former oil company executive who teaches management at George Washington University.

The businesspeople you're about to meet are not all religious or spiritual. But they all lead thriving companies that are guided by what I've called spiritual values. Tom Chappell, a Protestant minister, built Tom's of Maine from a two-person operation into a business that sells $35 million a year of all-natural personal care products. Jeff Swartz, the CEO of Timberland and an Orthodox Jew, leads a publicly traded company with $1.2 billion in revenues that sets the standard for community service. At Starbucks, as Howard Schultz and Orin Smith built a company that changed the way Americans consume coffee, they rewarded even part-time workers with health care benefits and stock options. Herb Kelleher and Colleen Barrett of Southwest Airlines have been shaped by a management philosophy called servant leadership that stresses modesty and teamwork; despite the woes of the airline industry, Southwest has been one of the top-performing companies of the last thirty years. UPS and Herman Miller have endured even longer, since the early 1900s, because their founders, and their successors, saw the dignity in every worker and found satisfaction in serving customers.

Not all the leaders in this book are CEOs. Barbara Waugh of Hewlett-Packard, a self-styled corporate revolutionary, used her skills as an organizer to persuade HP to develop technology for the world's four billion poor people. Environmentalist Mark Buckley is helping to turn Staples green. Social investor Amy Domini uses the power of finance to serve the common good. From each story, we'll try to learn more about what it means to bring spiritual values to work—both for companies and for those of us who go to work in search of creative fulfillment, meaningful relationships and the sense that what we do is both valued and valuable.

This book chronicles my search to understand how companies like UPS, Southwest Airlines, Starbucks, Herman Miller and Timberland are able to marry profit and purpose, and to see how their success can be replicated. What follows is an argument on behalf of a new and better way to do business. I'm not going to suggest that living one's faith at work is easy, because it's not—although ignoring or suppressing one's values is, in the long run, even more difficult. But I do hope to persuade you that it's worth the effort. In the pages ahead, as we visit some of the places where spiritual values are reshaping business in America—from a bakery in Yonkers, New York, to a high-tech start-up in Silicon Valley—I will do my best to capture the magic that happens when goodness and business live in harmony.

1

A QUIET REVOLUTION

In 1924, the president of the J. C. Penney Co. wrote to the manager of a company store in Eureka, Oregon, to praise him and his team for a job well done. "You did the most business that has ever been done in Eureka, and made the most money that has ever been made. I congratulate each and every one of you," said the executive. Then he delivered a gentle rebuke. "I don't want you to get the idea, Mr. Hughes, that we want you to make too much profit. There is danger in doing that very thing. There is a certain service that we owe to our community. Now, don't misunderstand me, I am not censuring you, but somewhere in the operations of the Eureka business there is a profit that we owe to the public."

Profits mattered to James C. Penney Jr., the company's founder and its guiding spirit for fifty years, but his Christian values mattered even more. The son, grandson and great-grandson of preachers, Penney had started his chain of stores, which were originally called the Golden Rule stores, with a single outlet in Kemmerer, Wyoming, in 1902. Operating in small towns at first, he dedicated the company to service—service to its working-class customers, who expected quality goods at fair prices, and service to its employees, whom he treated like family. Long before the advent of stock options, Penney gave every one of his store managers shares in the parent company so that they could share in its profits and success. "Business never was and never will be anything more or less than people serving other people," Penney wrote in *Fifty Years with the Golden Rule,* his autobiography.

So committed was Penney to his values that Penney Co. stores did not offer credit for many years because he believed that his customers needed to cultivate the virtue of thrift. When the company's board of directors finally voted to make credit available in 1957, long after rivals like Sears had done so, Penney continued to voice his reservations. "You will end up encouraging people to buy things they can not afford and should not buy," he told the board. "By offering credit, we encourage them to overbuy. With me, it is a moral issue of getting people in financial trouble." His ethic of service proved to be good for business. By the time of his death in 1971, the J. C. Penney Co. employed 162,000 people in 1,570 stores that rang up sales of $4.7 billion.

For Milton S. Hershey, too, business was about more than making money. What excited the inventor of the nickel candy bar was the opportunity to make the world, or at least his little corner of it, into a happier place. To that end, he transformed twelve hundred acres of rolling Pennsylvania farmland into America's most famous company town, a place where, as he put it, "the things of modern progress all center in a town that has no poverty, no nuisances and no evil." In contrast to the faceless company towns erected by nineteenth-century industrialists, Hershey, Pennsylvania, offered parks and swimming pools, a golf course and a roller coaster, a hotel, a sports arena, an ice-skating rink, a library and a two-year junior college where tuition was free.

Raised by his mother, Fannie, a dour Mennonite who disdained worldly pleasures, Milton Hershey rebelled by starting a business that brought smiles to the faces of millions of children. His bedrock values included charity, modesty and service. "Business is a matter of Human Service," read a sign on his office wall. After his wife, Kitty, died in 1915, Hershey gave all of his shares in the company to a school for orphan boys that he and his wife had started. "I have no heirs—that is, children," he explained. "So I decided to make the orphan boys of the U.S. my heirs."

Hershey's paternalistic dream faded over time. To his dismay, workers seeking higher wages struck the company in 1937. After his death in 1945, professional managers began to separate the company from the town. They cut back on the services provided by the company, and turned a public park, lake and gardens into a Disney-style theme park that charged admission. But Hershey's legacy persisted. When Hershey Foods was put up for sale in 2002, the people of Hershey knew what to do. Arguing that the company had an obligation to support the town and the school, they hired lawyers to oppose the deal, petitioned state legislators and marched in protest under the Kiss-shaped streetlights on Chocolate Avenue. They won—the nonprofit trust that still owns most of Hershey Foods turned down a $12.5 billion offer from Wrigley and elected to stay independent. "For once," my colleague John Helyar wrote in *Fortune,* "the almighty dollar had lost."

Born in the nineteenth century and shaped by small-town America, James C. Penney and Milton S. Hershey were old-fashioned men who lived traditional values at work. The ideals that guided them—industry, thrift, charity and service—are not often spoken of anymore in corporate America. But as architects of great companies, Penney and Hershey were in some respects ahead of their time. Each man imbued his company with a purpose that was more inspiring than making money. Both knew that profits were essential, but profits were not the reason to do business. They saw their role as serving their workers and their customers, as well as making money for themselves and their owners. And, in contrast to many executives, then and now, they did not think about business as a series of discrete transactions. Instead, their companies built long-lasting relationships with workers, customers and communities that depended on fairness and trust. Relationships mattered to Penney and Hershey because they focused on the long term. They managed not for the next quarter, but for the next quarter of a century.

In the wake of Enron, WorldCom, Tyco and too many other corporate scandals to enumerate, and at a time when most CEOs are grossly overpaid, workers are seen as expendable and production is shifting to so-called third-world sweatshops, the notion that corporations exist, above all, to provide service to others and to society may sound outdated or naive. It is not.

Forget about the headlines for a moment. You've surely had personal experience with businesses that are driven by an ethic of service. Most are small. Think of your favorite neighborhood merchant, the auto repair shop known for square dealing, or a family-owned restaurant that employs local teenagers. Their owners understand that doing the right thing is good for business, and that reputation is a valuable asset. There's nothing surprising about this. When people say "It's good business to treat your employees well" or "It's good business to go the extra mile for a customer" or "It's good business to give back to the community," we understand what they mean. What is surprising is that more big companies don't think that way.

That has begun to change—dramatically. A growing number of big corporations now believe that doing good is good business, and they are acting accordingly. Some are guided by leaders with spiritual values or by a sense of social responsibility that has been built into their corporate cultures. Others have been rocked by outside forces and all but required to rethink their obligations. Implausibly, the corporate scandals have turned out to be a boon for those who want business to serve the common good. A senior executive at a big software company recently told me: "Companies need to show that they are not just greedy institutions."

You may not have read or heard much about the ways that corporate America is changing for the better. The bad news about business gets more exposure than the good. But consider these examples:

• The industrial giant DuPont, which was once labeled America's worst polluter, is remaking itself from an old economy oil-and-chemicals company into an environmentally friendly life sciences firm. DuPont is committed to a strategy called sustainable growth—that means building businesses that can grow, indefinitely, without depleting natural resources—and so it sold off Conoco, its oil-and-gas unit, and bought Pioneer Hi-Bred International, the world's largest seed company. DuPont also sharply curbed energy usage, emissions and waste and set the gold standard for industrial safety. This $25-billion-a year company, which got its start in 1802 as a manufacturer of gunpowder, now makes soy protein, a corn-based stretchable fabric called Sarona and Tyvek, a versatile material that's made into home insulation and thin, lightweight, hard-to-tear envelopes for FedEx. (Using lightweight envelopes saves fuel in trucks and planes.) Paul Gilding, a former executive director of Greenpeace International who now consults for DuPont, makes the argument for going green in business terms. "It's almost a complete waste of time to talk about ethics and moral values if you want to change business behavior," Gilding told me. "The only thing that's going to drive sustainability in a lasting way is if it leads to profit and growth in big corporations."

• In another remarkable turnaround, Chiquita Brands has become a social and environmental leader in the $5-billion-a-year banana industry. That's an unexpected twist in the story of the 103-year-old company once known as United Fruit, which backed a military coup that toppled the elected government in Guatemala in 1954. (Back then, "banana republic" did not mean the place to shop for khakis.) In 2001, Chiquita, which provides 25 percent of the bananas sold in the United States and Europe, signed a historic labor agreement with a global coalition of banana workers' unions, promising to provide safe and healthy workplaces, eliminate child or forced labor and protect workers' rights to organize. The company also has promised to abide by a set of environmental practices, including eliminating deforestation and reducing pesticide use. "Chiquita has been gradually reinventing the banana business," said Tensie Whelan, executive director of the nonprofit Rainforest Alliance. Chiquita has arranged for third-party verification of its workplace and environmental practices, and the company issues a detailed corporate social responsibility report every year, complete with the photos and phone numbers of senior executives.

• David Pottruck, the hard-charging CEO of the Charles Schwab Co., has become one of a new breed of corporate leaders—humble and collaborative, empathetic, a good listener and focused on values. Speaking at a conference called Spirit in Business 2003, he argued that great companies need to talk more and do more about values, spirit and service. "Serving, serving, serving," he said. "It is the heartthrob of a company that works." Although Pottruck is by no means a touchy-feely guy—he wrestled and played football at the University of Pennsylvania and earned a Wharton MBA—he now believes that the best way to lead people is to inspire them to find meaning in what they do. For Schwab, that means helping people to save and invest their money so they can put their kids through college or enjoy retirement. "What are we doing? What difference are we making?" Pottruck asked. "To me, spirit in business is about that larger context." Pottruck's vision of business goes beyond the bottom line. "There's an enormous gravitational pull on every CEO in America, including me, to view the company just as an economic machine," he said. "But companies are also communities. They are communities of like-minded people who get together to, hopefully, accomplish something extraordinary."

• At the Container Store, a chain of about thirty big-box stores that sell stuff to help people get organized, the Golden Rule—treat people as you want to be treated—is given policy status. So its employees actually feel like they are the company's most important assets. Why? For starters, first-year employees get about 235 hours of training, in an industry—retail—where the average is about 7 hours. Salespeople get wages that are well above industry norms, a 401(k) plan with a company match, health and dental benefits and, most of all, the good feeling that comes from working at a place where they are valued. For four years in a row, the company placed number one or number two on *Fortune*'s 100 Best Companies to Work For list, which is mostly based on worker surveys. Not bad for a place where most people work selling boxes, shelves and garbage cans, albeit in designer hues.

• Led by the fast-growing supermarket chains Whole Foods Markets and Wild Oats, as well as such food manufacturers as Stonyfield Yogurt and Horizon Organic, the U.S. organic food industry has grown from a niche business with $1 billion in sales in 1990 to a $13 billion industry in 2003. More than 2.3 million acres of farmland have been certified as organic, according to the U.S. Department of Agriculture, a figure that's growing by nearly 20 percent a year. Although there's no definitive proof that organic foods are actually better for you, organic farming reduces the use of pesticides and chemicals that get into the air, earth and water, and it provides a lifeline for many small farmers. "I started this business because I wanted to make the world a better place," said John Mackey, the CEO of Whole Foods, who began with one health food store in Austin, Texas, in 1980. Today there are more than 120 Whole Foods Markets. A vegetarian baby boomer, Mackey said: "Food has been altered tremendously over the last hundred years with chemical fertilizers, pesticides, growth hormones and antibiotics. Whole Foods stands, not politically against that, but as an alternative for people who want to eat food as close to its natural state as possible. I believe that's a better way to live." His customers, who are willing to pay inflated prices for their groceries, evidently agree.

- Even Wal-Mart Stores, the nation's largest private employer and a company better known for its conservative mores than for an expansive sense of social responsibility, revised its antidiscrimination policy to include gay and lesbian employees in 2003 after a coalition of socially responsible investors brought pressure on the firm. The decision by Wal-Mart, which employs 1.1 million workers, means that nine of the ten largest companies in America, in terms of revenues, have rules barring discrimination against gay employees. (Exxon Mobil is the exception.) More than three hundred of the Fortune 500 companies have antidiscrimination policies protecting gays, and nearly two hundred, including General Motors and Ford, provide domestic partners with medical benefits. By contrast, the federal government offers no special protection for gay and lesbian employees, and only thirteen states bar workplace discrimination against gays. "It's very gratifying to see corporate America taking the lead on this," said David Smith of the Human Rights Campaign, a gay and lesbian advocacy group.

These are examples of companies that are becoming more socially and environmentally responsible. I could cite many others—Merck with its giveaway of Mectizan, a drug that treats river blindness, in Africa and Latin America, McDonald's with its demand that antibiotic growth hormones be removed from the diet of chickens, American Electric Power with its projects to plant trees in Bolivia, Brazil and southern Louisiana to offset carbon emissions and slow down global warming. None of these companies is perfect, and some are far from it. Wal-Mart buys goods from sweatshops, pays poverty-level wages and faces thousands of sex-discrimination lawsuits. Chiquita upgraded its own banana farms, but it buys fruit from farmers who don't meet its high standards. Investors in DuPont have not fared well since the company began its pursuit of sustainable growth, and Schwab laid off thousands of people after the stock market bubble burst. Whole Foods has battled union organizers.

But if you take a long-term view of where business is coming from and where it is going, you cannot help but see that corporate

America is changing for the better in some important ways. Start with the environment. Earth Day was celebrated for the first time in 1970, and for nearly two decades afterward environmentalists and corporations saw each other as the enemy. Today, many big companies—Citicorp, Home Depot and Kinko's, as well as DuPont and McDonald's—have formed lasting partnerships with environmental groups in an effort to reduce their environmental footprint and share best practices.

Next consider the workplace. Not long ago, many, if not most, bosses and workers experienced the factory or the office as a battleground where management and labor fought, sometimes bitterly, over pay and working conditions. A hierarchical, command-and-control approach prevailed. Today, although many workers remain alienated—otherwise *Dilbert* would not strike such a chord—most companies recognize that they have to compete for talent. A growing number, like the Container Store and Schwab, see their employees as partners who should be valued, respected and given the opportunity to find meaning, as well as make money, at work.

Progress has been dramatic as well for the women, African Americans, Hispanics, gays, lesbians and disabled people who have entered the ranks of corporate America. My company, Time Warner, has an African American CEO, Dick Parsons, and nobody makes a fuss about it. When the U.S. Supreme Court took up the issue of affirmative action in 2003, dozens of big companies, including Coca-Cola, General Mills, General Motors, Intel and Microsoft, filed briefs supporting the University of Michigan, which grants preferences to applicants from minority groups. (The federal government opposed preferences.) Many obstacles to equality remain, of course, but there's no going back to the days when minority groups were largely excluded from business.

Finally, there's the emerging issue of human rights. Until recently, few consumers knew or cared much about where products came from or under what conditions they were made. Most still don't know or care, but enough have begun to pay attention so that many companies want to do what they can to avoid exploiting workers in the so-called third world. They learned from the experience of Nike, Gap and the talk show host Kathie Lee Gifford, whose reputations were damaged when it became known that they did business with sweatshops.

These changes are not disconnected. Taken together, they add up to nothing less than a quiet revolution that has begun to transform corporate America. Big companies are gradually remaking themselves so that they can do more to serve the common good—by enabling workers to flourish, by producing goods and services that improve people's lives, by minimizing environmental damage and by trying to solving a wide range of social and economic problems. To be sure, only a Pollyanna would say that all companies are changing this way. Plenty of scoundrels work in business and, as we're reminded almost daily, greed drives all manner of irresponsible, antisocial corporate behavior. Even well-meaning companies must contend with pressures from Wall Street to increase their earnings every quarter, which makes it difficult for them to think about their impact on the public good. But I have come to believe that most companies, like the ones in this book, are moving toward a more humane vision of what business should be.

Certainly in their public pronouncements, most global corporations now acknowledge that they have obligations that go beyond the bottom line. Dozens of big public companies publish annual reports, usually called corporate social responsibility or corporate citizenship reports, in which they describe their efforts to meet social and environmental goals. "Replicating the business model of the past will not work," writes William Clay Ford Jr., the chairman and CEO of Ford Motor, in his company's 2002 report. "A genuine concern for customers, employees, business partners and the community not only is the right thing to do, it's also a powerful business strategy. It's what will drive the most successful companies in the 21st century." Such rhetoric is not always matched by action: despite Bill Ford's professed concern for the environment, Ford Motor churns out gas-guzzling SUVs and lobbies the government to oppose higher fuel efficiency standards. But the rhetoric by itself exerts a pull on corporate behavior. Perhaps unintentionally, every company that publishes a corporate social responsibility report—among them are such blue-chip companies as Alcoa, Hewlett-Packard, Intel, Johnson & Johnson, McDonald's and Procter & Gamble—reinforces and advances the idea that corporations have moral responsibilities. As more companies promise to do good, people expect them to live up to their promises. They become part of a never-ending spiral of rising expectations. They are expected to care.

To GET a better sense of where business is going and why, let's take a brief look backward. Today's conventional, hard-nosed approach to commerce—driven as it is by the belief that business is business and that companies have no obligations other than to make money and obey the law—may feel preordained and permanent. But it has been the dominant view for only about a century. What's more, for much of the century, business leaders have engaged in spirited debate with one another and with their critics about how corporations should be run and what their role in society ought to be.

Corporations today have such a miserable reputation that it's easy to forget that America was founded by people who believed firmly that business existed to serve God. The Puritans acknowledged no boundaries between their faith and their worldly affairs. Hard work, they believed, was a religious obligation, and church elders regulated wages, prices and interest rates in the Plymouth Colony. When a Massachusetts merchant named Robert Keayne allegedly charged too much money for horse bridles and gold buttons, he was fined by the Church, publicly censured and forced to apologize for his sin. God and business were inextricably intertwined.

So long as farmers, neighborhood merchants and small-scale factories dominated the economic landscape, the idea of business as a moral enterprise prevailed. People understood that their customers and their neighbors would hold them responsible for their actions, just as local merchants are held accountable today. In his *Autobiography*, Benjamin Franklin—an entrepreneur as well as an inventor, diplomat, moralist and politician—attributed his success in life to a practice, which he adopted at an early age, of faithfully cultivating twelve virtues: temperance, silence, order, resolution, frugality, industry, sincerity, justice, moderation, cleanliness, tranquility and chastity. Nowhere did Franklin commit himself to making money, though that was surely one of his goals; to the contrary, he promised himself to avoid "any foolish project of growing suddenly rich." As America's greatest self-help writer and a champion of middle-class morality, Franklin counseled his readers that living a virtuous life was the key to worldly success. This was pragmatic advice, well suited for an era when most Americans did business with people they knew. When commerce operates on such a personal level, as it did for most of the eighteenth and nineteenth centuries, character and reputation matter.

By the dawn of the twentieth century, though, industrialization had disrupted the bonds among owner, worker, customer and neighbor. Between 1880 and 1930, the rise of big business transformed commerce in America—it was urbanized, depersonalized and secularized. Beginning with the railroads, large-scale economic enterprises amassed enormous wealth and power. By 1920, General Electric, Ford, U.S. Steel, DuPont, Eastman Kodak, Procter & Gamble, B. F. Goodrich and International Harvester had emerged as leaders in their industries. Coca-Cola, Wrigley, Quaker Oats, Pillsbury, Heinz and Nabisco had become well-known brands. By 1929, the two hundred largest corporations in America owned nearly half of all corporate assets. Mass retailing and advertising ushered in a culture that valued status and consumption over self-restraint and frugality, the Protestant virtues prized by Franklin as well as Penney and Hershey.

New skills, known as management, were required to direct the sprawling new industrial enterprises. Because business on such a vast scale was unprecedented, the early industrialists looked to the military, the biggest organization they knew, and adapted its top-down, regimented structure. Workers were seen as interchangeable parts, and efficiency was valued above all else. At the Ford Motor Co., the invention of the assembly line reduced the amount of time needed to build a Model T from twelve hours to one hour and thirty-three minutes. Reflecting the mind-set of his day, Henry Ford asked: "Why is it that I always get the person when what I really want is a pair of hands?" The famed efficiency expert Frederick W. Taylor, who invented time-and-motion studies, advised industrial companies as they organized their factory floors to maximize output, no matter what the human cost. "In the past, the man has been first," Taylor wrote in 1911 in *The Principles of Scientific Management.* "In the future, the system must be first."

Industrialization spawned fierce resistance, setting off an intense debate about the power and accountability of big business. Labor leaders Samuel Gompers and John L. Lewis, muckrakers Upton Sinclair and Ida Tarbell and church-based reformers Washington Gladden and Walter Rauschenbusch all argued that companies had obligations to their workers and to their communities, a claim that these days can be heard from the likes of Ralph Nader and Greenpeace. A number of corporate leaders—among them Penney, Hershey, UPS founder Jim Casey and D.J. DePree of Herman Miller—also took the view that businesses ought to serve their workers and the broader society, as well as produce profits for owners. The so-called statesmen CEOs of the 1970s, men like Chase Manhattan's David Rockefeller and General Electric's Reginald Jones, shared similar beliefs. "Too many managers feel under pressure to concentrate on the short term in order to satisfy the financial community and the owners of the enterprise—the stockholders," Jones told *U.S. News and World Report* in 1981. "Boards of directors have to understand that they must shelter management from these pressures." They should do so, he declared portentously, "in the interest of the nation."

For most of the twentieth century, this view belonged to a distinct minority. Most executives of big companies adopted what academics called the "finance model" of the corporation, which says that companies exist solely and exclusively to benefit their owners. These businesspeople believe that their only obligation to society is to follow the law. They regard the corporation as an amoral institution, one that is duty-bound to maximize profits by responding to the demands of the marketplace. Free markets, they say, will then create economies that serve the common good. The eighteenth-century moral philosopher Adam Smith, a towering figure in the history of economic thought, provided moral support for free markets. In *The Wealth of Nations,* Smith argued that the forces of self-interest, unfettered competition and the "invisible hand" of the market would ultimately benefit laborers, manufacturers, landlords, peasants and society as a whole.

The Nobel laureate Milton Friedman remains the most influential twentieth-century advocate for the primacy of the shareholder and against an expansive view of corporate social responsibility. In *Capitalism and Freedom,* Friedman asked: "If businessmen do have a responsibility other than making maximum profits for their shareholders, how are they to know what it is? Can self-selected private individuals decide what the social interest is?" Friedman argues that private corporations are ill-equipped to solve social problems and, what's more, that they do not have the legal or moral right to spend their owners' money for any purpose that does not directly serve the corporation. To the degree that business executives spend more money than they must—to reduce their emissions of greenhouse gases, pay workers in the developing world, invest in their community or even donate corporate funds to charity—they are spending their shareholders' money to further their own agendas. Better to pay dividends and let the shareholders give the money away if they choose, or so the argument goes.

In the corporate world, the loudest cheerleader for shareholder primacy has been Reginald Jones' handpicked successor at General Electric, Jack Welch. Welch blew up the GE bureaucracy, fired thousands of workers, and dumped underperforming units, all in the name of generating value for shareholders. He had just one yardstick for success—GE's stock price. Corporate raiders of the 1980s and CEOs of the 1990s—"chainsaw" Al Dunlap is the most extreme example—went on to squeeze workers, suppliers and communities, driving up stock prices for the short term while chanting the mantra of shareholder value. What no one knew until it was too late was just how many corporate CEOs were lining their own pockets at the expense of their shareholders. But that's another story.

There are at least two problems with the claim that the best way for corporations to create value for shareholders is to keep a laser-like focus on the bottom line. The first problem is that money spent to provide generously for employees, to protect the environment or to support charities can serve valid corporate purposes. Such spending, when carried out wisely, enhances a company's reputation and brand, and especially its standing in the eyes of the people who work there. Reputation and brand may be intangible assets, but they deliver substantial value to shareholders over time. The second problem is that what's good for business in the short run can be bad for society and the natural environment—and therefore for business—in the long term. Several years ago, McDonald's helped to form a coalition of companies to pressure fisheries to stop depleting the oceans of fish. If the effort succeeds, fish will cost more, at least for now. So, I asked a McDonald's executive, why worry about the fish? "Simple," he replied. "We want to be able to buy fish ten years from now." This tension between short-term and long-term thinking is a key theme of this book: a willingness to think about the long term sets exemplary companies apart from those that conduct their business with an eye on the day's closing stock price. Forward-looking companies are willing to take responsibility for their long-term impact, not only on their workers and customers but on fish, global warming, pollution, poverty, AIDS, our dependence on Mideast oil and the threat of terrorism, all of which pose potential risks to business. Companies, no less than people, have an interest in promoting a healthy, safe and just world so that they can thrive for years to come.

The sheer scale of twenty-first-century business helps explain why companies have come under pressure to take this broader view of their obligations. The world's five largest corporations—Wal-Mart, General Motors, Exxon Mobil, Royal Dutch Shell and BP—had revenues ranging from $179 billion to $246 billion in 2002, which is more than the gross national product of all but about two dozen countries. Global corporations are more than economic entities or places to work. They have become as inescapable, and as vital to our well-being, as air. Indeed, they affect the air we breathe, the water we drink, the food we eat, the cars we drive, the places we live, the culture we consume and the government with which we live. Experience has taught us that big corporations are too important to be ignored and too powerful not to be held to high standards of behavior.

That, in a nutshell, is what is driving this quiet revolution in corporate America: new, radical and ever-increasing expectations of business. Living by spiritual values or, if you prefer, practicing social responsibility has become good business because people today—whether in their roles as workers, consumers, citizens or even, sometimes, shareholders—expect big companies to do more than obey the law. In a groundbreaking 2003 book called *Value Shift*, Harvard Business School professor Lynn Sharp Paine makes the case that society has in recent years come to endow the corporation with a moral personality. Leading corporations, she argues, are now expected

> to conduct themselves as "moral actors"—as responsible agents that carry out their business within a moral framework. As such, they are expected to adhere to basic ethical principles, exercise moral judgment in carrying out their affairs, accept responsibility for their deeds and misdeeds, be responsive to the needs and interests of others, and manage their own values and commitments.

There's plenty of anecdotal evidence to support this argument, as we'll see in the pages ahead. People prefer to work for companies and to support businesses, large or small, that they believe to be good citizens. And they tell pollsters that they are inclined to punish those that do wrong. A 2002 Corporate Citizenship Study commissioned by the Cone public relations firm found that when consumers learn about a firm's negative practices, 91 percent say they would consider switching to another company, 85 percent say they would pass the information to family and friends, 83 percent say they would refuse to invest in that company, 80 percent say they would refuse to work at that company and 76 percent say they would boycott that company's products. Whether people actually behave that way is a different question. But, at least in the court of public opinion, Milton Friedman has lost the argument about whether companies have a social responsibility that goes beyond the bottom line. In twenty-first-century America, they do. This is a verdict that no business can afford to ignore.

WHAT we are now witnessing in America, as a result, is a decisive shift in the long-running debate about the proper role of business. The climate in which business operates has changed, and there's no turning back. Even now, powerful forces continue to drive business to define its obligations more broadly. What are those forces? They include the spirituality-at-work movement, the changing nature of work itself, government regulators, advocacy groups and socially responsible investors. Interestingly, they can be traced back to the politics and culture of the 1960s—the era of civil rights, feminism, environmental activism and doing your own thing. Ben & Jerry's is by no means the only company to emerge from the values of the 1960s. Those values are shaping the executive suites of the Fortune 500 as well.

Consider, first, the impact of baby boomers. Unlike the generation that came of age during World War II, people who were shaped by the 1960s, as well as those who followed, entered the workplace looking for more than a paycheck and a secure job. They are, to this day, exerting a strong pull on companies to behave better. Business-people, like clergy, teachers, social workers, doctors, nurses, police officers, firefighters or soldiers, want to be able to find meaning and purpose in what they do. They want to work for companies they respect, admire and trust. They want to live their faith and values at work. This is what the spirituality-at-work movement is all about.

This movement has grown apace in recent years. Best-selling books, conferences, lecture series, Internet newsletters, church gatherings and meditation rooms or prayer meetings at work all reflect and encourage people's strong desire to close the Sunday-Monday gap—the idea that faith is one thing, business is another and never the twain shall meet. Spirituality-at-work initiatives turn up in unexpected places. In Hollywood, Robert Johnston, an evangelical Protestant minister who teaches at the Fuller Theological Seminary, leads a group called Reel Spirituality for Christians who work in the movie business. The group supports a festival of spiritual films and hosts dialogues between theologians and directors. "Film can be a resource for understanding faith, and vice versa," Johnston says. In Boston, Will Messenger, a former management consultant, leads a group called the Business Leadership and Spirituality Network, which brings small groups of CEOs to confidential monthly dinners where they can talk in a supportive environment. An Episcopal priest with a Harvard MBA, Messenger told me that his agenda is to reform business practices, not merely to leave executives feeling good about themselves. "A lot of the spirituality movement's basic message is 'You're a good person, just love yourself more,'" he says. "I don't think that is going to challenge insider trading or cooking the books." Several years ago, I attended a conference on spirituality and leadership at the business school of the University of Santa Clara, a Jesuit institution in Silicon Valley. For two days, business people, academics and theologians practiced silent meditation, listened to spiritual readings and talked about such topics as how to find one's true calling. "There were two things I thought I'd never see in my life," said André Delbecq, a management professor who organized the event. "The fall of the Russian empire and God being spoken about at a business school."

Baby boomers are responsible for much of this self-examination. As Greg Pierce, a leader of Business Executives for Economic Justice in Chicago and author of a book called *Spirituality @ Work,* said: "We've always been a very introspective group—which is the polite way of putting it. Actually, we think the world revolves around us. We're reaching the top of our careers, we're kind of where we are going to be, and now we are saying, 'What's it all about, Alfie?'" Or, as a Silicon Valley executive said at the Santa Clara conference: "You get to the top of the ladder and find that it's leaning against the wrong building." Stories about the meaning of work now appear regularly in the business press, particularly in *Fast Company,* a magazine founded in 1995—by two baby boomers, of course. One of the magazine's bedrock principles is that work is "the ultimate expression of a fully-realized self." Or, as *Fast Company* founding editor Alan Webber has said: "If it's not fun, don't do it. Time to get another job."

Such aspirations reflect the changing nature of work. In the industrial era, companies could and did ignore their employees' thirst for meaning. Recall Henry Ford saying that he wished he could hire just a pair of hands. But a pair of hands won't get you very far anymore. Manufacturing, construction, mining and agriculture now employ fewer than one in four U.S. workers—jobs in manufacturing, which peaked in 1979, have declined sharply since 1998—and even people who work on farms and in factories use their heads as much as their hands.

In today's knowledge-based economy, companies want and need the whole person. "Knowledge has become the most important fact of economic life," writes Thomas Stewart, my former *Fortune* colleague, in his 1997 book *Intellectual Capital:* "In the new economy, intellectual capital—not natural resources, machinery or even financial capital—has become the one indispensable asset of corporations." Business's most important task, he argues, is therefore to manage its intellectual capital. Companies own some intellectual capital in the form of brands, patents, software and content, but a vast store of valuable knowledge belongs to employees. Their knowledge, creativity, energy and relationships can make or break companies. These assets, it's often been said, leave the building every night.

As a result, the balance of power in the new economy has tilted away from the owner and toward the employee. As Peter Drucker wrote in *Management in a Time of Great Change*:

> The industrial worker needed the capitalist infinitely more than the capitalist needed the industrial worker. . . . In the knowledge society, the most probable assumption—and certainly the assumption upon which all organizations have to conduct their affairs—is that they need the knowledge worker far more than the knowledge worker needs them.

In other words, successful companies need to behave as if people are their most important asset—because, in fact, they are. Companies that want to attract, retain and engage the best people know that they have to offer them more than a paycheck. They have to provide their workers with a sense of purpose as well. Good leaders understand that. When I ask executives why they won't cut corners when it comes to the quality of their products even if consumers wouldn't notice the difference, or why their environmental programs go well beyond compliance, or why they want to help alleviate poverty in their community, the answer is almost always the same: "Our people have high expectations of the company."

So there's no doubt that employees with strong values exert a powerful effect on their companies, particularly as they rise in the ranks. They can accomplish a lot operating on their own. But they are not operating on their own—far from it. Government regulators, tort lawyers, corporate critics and especially activist groups all have pushed business to behave more responsibly since the beginning of industrialization, and they have gathered momentum in the decades since the 1960s.

So strong was the flood tide of liberalism during the 1960s that it left us with a Republican president, Richard Nixon, who changed the rules of the game for business. Prodded by civil rights organizations, environmentalists and consumer groups, Nixon and the Congress between 1969 and 1972 created four important regulatory agencies—the Environmental Protection Agency (EPA), the Equal Employment Opportunity Commission (EEOC), the Consumer Product Safety Commission (CPSC) and the Occupational Safety and Health Administration (OSHA)—that raised the bar for business conduct. Even when they later came under the influence of pro-business Republican administrations, these agencies pushed business to do better. Only after the EPA collected and published emissions data, for example, could environmental groups bring pressure on DuPont by labeling the company the nation's worst polluter. Because the EEOC collects data on hiring of blacks and Hispanics, victims of discrimination can sue under 1960s civil rights laws; such lawsuits dramatically changed the way companies such as Texaco and Advantica, parent of Denny's, treat minorities. Many more companies surely have mended their ways to avoid regulatory hassles or lawsuits that would cost them money or damage their reputations.

Public interest groups have also had an enormous impact on corporate conduct. Social and environmental activists who once focused on government policy now work directly—and sometimes cooperatively—with business. They find they can make more of a difference that way. "There's a great political framework in this country," says John Passacantando, executive director of Greenpeace USA, "but so much of it has been undermined by smart, savvy corporations who have found ways to end run regulations. We have to take the pressure straight to these corporations." Greenpeace delivered vats of contaminated water from Bhopal, India, site of the world's worst industrial disaster, to the headquarters of Dow

Chemical, which acquired Union Carbide, and responsibility for Bhopal, in 2001; it temporarily shut down gas stations owned by Exxon Mobil to protest the company's stand on global warming; and it parked buses in front of a Shaw's supermarket distribution center to block deliveries of genetically engineered food.

Few companies want to sit down with vocal, grassroots organizations like Greenpeace. But their protests open doors for nonprofits that are ready to do business with corporate America. Environmental Defense, a New York–based group that pioneered this collaborative approach, forged a partnership with McDonald's in 1990 that has lasted more than a decade; it helped the fast-food giant eliminate Styrofoam packaging, reduce waste, curb energy consumption and buy more recycled products. More recently, Environmental Defense organized the Partnership for Climate Action with Alcan, BP, DuPont, Entergy, Ontario Power Generation, Pechiney, Shell International, and Suncor Energy. (If these companies were a country, they would rank twelfth in the world in emissions of greenhouse gases.) Each firm has publicly pledged to reduce emissions and to report on its progress. "We are results-driven," says Fred Krupp, the president of Environmental Defense. "You have to move multinational corporations if you are going to protect the global environment."

Sometimes the activists are amazed by their own power. The Rainforest Action Network (RAN) has just twenty-two full-time employees and a budget of $2 million, but it helped to convince Home Depot, the big home builder Centex and the New York Times Co. to stop buying timber from old-growth or endangered forests. Its tactics range from quiet negotiations to no-holds-barred public protests that target a company and its brand. "We make a pitch to a company on why they should change, from an ethical, environmental or social perspective," explains Michael Brune, the executive director of RAN. "But if they don't take to the message, we give them the 'you can do this the easy way or you can do this the hard way' speech that my dad used to give to me." To get Home Depot, the nation's biggest retailer of wood, to stop buying old-growth timber, the Rainforest Action Network picketed stores, ran full-page newspaper ads and organized local environmentalists to testify against Home Depot in communities where the retailer wanted to open new outlets. Largely as a result of campaigns by RAN and its allies, eight of the ten biggest home-improvement retailers and three of the five biggest home builders in America have agreed to stop using timber from endangered forests.

Companies that ignore activist groups do so at their peril. One example: Monsanto, which in its haste to get genetically modified agricultural products to market in the late 1990s angered a swarm of environmental groups in Europe. Monsanto's CEO, Robert Shapiro, later backtracked, telling a Greenpeace gathering: "Our confidence in this technology [genetic engineering] and our enthusiasm for it has, I think, widely been seen—and understandably so—as condescension or indeed arrogance." But it was too late, and the company's big bet on biotech agriculture failed. "Gone are the days when you could hatch things in a back room, foist them on the world, and expect people to swallow them," says Stuart L. Hart, a professor of strategy at the Kenan-Flagler Business School at the University of North Carolina. Hart, an authority on sustainability, has studied the interplay between nonprofits and corporations; he notes that the Internet has made it much harder for multinational corporations to avoid scrutiny and easier for activists to spread the word about corporate misconduct. "It has become very difficult for large institutions to run and hide," Hart says. "You see, increasingly, this demand for accountability and transparency." In this way, big companies have to guard their reputations in the global village much as local merchants do in their neighborhood.

Compounding the pressures on corporate America are investors who use their wealth to sway business behavior. No one knows exactly how many there are, or how rigorously they align their investments with their beliefs, but they include wealthy individuals, people who entrust their money to socially responsible mutual funds and institutional shareholders, particularly those managing union and government pension funds and foundation assets. Social investing as we know it today is yet another legacy of the 1960s. In

1971, two Methodist Church peace activists launched the Pax World Fund, the first diversified mutual fund to use social screens; they did so because they wanted to invest church members' funds without supporting industries that benefited from the Vietnam War. While social investors today continue to avoid companies they deem unpalatable—typically those involved in weaponry, tobacco, alcohol, gambling and nuclear power—these so-called negative screens do not have much effect on corporate behavior. Social investors have more impact when they become active shareholders, by lobbying companies on such issues as diversity, inner-city lending, corporate governance, and recycling.

Social investors had their greatest victory during the 1980s when they pressured big U.S. companies to report on their conduct in South Africa. Their efforts helped to convince U.S. companies to stop investing in South Africa, which led to dramatic declines in capital inflows and, eventually, helped topple the apartheid system. More recently, social investors have put the issue of global warming on the corporate agenda. Were it not for their work, it's unlikely that oil, utility and automobile companies would be taking steps—as tentative as they are—to report on and reduce their emissions of greenhouse gases. Social investors also led the coalition that lobbied Wal-Mart for two years to get the company to prohibit discrimination based on sexual orientation.

Social investing has grown rapidly. In 1980, just two socially responsible funds had about $66 million under management. In 2003, about two hundred social funds manage about $162 billion in assets, according to the Social Investment Forum, an industry group. Even so, social investing remains little more than a blip on the screen of most CEOs. Its potential is largely untapped. Later in this book, we'll look at social investing in more detail and meet Amy Domini, who runs the Domini Social Index Fund, which, with about $1 billion in assets, is one of the biggest socially responsible funds.

Taken together, these forces—the growing expectation that business should act morally, the desire of people to find meaning in their work and the pressures brought to bear by activists and social investors—are driving the quiet revolution to reform business. Much work, of course, remains to be done. Millions of workers care about living their faith and values at work, but many corporate leaders are too focused on the short-term bottom line to listen. While corporate social responsibility has claimed a place on the agenda of global corporations, it is not an integral part of what most companies do. Few CEOs wake up in the morning and worry about the sustainability of the planet—or even the sustainability of their company. They are more likely to worry about delivering earnings growth in the current quarter, and the next one, to Wall Street. So much of the argument over how best to do business comes down to time horizons—whether it is worth absorbing a short-term hit to build a better company, or a better world, over time. "We believe that a company that pollutes the environment or mistreats its workers can get away with it for a while," says Julie Fox Gorte, director of social research for Calvert Asset Management, a social investing firm. "But eventually it's going to come back to haunt them."

The market will eventually settle this debate. Some companies will stick to business as usual. Others will be guided by their faith and embrace a broader view of their social responsibility. We'll see which ones perform better. Of course, there's no one "market." Businesses operate in many markets, none of them static—labor markets, stock markets, markets where they buy and sell goods, and the marketplace of public opinion, where reputations can be built or destroyed. Markets shape companies, but companies can change markets, too, as we'll see.

I believe that the business case for doing the right thing has become so compelling that companies that do good will also do well. We will look at some of the best of them in the pages ahead, beginning with a bakery in the struggling city of Yonkers, New York. You've probably tasted its brownies.

2

WHAT IS A SPIRITUAL BUSINESS?

GREYSTON BAKERY AND TOM'S OF MAINE

Walk along the waterfront in Yonkers, New York, and you notice two things right away: the dramatic cliffs of the Palisades across the Hudson River, and a neighborhood that is exhibiting unmistakable signs of rebirth. Yonkers, a working-class city of 196,000 people, has come through hard times. Some of the riverfront structures are dreary or worse—the aging city jail, an abandoned oil terminal and the ugly, low-slung offices of the state department of social services. But next to the railroad station stands a brand-new city library, and nearby, construction has begun on a waterfront park. There's talk of a minor-league baseball stadium. And just up the street, the Greyston Bakery is celebrating the opening of a $9.6 million plant and retail store, designed by the renowned architect Maya Lin. This is the most delectable ribbon cutting I've ever attended. Bakery workers serve carrot cake, cheesecake and pecan pie to hundreds of friends of Greyston who have come to join the celebration.

Most everyone in Yonkers loves Greyston. Two Republican mayoral candidates, bitter opponents in a recent primary, shared the stage at the ceremony with Nita Lowey, a Democratic congresswoman. "Greyston produces all this food to nourish the body," said Andy Spano, the Westchester County executive. "What they're really doing is nourishing the soul of a community."

The Greyston Bakery makes "sinful desserts that support saintly causes," a Zagat guide once said, and that's a good way to sum up this unique enterprise. Founded in 1982 by Bernard Glassman, a Brooklyn-born mathematician and Zen Buddhist priest, Greyston is now the center of a "mandala"—that's a Sanskrit word for circle—of organizations that serve the needy in Yonkers. These organizations provide apartments for the homeless, care for people with HIV/AIDS, furnish job training, child care and a community garden, all under the umbrella of the nonprofit Greyston Foundation. The foundation owns the bakery. But the bakery itself has always been and still remains a for-profit business, albeit one guided by carefully considered spiritual principles. It generated sales of $4.7 million and profits of $260,000 in 2002. More than any other company I've found—Tom's of Maine, whose story follows this one, comes closest—Greyston strives to do what could be called God's work. That's why Greyston is the first business we'll examine in some detail.

In essence, Greyston serves the poor by feeding the rich. A producer of gourmet cakes, tarts and brownies, Greyston hires Yonkers residents on a first-come, first-served basis because the company believes that everyone deserves a shot at a job. Once hired, workers get intensive training. They also get help with personal and family problems, whether or not those are job-related. Meetings at Greyston begin with a moment of silence. And all profits go to help the needy. Julius Walls Jr., the CEO of Greyston, is a forty-two-year-old African American businessman who as a teenager had dreamed of becoming a priest. Now, he says: "I think of a lot of what I do here at Greyston as my ministry."

At the ceremony, Walls spoke with emotion about how he and

his brothers stuck together when they grew up in a tough section of Brooklyn. He said he thinks of the fifty-five Greyston workers he leads as a family. "It's all right to want and need and ask for and get support," he told them. "We all need it. I promise you that, like a responsible big brother, I'll support you when you need it. I'll also challenge you when you need it. I love you. You inspire me. God bless you."

No one spiritual tradition shaped Greyston. Glassman, the Buddhist teacher who got it started, was raised as a Jew by parents who were devout socialists. Walls grew up as a Catholic and now worships in a Baptist church. No religion is practiced inside the bakery. But when Glassman and the Zen community he founded created Greyston, they did so with what Buddhists call "mindfulness"—that is, they considered the spiritual implications of every decision they made. "I was looking for a way for business itself to be a force for social change, and a way of spiritual transformation," Glassman said.

Glassman took a roundabout route to Greyston. Born in 1939 in the working-class neighborhood of Brighton Beach, he was the child of Eastern European immigrants. His parents' idealism, and the prejudice against both Jews and blacks that he witnessed as a kid, planted the seeds of his activism. But his first love was airplanes. So, after getting his college degree in engineering, Glassman became an aerospace engineer for McDonnell-Douglas, working on unmanned missions to Mars.

In the early 1960s, Glassman began the formal study of Zen at a temple in Los Angeles's Little Tokyo. Twenty years later, after becoming a Zen master, he moved back east to start the Zen Community of New York in Riverdale, an attractive section of the Bronx. With the goal of combining social activism with Zen Buddhism, Glassman and his students decided to start a business that would provide them with what Buddhists call a "right livelihood." By that, they meant a way of earning a living that does no harm to people or the earth, that provides an opportunity for personal and spiritual growth, and that benefits others. They chose to start the bakery. "Bakers," Glassman explained, "need many of the same qualities we were developing in our Zen practice: detailed care, mindfulness, meticulous attention and harmonious interaction among all the persons involved." Some community members wanted to make wholesome breads rather than fancy desserts, arguing that fancy cakes did not fulfill basic needs. But Glassman was not as doctrinaire. He had worked on weapons projects at McDonnell-Douglas, and he knew that some people sincerely believed that weapons could help preserve peace. Besides, he said: "There's a large population that enjoys cakes—including me—and I felt that if we could create the most delicious, healthiest cake possible, using real ingredients instead of harmful chemicals, then we'd be helping the cake-eating people."

Once the bakery did well enough to support the Zen community, Glassman and his students looked for a larger family to sustain. They moved Greyston to Yonkers to train homeless and chronically unemployed people. Training poor people, most of whom had never held a steady job, proved difficult, costly and time-consuming, and the Zen students struggled as they learned how to do it. "Emotionally, it was taxing," says Glassman. "People would not show up because their kid had been shot. There were lots of dysfunctional families, and drug problems." Patience and persistence were required from both the Buddhists and the new Greyston workers.

A turning point for Greyston arose after Glassman attended a gathering of socially conscious businesspeople and investors in Gold Lake, Colorado, in 1987. (This group formed the Social Venture Network, the trade association for socially responsible businesses.) At Gold Lake, Glassman met Ben Cohen of Ben & Jerry's. They found that they had lots in common besides desserts—they were about the same age, they'd grown up in Brooklyn and they were committed activists. They strolled around the lake and talked about how they might work together. In time, they devised a plan: Greyston would bake brownie wafers to go into Ben & Jerry's ice cream sandwiches.

Everyone at Greyston worried about whether they could make the transition from baking fancy pastries and custom-made cakes to mass-producing brownie ingredients. Greyston had to raise $500,000 to expand, and there was no guarantee that the Ben & Jerry's deal would pay off. Only after months of costly experimentation did Greyston secure a long-term contract from Ben & Jerry's. "It almost destroyed us," said Glassman. "Then it turned out to be a wonderful thing." Buddhists don't believe in God, but faith, or at least a deeply felt optimism—which may be the same thing—helped keep Greyston alive. Ben & Jerry's remains Greyston's biggest customer by far, generating about 80 percent of the bakery's revenues. Next time you buy Chocolate Fudge Brownie ice cream or frozen yogurt, two popular flavors created expressly to use Greyston's brownies, you'll be supporting Greyston.

Bernie Glassman left Greyston in 1996. The bakery was on a solid footing, and the Greyston Foundation had become a force in Yonkers, using government and private grants, as well as the bakery's earnings, to create a flourishing network of social service organizations. "Everything was in very good hands," he said. Glassman told me he felt called to do interfaith work on peace, social justice and environmental issues, and so he began a new organization called the Peacemaker Community, to which he still devotes his energies.

Right about then, Julius Walls Jr. found Greyston. He discovered the place almost by accident, although, not surprisingly, he sees a greater power at work. "I was supposed to be here, honestly," he said. Walls was working for the Cocoline Chocolate Co. when he made a sales call at Greyston. He didn't make a sale, but Greyston made a big impression on him. "It was all about providing jobs and opportunity," he said. "I loved it." Walls was ready for a change because he chafed at the way traditional companies did business. "It was a matter of us versus them," he said. "You paid the least amount possible to your employers and suppliers, and you charged the most you could to your customers." So Walls kept in touch with Greyston, did some fund-raising with the bakery and got hired as a marketing consultant in 1995. Two years later, he was named CEO.

Like Glassman, Walls hails from Brooklyn. The son of a corrections officer who worked for thirty-three years at Riker's Island, he grew up in a public housing project in Bedford-Stuyvesant. Walls was educated in Catholic schools—his African American parish paid his tuition—and he was studying for the priesthood at a small Brooklyn seminary called the College of the Immaculate Conception when he decided that he wanted to have a family. (He and his wife, Cheryl, now live in Yonkers with their three children.) He switched to Baruch College, a branch of the City University of New York, where he could go to school at night while working days. He studied business and was elected president of the student body.

An outgoing and opinionated man, Walls has taken Greyston to new heights. He made a concerted effort from the start to raise expectations and deliver the messages that sales, efficiency and profits all matter. "There used to be a mentality on the part of the employees who came here that if you're really nice, we'll figure something out to keep you and it doesn't matter if you're producing or if the business is doing well," Walls said. That's no longer the case. "You must perform," he said. "We have very strict standards." By taking a disciplined approach to its business, Greyston is better able to fulfill its core mission, which is to be a "force for personal transformation and community development." The business and social agendas, in other words, go hand in hand.

Walls instituted "open hiring" at Greyston, both to eliminate favoritism and because he believes everyone deserves the opportunity to work. Many of Greyston's fifty-five or so employees are formerly unemployed or homeless, recovering from substance abuse or returning to the city from prison. "People can change their life, change their habits, change their behavior and move forward," Walls said. "We won't hold your past behavior against you." Interestingly, Walls has learned from the open hiring practice that it's all but impossible to predict who will succeed and who won't. "There are people I would not have hired who are managers now," he said.

As the son of a prison guard, Walls is unsentimental about the problems associated with poverty, drug abuse and crime. So he takes a no-nonsense approach to the Greyston workforce. New workers enter a twelve- to sixteen-week apprenticeship program during which they are regularly graded on attendance, punctuality, attitude and productivity. "Yes, they will have learned something about baking, mixing, depositing, cutting brownies," Walls says. "But the goal of that program is that they learn how to work." Trainees meet as a group with Walls every two weeks and are reminded that they will be held accountable for their performance. Most workers meet the standards, but those who fall short quit or are fired.

Still, Walls preaches accountability in the context of a compassionate workplace. "We talk about self-sufficiency within community," he said. When he saw that Greyston workers were asking their supervisors to help them with personal and family problems, he worried that it was too much to ask managers to be the "momma and poppa and counselor and therapist" for their people. But the company didn't want to turn its back, either. So Greyston created a department called Pathmaker Services, run by a social worker, to help workers with their problems, whether or not they are job-related. (Some big firms offer a corporate version of Pathmaker in the form of confidential employee assistance programs, but Greyston goes further, helping with issues ranging from finding apartments to collecting child support.) Greyston also will lend money to its workers, give them small grants to pursue their education and help them prepare resumes if they decide they want to leave. The underlying message is clear: Greyston's people are valued for who they are, not just for what they can do for the company.

I talked with several Greyston workers at the opening of the new bakery. Before joining Greyston in 2000, Steve Gill, who is thirty-four, had struggled to make ends meet and take care of his two daughters. He began as an entry-level baker, became an assistant in purchasing and now works as purchasing manager. "I continue to grow," he said, and the company is helping him to pursue a college degree. Vernate Miller, 52, joined Greyston in 1999, as part of the federal welfare-to-work program. He'd been unable to hold down a job for most of his life. "I'll be honest with you," he told me. "I didn't want to work." Now, he said, he never misses a day at Greyston, and he convinced his brother to get a job there, too. Somehow he supports his wife, who has lupus, and three children on a salary of about $330 a week.

With its new facility and expanding payroll, Greyston will have to do a better job of marketing its cakes and tarts, which account for about 20 percent of revenues. Some are sold retail, but they are pricey—$18 for a New York cheesecake, $25 for a triple chocolate mousse cake. Most are purchased by Manhattan restaurants that want to provide fine desserts but can't afford to hire their own pastry chef. Walls would eventually like to market Greyston as a brand so that eateries could proudly tell their customers they are serving desserts by Greyston. "We'll market the product first, but we will also market the mission," says Walls. The product is already a hit: when Zagat's rated the bakery, it was ranked along with several others as number two out of 160 bakeries, just behind Paillard, a chic French patisserie on the Upper East Side.

The Greyston story demonstrates that it is possible to create and operate a successful business that embodies spiritual values. Greyston has been shaped by the principle that people should be valued for who they are, by the belief that we are all interconnected, by the desire to serve others and by the hope that the work we do can nourish our souls.

Is Greyston's model replicable? In theory, it is—but Glassman and Walls both note that very few of Greyston's achievements have come easily. The bakery is a small workplace that has benefited from patient, charismatic and deeply committed leadership. Companies that required highly skilled labor can't hire the majority of their workers from the ranks of the poor. And Greyston has been sustained by the Ben & Jerry's deal, which took root because of the common vision of Bernie Glassman and Ben Cohen.

Still, other companies can learn from Greyston's deep commitment to its people. They can hire and train more people who are mistakenly labeled as unemployable, and get a lifetime of loyalty in return. Or they can simply invest more to develop their people. Such investments pay off, Julius Walls believes firmly. "As we've taken care of our employees, our employees have taken care of this business," he said. Of course, the ultimate payoff—for Greyston and its people—goes well beyond taking care of business.

IT's a long way from Yonkers to Kennebunk, Maine, a bucolic coastal resort of 10,400 year-round residents. While tourism is the bulwark of the local economy, Tom's of Maine, with about 150 employees, is the biggest business in town. A family-owned firm, Tom's makes all-natural personal care products in a small factory that was formerly the town railroad station. (Here the scent is not of chocolate brownies but of toothpaste.) Nearby, the firm's headquarters occupy a renovated shoe factory overlooking the picturesque Mousam River, with its gurgling waterfall. It's no wonder that Tom's has launched an ambitious promotional campaign that connects its products to the protection of America's rivers.

By any measure, Tom's of Maine is a successful enterprise. Tom and Kate Chappell, who have been married for thirty-seven years, started the company in 1970 with a $5,000 loan and a single product, a biodegradable laundry detergent that might have been successful, except that it did not do a very good job of cleaning clothes. From that inauspicious beginning, they built Tom's of Maine into a trusted brand, albeit for a niche market of health-conscious and socially aware consumers. In 2003, Tom's sold more than $35 million of toothpaste, mouthwash, deodorant, soap, shaving cream and wellness tonics—enough to get the attention of industry giants like Procter & Gamble, Colgate and Unilever, which at one time or another have expressed interest in acquiring the privately held firm.

But what makes Tom's of Maine worth our attention is that the Chappells have explicitly made values, not toothpaste or deodorant, the driver of their business. Tom Chappell, the company's chairman and CEO, is a devout Episcopalian and a midlife graduate of the Harvard Divinity School; his years there reshaped his thinking about how to run the company. He has written two thoughtful books about business and values, and he founded the nonprofit Saltwater Institute, which helps leaders to live their values at work. Most importantly, he is both earnest and disciplined about his efforts to infuse spiritual values into every corner of Tom's of Maine: The company makes all-natural products that are safe and effective. It seeks to cultivate fulfilling relationships with its workers. It treats its customers with respect. It tries to minimize its environmental footprint. And it donates 10 percent of its pretax profits to charity. (The norm is less than 2 percent.) Those practices reflect the values that have sustained Tom's for more than three decades, Chappell said: "Do what's good for people. Do what's good for the environment. And make money doing it. Those are the goals that we began with, and they haven't changed."

Tall and lean at age sixty, wearing a woolen shirt and khakis on the day we met, Chappell looks like the Yankee he is. He has a long face, a shock of white hair, a ready laugh and the deep voice of an old-time country preacher. Given his age and the fact that Kate has decided to devote herself to painting, Tom has begun to think seriously about how the company will fare without him. He hopes to pass control of Tom's on to others who will preserve its values. "We are not going to sell to a P&G or a Colgate," Chappell declared. "We're not the least bit interested." Selling would make sense only if financial security were uppermost in his mind. "The money would be unbelievable," he said. The Chappells still own a majority of the shares, although they have parceled out small stakes over the years to a number of like-minded investors, notably John Whitehead, the retired chairman of Goldman Sachs. In the mid-1990s they briefly pondered selling, going so far as to hire an investment banker to value the firm. But they decided to stay the course, for several reasons. Their five children, who range in age from twenty to thirty-seven, have all worked at Tom's, and several are now executives who might one day want to run the place. The Chappells also felt an obligation to their workers. "There's no guarantee, with a sale, that these people would have a job and a factory in Kennebunk, Maine," Chappell says. "And there's no assurance that the brand will have the same value, because of its values, that it has today." One of Chappell's heroes, the maverick CNN founder Ted Turner, sold his cable networks to Time Warner and quickly came to regret it. Chappell does not want to make a similar mistake.

Besides, he has bigger things in mind than Tom's. Chappell believes that he is pioneering a new paradigm for American business—one that seeks to build long-term value by integrating the pursuit of the common good with the pursuit of profit. "Creating values-driven companies is a whole new way of looking at a brand of capitalism that has been in history's driver's seat since the middle of the 19th century," Chappell has written. "We must create a new kind of capitalism—with a heart and soul." To make his case that values can build value, Chappell wants to build Tom's into an even bigger success and then take the company public, so that more business-people recognize what he has done. "If social responsibility is going to work," he told me, "it has to work in the financial marketplace. People are going to have to see this as an attractive financial asset."

Chappell himself never doubted that business could be a moral pursuit. While Tom's of Maine is a product of the back-to-nature ethic of the 1960s, he is a child of the 1950s. His belief in the goodness of business, his religious faith and his love of the outdoors can all be traced back to his boyhood in Pittsfield, Massachusetts, where his father owned a textile business and Tom sang in the church choir. Chappell literally enjoyed a Norman Rockwell childhood—at age ten he was painted by Rockwell and appeared, as an altar boy, on the cover of the *Saturday Evening Post.* After boarding school and college, he worked as a salesman at the Aetna Insurance Co. before relocating to Maine. There, he and Kate, who is an artist and writer, got into organic gardening, helped develop an alternative school and launched a company that was then called Tom's Natural Soaps.

They struggled at first. Their nonpolluting laundry detergent, called Clearlake, was sold in reusable containers, complete with prepaid postage, so they could be mailed back to the company. "It had all the social responsibility you could want," Chappell said. It just didn't get clothes clean. Chappell remembered telling a skeptical buyer for Hanover's supermarkets that his customers would want the product, and that if they didn't, the store ought to tell them that they should want it. The buyer looked him in the eye and said quietly: "We don't tell people what they should want here." Today, Chappell laughs out loud at the memory of his youthful arrogance. "I was so indignant that he didn't get it," he said.

The story is revealing. Like many successful entrepreneurs, Chappell has struggled over the years to harness his ego. It's a tricky business, knowing the difference between the boldness that leaders need to take risks and the arrogance that blinds them to mistakes. In 1975, for example, Chappell read a bunch of toothpaste labels and somehow became convinced that consumers had an appetite for natural toothpaste, free of the chemicals that went into Crest or Colgate. Others doubted him, especially because chemicals like saccharine give most toothpaste its familiar sweetness. He didn't care, and he was right. Natural toothpaste quickly made the company a success, and to this day, an array of toothpastes that come in such flavors as apricot and fennel generate more than 60 percent of the firm's revenues. Chappell was also advised not to expand into deodorants; he did so, and they, too, sold well. "Had I listened to my advisors and friends, even Kate, we never would have created the products that turned Tom's into a competitive presence on the shelves," he said. His audacity enabled Chappell to start Tom's, create new products and buck conventional thinking about how business should be conducted.

The trouble is, when left unchecked, the sheer force of Chappell's passion and personality can intimidate others, and his pride can leave him impervious to critics. He writes: "Even after almost a decade of lecturing and writing about my belief that corporate

America has to junk its autocratic, know-it-all tendencies and partner up with our so-called subordinates, I am still as naturally self-
interested, overconfident, full of pride and eager to control a
meeting as any CEO in America." For years, Chappell made virtually all of the big decisions at Tom's by himself, even though he had
never run a company before.

As Tom's grew from a mom-and-pop operation into a bona fide
company, Chappell needed help. He hired a bunch of hotshot MBAs
to assist him with the nuts and bolts of the business—expanding
distribution, refining the business model and improving margins.
The new crop of executives moved the company beyond natural
foods stores, most in New England, and into drugstores and supermarkets across the country. But they did not share Chappell's commitment to values. Too often, he thought, Tom's operated like any
other business. Men dominated the firm, even though most of its
customers were women. Aggressive competition, turf battles and
making the numbers took precedence over caring about people.
Tom's was growing fast, and its success had made Chappell a
wealthy man. But the business was not as much fun, and his discon-
tent set off some intense self-examination. "My everyday business
life had gone stale," he said. "It was one calculation after another."
He wondered out loud whether he wanted to devote the rest of his
life to selling toothpaste, even of the chemical-free variety. He asked
himself if he should leave business altogether.

He sought answers in divinity school. Beginning in 1986, Chappell spent two days a week attending classes at Harvard, juggling his
academic work with his responsibilities as a husband, a father of five
and a CEO. Spending one or two nights a week at a retreat center in
Cambridge, he took time to think anew about himself, his values,
his company and how they all fit together. He was surprised to discover how much the great moral and religious teachers had to say
about his desire for meaningful work. Reading the sermons of the
eighteenth-century preacher Jonathan Edwards, for example, Chappell was struck by Edwards' idea of "being as relation"—the notion

that while each of us is an individual, our identity is defined primarily by our relationships to others and to God. As a New Englander, Chappell had always thought of himself as proudly self-reliant. Now, he realized, he could not see himself as separate from God, from Kate, from his family, his friends, his company and his community. Business, he thought, could be best understood as a network of relationships, connecting owners, workers, customers, suppliers and communities, all of them interdependent.

Chappell was fascinated, too, by the twentieth-century Jewish philosopher Martin Buber, whose landmark book *I and Thou* distinguished between "I-it" relationships, where other people are treated as objects to be used, and "I-thou" relationships, where others are respected, honored or loved for who they are. Too many business transactions, Chappell thought, were dominated by an "I-it" way of thinking, in which one party or another tried to get the upper hand. Too few took an "I-thou" approach, where each person honored the other. He and Kate had begun by thinking about their customers as individuals, as neighbors or even friends, but the marketing professionals he had hired lumped people into demographic and psychographic groups, to be targeted with clever messages. The very word *targeted* dehumanized the consumer.

Chappell left divinity school with a master's degree and the firm conviction that Tom's had gotten off track. He distributed writings by Edwards, Buber and Immanuel Kant to his board of directors and senior managers, and he invited H. Richard Niebuhr, a scholar of religion, to speak at a corporate gathering. The company rewrote its mission statement to put values at the center. Tom's promised, among other things, "to respect, value, and serve not only our customers but our co-workers, owners, agents, suppliers and community; to be concerned about and contribute to their well-being, and to operate with integrity so as to be deserving of their trust." Chappell wrote a book, called *The Soul of a Business,* about managing for profit and the common good. "I had to spend four years at the Harvard Divinity School," he wrote, "to find out that my religious

beliefs, my respect for people and the environment—my values—
did not have to get in the way of making a profit."

Still, doing the right thing can sometimes conflict with business
goals. In 1993, chemists at Tom's reformulated the firm's honey-
suckle deodorant by adding lichen, a natural antimicrobial. Complaints poured in: fully half of the customers said the deodorant
made them smell worse. Tests showed they were not mistaken.
Recalling the deodorant would cost $400,000, wiping out 30 per-
cent of the firm's projected annual profit that year. "We had a genuine moral dilemma—profits versus values," Chappell said. With
some reluctance, Chappell ordered the recall and sent free samples
of an improved formulation to two thousand customers who had
complained. Another time, Tom's spent about $300,000 to test its
toothpaste on humans, in order to get the American Dental Association's seal of approval. (Most toothpaste is tested on rats, which
costs much, much less.) Tom's won't test its products on animals.
Chappell conceded that letting values drive the business costs more
in the short run; he hopes and believes that doing the right thing
will pay off over time with employees and customers.

The argument that a company's values help attract, retain and
engage employees is relatively straightforward. Tom's is a good
place to work: it offers its workers three months of paid maternity
leave, subsidized child care, time off to do volunteer work and exercise classes in a company-owned wellness center. No one can be
required to work nights or weekends and, when possible, people set
their own schedules. Jill Schmidt, a longtime employee who oversees the laboratory, works a thirty-two-hour week so that she can be
with her children when they come home from school. "The flexibility has been fabulous," she said. Everyone gets Friday afternoons off
in July and August, to enjoy the brief Maine summer. "Treat an
employee as a cog in the machine, and you'll get a cog's work,"
Chappell writes. "Treat that same person as a member of your family, and you'll get eternal loyalty." Providing good wages and benefits
is a relatively simple, if costly, way to do that.

Creating a great workplace culture is harder. Chappell would like Tom's to be both a community of people who care for one another and a high-performing organization. So, on one hand, he encourages his employees to get to know and value one another as people. People work in teams, with lots of listening and sharing of ideas. Executives go on retreats to build closer relationships, and the company regularly gathers for picnics, birthday celebrations and retirement parties. None of that, though, means that the company can accept substandard work or tolerate an executive who does not grow along with the firm. "Without competency, everything breaks down," Chappell said. With that in mind, he recently instituted 120-day performance reviews during which employees have to meet exacting standards. "If someone is not performing, that's not just a problem for them," he said. "It creates a dysfunction that goes beyond them." The needs of the business, in other words, must take precedence over building a caring community because without a thriving business, there can be no community.

Whether Tom's can turn its values into a selling point with customers is a more difficult question to answer. Like any good salesman, Chappell would like to build long-lasting relationships with the people who buy his products. Boxes of toothpaste and deodorant sticks are jam-packed with information—not merely lists of ingredients but also exhortations to support environmental causes that are signed, "Your friends, Tom and Kate." This may sound cloying, but it reflects the reality that at least some of Tom's customers feel an affinity for the company and its causes. Every year, Tom's gets about forty thousand letters, phone calls and e-mails from customers, and about 85 percent are positive. That's an astonishing ratio. (The most frequent message is a letter or e-mail thanking the firm for not testing its products on animals.) Each letter and e-mail gets a personal response, a standard that pushes the limits of the creativity of a five-person team devoted to consumer dialog. "There are only so many ways to say thank you for calling, but we do try to avoid canned text," says Patti Murphy, who leads the group. The point is, treat people the way you'd like to be treated—and no one likes getting a form letter.

Chappell wants to get the word out about Tom's efforts to serve the common good because he believes that customers do care about where their money goes. "In spite of the cynicism they are justified in feeling," he said, "consumers still are hopeful that they can believe in something and somebody. We think you can build a brand on shared values." This is a big idea that is, for the most part, untested; several companies in this book are trying to figure out how to incorporate their values into their marketing. But clearly, some consumers—how many, no one knows—do care about how corporations conduct themselves, and adjust their buying habits accordingly. To that end, Tom's has launched its biggest promotion ever around the National Rivers Awareness Project, a five-year partnership with the National Parks Service and two environmental groups, River Network and the Nature Conservancy. Designed to draw attention to the plight of American rivers—most are polluted to some degree—the campaign encourages people to work with local cleanup and advocacy groups. Thousands of people who buy Tom's toothpaste will get a free DVD explaining how they can get involved. If all goes according to plan, Chappell said, the partnership will build the Tom's brand and serve the common good.

Tom's could use a boost. Several years ago, the company bought an organic farm in Vermont and entered the herbal supplements business. But the field is crowded, and new products such as a valerian tonic and echinacea extract have been slow to catch on. "We got in over our head," Chappell said. "We lost our focus." The company, which had been consistently profitable, lost money for about eighteen months. Chappell's commitment to values may have caused him to lose business focus. "I keep urging Tom to focus on sales and profits first and social responsibility next," an investor in the firm, who requested anonymity, told me.

Meanwhile, Tom's growth curve has flattened. Revenues have been increasing by 5 or 6 percent a year. Chappell would like to drive the growth rate up closer to 30 percent. "Growth is our only defense," he said, with some urgency. "I've watched toothpaste niches grow to 3 or 4 percent market share and then fade to nothing. You need momentum. You need scale. Without scale and momentum, you are highly vulnerable." Moreover, Chappell wants to take the company public, to prove that a business driven by values can consistently deliver the earnings growth that Wall Street demands. With few exceptions—most of them companies that pay a steady dividend—businesses need growth to attract investors. Only by driving growth and going public, Chappell said, will he be able to prove that his new business paradigm is replicable.

But is it replicable? The problem facing Tom's is what entrepreneurs who start socially responsible companies describe as the legacy problem—the challenge of preserving the values, as well as the business, when the founder steps down. It's a vexing challenge, as companies like Ben & Jerry's, which is now a unit of the global food giant Unilever, or Odwalla, which was sold to Coca-Cola, have learned. Like Greyston, where the social mission preceded the business, Tom's of Maine, with its divinity school grad at the helm, is a unique enterprise. I have told their stories because Greyston and Tom's are among the very few companies that are explicitly guided by spiritual values. They set standards that others are unlikely to meet. But they are also small companies where the influence of the founders remains strong. Next we will visit a much bigger company, Southwest Airlines, which employs thirty-five thousand people. It had a legacy problem of its own when its founder, Herb Kelleher, stepped down in 2001, just before the airline industry entered the worst crisis in its history. That would test the spirit of Southwest as never before.

3

CAN A BIG COMPANY HAVE A HEART?

SOUTHWEST AIRLINES

September 11, 2001, began like any other morning for Colleen Barrett, the president and chief operating officer of Southwest Airlines. Barrett, who is the highest-ranking woman in the U.S. airline industry, got up at 4 A.M. and spent about an hour and a half reading mail from customers and employees, as she does most mornings. She arrived at company headquarters in Dallas by 7 A.M. and had another quiet hour to herself before her daily round of meetings was to begin. The single mother of a grown son, Barrett is, by her own admission, a workaholic—one who has devoted her energies to Southwest since the late 1960s, even before its first plane took flight. She will tell you that she loves the airline and its people like family. "We use the word *love* a lot around here," Barrett says. "That's pretty edgy in corporate America." Southwest's home base is Love Field in Dallas, and its stock symbol is LUV.

In September of 2001, Barrett and Jim Parker, the CEO of Southwest, had a lot to prove. They had taken over the top jobs at the airline just three months earlier, when Herb Kelleher, Southwest's flamboyant president, CEO and chairman, stepped back from day-to-day operations. Kelleher, who remains chairman of the board, has gotten much of the credit for Southwest's success, and deservedly so—he is a shrewd executive and a charismatic leader whose bighearted, fun-loving approach to business personifies the Southwest spirit. (Herb, as everyone calls him, has appeared in public dressed as Elvis and the Easter Bunny, and he once arm-wrestled the CEO of another company for the use of an advertising slogan.) Southwest was so closely identified with Kelleher that people wondered how the airline would fare without him. It was up to Parker, a low-key lawyer, to demonstrate that Southwest's pioneering business model—it was the first low-cost, low-fare, short-haul, point-to-point airline in the United States—could continue to spread across America, and perhaps eventually to the rest of the world. Barrett had to prove that Southwest's caring culture, which is every bit as unique, could be sustained without Kelleher as the company kept growing. Southwest had fewer than 200 employees when it began flying in 1971; three decades later, it employed 31,500 people.

On September 11, one of those people interrupted Barrett's first meeting with the news that a plane had hit the World Trade Center in New York. She turned on CNN, called Kelleher at home, then headed for the boardroom for an emergency gathering of Southwest's senior executives. Within an hour, the Federal Aviation Administration had shut down the airspace over the United States for the first time ever. In the boardroom, Greg Wells, a vice president for safety, security and flight dispatch, began counting down the number of Southwest planes that remained in the air; one plane was unaccounted for, for what seemed like hours, until they discovered that it had been diverted to Grand Rapids, Michigan. "That's when it really hit me," Wells said later. "I knew we were out of danger. Yet I knew the real battle had just begun."

Southwest was out of business, like every airline, and no one knew when commercial planes would fly again. The company had to deal with unprecedented challenges—logistical, financial, security-related. Recalled Barrett: "I basically spent the next three days in the boardroom, with very little time for sleep or anything else."

Southwest and its people were tested as never before that week. No one in the industry could have anticipated a terrorist attack that would turn airplanes into weapons of war. Nor could executives huddled in Dallas deal with every contingency as Southwest jets landed unexpectedly in cities across America. But, as Barrett and Parker and others realized later, Southwest turned out to have been extraordinarily well prepared for 9/11 and its aftershocks.

For one thing, Southwest's people were accustomed to solving problems on their own. This isn't an airline that runs by the book. Reservations agents, ticket agents, flight attendants, even pilots and baggage handlers are trained to help customers first and ask questions later. "We've got rules," Barrett says. "You can't have a company and not have rules. But basically we talk ten times more about doing the right thing than we do about rules and procedures."

So, for example, when Terry Taylor, a Chicago-based captain, learned that the Southwest flight bound for Providence, Rhode Island, that he was piloting was being diverted to Grand Rapids, Michigan, he improvised. Because Grand Rapids is not served by Southwest, the airline has no ground personnel there. After Taylor landed the plane, he explained to his sixty-five passengers what had happened, commandeered a set of air stairs and led them into the terminal himself. Next, he and his first officer climbed into the cargo bins and unloaded the bags. They found hotel rooms for some people and arranged rental cars for others. The next morning, Taylor took the remaining passengers to the Amtrak station, where, using his personal credit card, he bought them tickets to return to Chicago.

Similar stories unfolded everywhere. Eighty-five of the 360 Southwest flights operating at the time of the attack were diverted. In Moline, Illinois, a captain escorted a boy traveling alone to a hotel room, where they played Nintendo; later he took his crew and customers to a movie. In Colorado Springs, a girl traveling alone shared a hotel room with a flight attendant. In Nashville, two children went to stay with the sister-in-law of a Southwest worker who volunteered to help. Southwest's people even reached out to competitors—they delivered home-baked cookies to reservations centers in Phoenix operated by United and American Airlines, the two carriers whose planes had been hijacked.

Southwest was well prepared financially, too. It had the lowest costs, the strongest balance sheet and the highest credit rating in the U.S. airline industry. This was Kelleher's legacy. A fiscal conservative, he had helped steer Southwest through a series of rough patches—the Arab oil embargo of 1973, a spike in jet fuel prices in 1979–80, and recessions in the early 1980s and early 1990s. Given the volatility of the airline business, he believed in anticipating worst-case scenarios. "If we manage in good times as though it is the bad times," Kelleher often said, "then when the bad times do come, we will be better prepared to weather the downturn." Even so, in the days after 9/11, Southwest had to borrow $1.1 billion and postpone the delivery of new aircraft to make sure it had plenty of cash on hand. Everyone knew that it would take months or years for air travel to return to normal—if indeed it ever would.

Facing brutal pressures, most airlines responded by squeezing both their employees and their customers. In the weeks after September 11, the industry laid off 122,000 people—about 20 percent of its workforce. The other big carriers eliminated flights, rolled back wages and benefits, reduced the size of crews and served fewer meals. Remarkably, Southwest did none of that—it did not cut back its flight schedule or lay off a single worker. (Eliminating meals was not an option since Southwest does not serve any.) While rank-and-file workers offered to give back some of their pay to help preserve jobs, their generosity was unnecessary. "We did not talk about furloughs," Barrett said. "It was a given that we would not lay anyone off." While the bonds of loyalty between a company and its employees have disappeared in most of corporate America, they remain strong at Southwest. "Nothing kills your company's culture like layoffs," Kelleher had said in a farewell interview as CEO with *Fortune.* "We could have furloughed at various times and been more profitable, but I always thought that was shortsighted. . . . The thing that would disturb me most to see after I'm no longer CEO is layoffs." His successors were not about to let him down.

Nor would they disappoint Southwest's customers if they could avoid doing so. Although the customer does not come first at Southwest—the employee does, as we'll see—an ethic of service is at the core of Southwest's culture. Kelleher, Barrett and others at the company talk about "servant leadership," a management philosophy developed by a former AT&T executive and practicing Quaker named Robert K. Greenleaf that says that the job of a leader is to serve others, enabling them to flourish. Everyone at Southwest is encouraged to think of his or her work as a form of service, either to customers, to fellow employees or to both. Immediately after the terrorist attacks, Southwest announced that it would offer full refunds to passengers who had bought tickets to fly anytime in September. That was the most accommodating policy of any major carrier. "If we are going to be true to who we are, we've got to give them their money back," said Gary Kelly, Southwest's CFO. It ended up costing the company $50 million to $100 million, he later estimated, but customers were grateful.

This underscored another way that Southwest was prepared for 9/11: it had the most loyal customers of any airline. Remarkably, some customers responded to the attacks by sending to Southwest the coupons they had earned for free flights or refund checks they were owed. "We want to try and give back something for the years of great service," wrote a California couple, who sent a $66 credit back to Southwest. Barrett was touched, although not entirely surprised, to read such letters. "Show that you care, and that you really want to take that extra step, and people will pay you back a million times over," she said. Parker calls it the "round world" theory—that what goes around comes around.

The Southwest slogan—"Freedom to Fly"—took on special meaning on the morning of September 14, 2001. About a thousand Southwest workers amassed behind a security fence at Love Field to watch the first plane take off. "It was almost as if, as a company, we wanted to get as close to that plane as possible," said one executive. People waved banners and flags, and someone began to sing "God Bless America." "Only then did I realize how quiet it had been," said Barrett. Out of pride, relief or exhaustion, or perhaps all three, she began to cry. So did Kelleher and most everyone else. It was Barrett's fifty-seventh birthday. "I couldn't have had a neater birthday present," she said. "It was an incredible moment." Southwest was back.

People say that character is not made in a crisis; it is revealed. Southwest's character had been built day by day, decision by decision, during three decades. It was revealed during three days in September of 2001.

W HEN I went to see Colleen Barrett about eighteen months later, as the Iraq war was winding down, the U.S. airline industry remained in dire straits. A perfect storm of bad news—the war, fear of terrorism, a sluggish economy, burdensome security procedures and a mysterious new disease known as severe acute respiratory syndrome (SARS)—had devastated the air travel business. Collectively, the airlines had lost $7.8 billion in 2001 and another $10 billion in 2002. Two big carriers, United and US Airways, had been forced into Chapter 11 bankruptcy, even after receiving federal aid. Despite slashing labor costs and curbing service, the major airlines were losing money. "Even in the best of times," wrote Jamie Baker, an industry analyst with J. P. Morgan, "we consider all airlines whose names start with something other than 'Southwest' to be bankruptcy candidates."

Southwest was not immune to the slump. Because the demand for air travel remained sluggish, its revenues were down. So were earnings. But at least Southwest *had* earnings. That, by itself, was a triumph. The airline had managed to eke out profits during every quarter of the downturn, including the September 11 quarter. In 2002, Southwest generated $5.5 billion in revenues and $241 million in profits, thereby preserving a remarkable streak for an airline— thirty consecutive years of profitability, dating back to 1973. (It kept the streak alive in 2003.) When *Money* magazine celebrated its thirtieth anniversary in the fall of 2002, it ran an article called "The 30 Best Stocks" that began like this:

> It was straight out of Ripley's. When *Money* asked Ned David Research this summer to compile a list of the 30 best performing stocks since our debut in 1972, it seemed obvious that the No. 1 performer would reflect the brawn-to-brains transformation of the U.S. economy. Probably a technology stock. Or a big name in pharmaceuticals.
>
> What we were not expecting was an airline—Southwest Airlines, to be precise. Since August 1972, Southwest has produced annualized returns of 25.99%, which means that had you invested $10,000 in Southwest 30 years ago, your stake would be worth a little over $10.2 million today. Southwest, of course, is not your typical airline.

No, Southwest is not your typical airline. I'd come to ask Barrett what has made it so atypical—and so successful.

I got my first clue as I walked down a long, wide-open hallway to Barrett's office. Southwest's headquarters do not look like any other corporate office I've seen. The walls are covered by framed photos of Southwest's people, banners commemorating company milestones, old advertisements or mementos from parties or celebrations. I felt as if I was walking through a life-sized family album; there's even a hallway lined with pictures of employees and their pets. Barrett's office, too, is homey, cluttered with photos and mementos, hearts of all kinds and a comfy couch. There's no pretense here. A white-haired, matronly woman with wire-rimmed glasses, Barrett looks like the grandmother she is. (She was divorced many years ago. Her son, Pat, is grown and the father of a six-year-old boy.) On the day of my visit, she was comfortably dressed in slacks and a Harley-Davidson sweatshirt. To understand Southwest, she told me, we need to start at the beginning.

Most Southwest employees know the story of the airline's birth: In a bar in San Antonio in 1966, a pilot and businessman named Rollin King proposed to his lawyer, Herb Kelleher, that they start a low-fare airline. If they kept it in Texas, King explained, they could start flying without having to get permission from federal regulators. King scrawled a triangle on a cocktail napkin, with the corners representing Dallas, Houston and San Antonio—Southwest's first route map. When Kelleher asked where they'd get the capital, King looked puzzled for a moment and said they'd just have to raise it. Kelleher shut his eyes in disbelief, and when he opened them, King was grinning wildly at him, like a man who knows that he's pushing the limits of common sense. "Rollin, you're crazy," Herb exclaimed. "Let's do it."

It would not be easy. For five years, the pilot and the lawyer and the lawyer's indefatigable legal secretary—that would be Colleen Barrett, who kept Herb organized and on time and in the process learned all there was to know about the airline business—shuttled from regulatory agencies to courtrooms to banks, trying to get Southwest off the ground. (King himself flew twenty-five to thirty hours a month during Southwest's early years and became a member of its board of directors.) Three entrenched carriers—Continental, Braniff and Texas International—sued to prevent the upstart from getting permission to fly, and the legal battle eventually reached the U.S. Supreme Court. The big carriers were so hellbent on squashing Southwest that they pressured bankers and vendors not to do business with Kelleher and his people. This was more than fierce competition: in 1975, the federal government indicted Braniff and Texas International for violating antitrust laws by colluding against Southwest. They pleaded no contest, and each paid a $100,000 fine.

Those battles turned out to be blessings, Barrett recalled, laughing at the memory. The free publicity alone was worth millions to a start-up like Southwest. "If those big, bad guys had just kept their mouths shut and had not been so arrogant and so sure that they could keep us on the ground, we would have been bankrupt in two years," she said. "That was what created our culture. That was what created our spirit." Early on, Southwest hired mostly people who had been laid off by other carriers; these people had the airline business in their blood, they did not want to do anything else and they did not take kindly to the idea that their bigger competitors wanted to shut them down. "There is nothing stronger in terms of building spirit than letting somebody think they are being challenged," Barrett said. "Did we grab on to that and take advantage of it? Hell, yes. Herb created the battle culture. He created the warrior spirit."

Southwest loved a good fight. Even after it was well established, the airline saw itself as an underdog. When United Airlines announced plans to launch a low-fare West Coast shuttle in the mid-1990s, Kelleher issued a call to arms that reflects the fighting spirit of Southwest:

Since the collapse of Russia's Aeroflot [he wrote to every Southwest employee] United Airlines has become the largest airline in the world, approximating seven times the size of Southwest, in terms of gross revenues per year.

The world's largest airline has recently announced that it will launch its initial direct assault against Southwest, in the western part of our route system. . . .

In addition to our stock price, our wages, our benefits, our job security, our expansion opportunities, and, foremost, our pride of accomplishment as our nation's best airline are all on the line, as the war begins with United Shuttle on October 1, 1994. . . .

I am betting on your minds, your hearts, your souls and your spirits to continue our success. Let's win this one and make aviation history—again!

To Kelleher, the competition between Southwest and its bigger rivals was nothing less than a battle between the forces of good and evil.

Kelleher could rally his troops this way because Southwest and its people saw themselves as fighting for something more important than the company's bottom line. Their cause—their higher purpose, if you will—was to keep airfares low so that more people could afford to fly. "Southwest is in the business of allowing people from every walk of life to see and do things they never dreamed of," said Roy Spence, the charismatic CEO of GSD&M, the Austin, Texas–based advertising agency that has created Southwest's ads since the 1980s. Southwest's long-running "Freedom to Fly" campaign, which uses the tagline "You are now free to fly about the country," is aimed at Southwest's own people as well as at its customers, Barrett said. "I tell the pilots and flight attendants that they must never think that our freedom campaign is just a campaign or propaganda," she said. "It is absolutely who we are. We have opened up the skies of America."

This is not just rhetoric; it is the reality, as people realize when they fly Southwest and talk to their fellow passengers. On a recent flight from Baltimore to Hartford, I sat with a couple from Maryland who spend every fall weekend in New England, watching their son play college football—something they couldn't afford to do if they didn't fly Southwest. My teenage daughters visit their grandmother more often because they can fly from Baltimore to Long Island for as little as $49. (Southwest's average passenger airfare is about $86.) Before Southwest came along, only about 25 percent of Americans had ever taken an airline trip; today, about 75 percent have flown. When Southwest enters a new market, traffic goes up and the fares charged by the other airlines go down.

To accomplish its mission, Southwest reinvented the airline business. It flies mostly short-haul, point-to-point routes, eschewing the hub-and-spoke system favored by others. It deploys only one plane, the Boeing 737; that reduces the costs of training, maintenance and spare parts. Southwest also gets its planes in and out of airports faster than its competitors; that means that the airline can use its gates more effectively, keep its people busy and keep planes in the air longer. It sells most of its tickets directly to customers, rather than through travel agents; nearly half of all Southwest tickets are sold very efficiently on the Internet. And, instead of meals, the airline serves snacks, typically a bag of peanuts on short flights. ("Still nuts after all these years" says a Southwest billboard.) These innovations all drive down costs. Today, Southwest's operating expense per passenger mile is about 7.4 cents; the industry average is about 10 cents a mile. Low costs, of course, enable Southwest to charge low fares and still make money. It's as simple as that.

Or is it? Most people who have analyzed Southwest have focued on these business innovations. No doubt they are essential to the airline's success; like every company in this book, Southwest has had to be smart about business as well as committed to good values. But Kelleher and Barrett will tell you unequivocally that they believe that Southwest's values, culture and spirit—the so-called softer issues—are what have truly set the airline apart. Kelleher has said so many times, in part because he believes the airline has not been well understood. "Southwest's essential difference is not machines and things," he once said. "Our essential difference is minds, hearts, spirits and souls." Another time, he said: "The culture of Southwest is probably its major competitive advantage. The intangibles are more important than the tangibles because you can always imitate the tangibles." In fact, as Barrett reminded me, United, Delta and US Airways have all tried to launch low-fare units to compete with Southwest. "People can buy airplanes, they can hire people and they can charge low fares, and, maybe, for a while, they can have low costs," she said. "No one, in my opinion, has ever matched our people in terms of culture, spirit or just customer service focus. . . . For us, it's a way of life. The way you treat people is a way of life."

Before we delve into the Southwest culture, a word or two about its origins. If you ask Kelleher and Barrett why they approach business the way they do, they talk about their families. Both grew up in Irish Catholic working-class homes, Kelleher in New Jersey, Barrett in Vermont. "Herb and I were both raised by strong women, mothers who were very sentimental. *Religious* is probably not the right word, but very Christian. They had strong ethical views," Barrett said. Kelleher remembers being a kid of eleven or twelve and sitting up half the night talking with his mother. "She talked a lot about how you should treat people with respect," he said. "She said that positions and titles signify absolutely nothing. They're just adornments. I was kind of her disciple." Later, he spent summers working on the floor at a Campbell's soup factory, which gave him a bottom-up view of the business world. Barrett was the oldest daughter of an alcoholic father and a mother who worked six days a week as a keypunch operator to support a family of five. "My mother worked every day, practically, of her life. She instilled in me that you get your rewards from hard work," Barrett said. "And we were raised with what has turned out to be the company mission statement. Respect other people, respect differences, don't ever think you are any better than anyone else . . . and don't ever be ashamed of who you are." Her Catholic-school education also shaped her. "I had all those knuckles broken by the nuns," she said, "and all that goes with it." Barrett graduated as the valedictorian of a junior college and would have gone to law school if she had had the money. Instead, she became a legal secretary and married her high school boyfriend, whose Air Force career brought them to San Antonio. There she went to work for Kelleher, beginning a partnership that has lasted for thirty-five years. "She got her MBA from Herb," a colleague says.

Barrett began at Southwest as the corporate secretary and steadily rose in the ranks. As president and COO, she oversees all of the airline's operations. "I never concentrated on careers or titles," she has said. "I just always wanted to really feel good about what I did every day." She has become, among other things, the steward of the Southwest culture. "Somehow she has helped Southwest and its people figure out how to be incredibly focused and disciplined, and still have fun doing it," said Kevin Freiberg, a former consultant to the company and coauthor of *Nuts!,* a book about Southwest. "She is truly one of the keepers of the values."

There's no mystery about what core value guides Southwest. "It's a simple as practicing the Golden Rule," Barrett says. "Internally or externally, it makes no difference, our culture is literally customer-service-driven. We tell people that from the date of their first interview, and we never stop." Even employees who rarely deal with airline passengers—say, people working in logistics or finance—are encouraged to think of other people inside the company as customers whom they are serving. Instinctively, Kelleher and Barrett practiced servant leadership, although they did not become aware of Robert Greenleaf or the servant leadership movement until the late 1980s, when they got a letter from a frequent Southwest flier named Anne McGee-Cooper.

Her letter, offering perceptive observations about Southwest and its workers, so impressed Barrett that she invited McGee-Cooper to lunch. A former art teacher with a doctorate from Columbia, McGee-Cooper is an expert on creativity and learning who worked with Greenleaf for the last fifteen years of his life. Before long, McGee-Cooper began to teach servant leadership at Southwest. Conceptually, the idea is simple: the most ethical, respected and effective leaders are those who begin with a heartfelt desire to serve others. Putting servant leadership into practice is more difficult. Servant leaders support, coach and reward others, listen at a deep level, communicate openly and often, share credit, admit mistakes and provide needed resources. "It's a totally different paradigm than corporate America has worked under," McGee-Cooper told me. Since Greenleaf's death in 1990, his work has been carried on by the Greenleaf Center for Servant Leadership in Indianapolis, which has worked with such diverse businesses as the publisher Meredith Corp., the lawn mower company Toro and the retailer Men's Wearhouse.

The Southwest model of servant leadership puts the company's workers first. Most everything at the airline depends on engaging their minds, hearts and spirit. As Barrett told me: "We have the pyramid upside down, compared to most companies, and we don't make any bones about it. Employees are first. Passengers are second. Shareholders are third." The logic behind this approach is simple: If the company treats its people right, they are likely to treat customers right. Satisfied customers develop a loyalty to Southwest. Their loyalty drives revenues and profits and ultimately creates value for shareholders. What's interesting about Southwest is that shareholders have done fabulously well, even though the company takes care of its workers and its customers first.

Putting its people first means lots of things at Southwest—no furloughs, competitive salaries, the airline industry's first profit-sharing plan, stock options for most employees, lots of psychic rewards and an operating philosophy that pushes responsibility down to the grassroots level. It means allowing—no, encouraging—people to have fun on the job. And it means that the customer is *not* always right; a passenger who abuses a Southwest employee is likely to be told that he or she is no longer welcome on the airline. "We are very, very caring," Barrett said, "and we will do everything we can to make the situation right. But you have to be willing to look a jerk in the eye and tell him, nicely, that he is a jerk."

Because Southwest is so strongly committed to its workforce, labor relations at the airline, which is about 80 percent unionized, have generally been harmonious. "We have been successful in negotiations," CEO Parker has said, "when we go in asking how much we can pay employees rather than how little we can pay." The airline industry slump has created stresses, though. Thom McDaniel, an eleven-year veteran of Southwest who is president of the flight attendants' union, was engaged in a difficult contract negotiation with the company as I worked on this book. His members, he told me, had been willing to work harder for less pay during other industry crises, but this time Southwest was asking for too much in the way of givebacks. "Eventually, you have to say, 'How much is enough?'" McDaniel said. "We can be happy working at Southwest, but we have to take home a paycheck we can be proud of." Initially, Southwest asked the flight attendants to work longer days, but management backed off when the union said the extra hours would make it difficult to deliver the level of customer service to which they are committed. "We've set a standard and we don't want to lower it," McDaniel said. Still, for all his frustrations—the contract negotiations lasted well over a year—McDaniel told me that he has enormous respect for the leaders of Southwest and that he is proud to work there. "We do love our company," he said. "I still think we do what we do at Southwest better than anyone else in the industry." This is not the way most union leaders talk about management when times are tough.

Certainly Southwest remains a desirable place to work. In 2003, the airline received 202,357 resumes and hired 908 new employees. Southwest hires very carefully because its culture is so important. "We hire for attitude and train for skills," Barrett explained. "That doesn't mean I'm going to hire somebody who can't fly to be a pilot. But we won't necessarily hire the most technically skilled pilot. He could have eight hundred medals hanging on his chest and five hundred letters of recommendation, but if he comes in and he's unpleasant, attitude-wise, that's it." Southwest has built behavioral profiles of successful pilots, flight attendants, ticket agents or reservations agents, and its recruiters have been taught to spot verbal and physical clues to character. (Note to applicants: be nice to *everyone* you meet at Southwest.) Unlike human resources departments in most companies, Southwest's "people department" can veto job candidates other divisions want to hire. This policy provoked a battle with flight operations, which hires pilots, but "it's one of the best decisions we ever made," Barrett says. "Piloting had been a good-old-boy thing." Southwest looks for pilots who have their egos in check, so much so that they can get along well even with the famously strong-willed air traffic controllers. "The people in the tower are amazed at the civility of our pilots," Barrett says, "and it pays handsome dividends." Remember, the controllers decide which airline's planes take off when during runway traffic jams.

So who gets hired at Southwest? Typically, people who are enthusiastic, who display a warm and outgoing personality and who enjoy working with others. Altruism is much admired—someone who's active in the PTA, Scouts or a church group gets an edge. "We're not for everybody," Barrett says. "If you're not a touchy-feely person, you're going to be kind of uncomfortable in our environment." Having a sense of humor is almost essential. "Laughing is healthy," says Barrett. "Laughing produces a more human environment." (An early recruiting ad, touting Southwest's casual dress policy, ran under the headline "Work at a Place Where Wearing Pants Is Optional" and said: "We're always looking for people who take their jobs seriously, but not necessarily themselves. So if you're a bit of a ham and unusually allergic to stuffy uniforms, call our People Dept. hotline. And come to a place where you'll enjoy working your pants off.") Frequent flyers on Southwest have all become accustomed to flight attendants who get their kicks out of amusing or surprising passengers; some flight attendants have been known to hide in the luggage bins and pop out as passengers board. (I once witnessed a contest to see which passenger had the biggest hole in his sock.) Everyone at Southwest seems to love a good laugh. When a competitor claimed to be tops in customer service, Southwest ran the following ad: "After lengthy deliberation at the highest executive levels, and extensive consultation with our legal department, we have arrived at an official corporate response to Northwest Airlines' claim to be No. 1 in customer satisfaction: LIAR, LIAR, PANTS ON FIRE!"

Once people are hired, Southwest encourages them to think of themselves as owners of the airline. The profit-sharing plan and stock options go a long way in that direction; employees own more than 10 percent of Southwest's outstanding shares. Barrett and Parker also communicate frequently about the business issues they face, so employees understand the contributions they can make to the airline's success. (Next time you fly Southwest, ask a flight attendant how the stock is doing; chances are good that she or he will know.) Since owners shouldn't be governed by policy manuals, Southwest keeps rules to a minimum. In any event, workers tend to police each other, especially when it comes to saving money. "There's peer pressure here not to be wasteful," CFO Gary Kelly told me. "People pay attention to every last dollar." There's also pressure to do whatever needs to be done to keep the airline moving and its passengers happy. To set an example, Kelleher used to help load baggage on busy holidays, and Barrett says she had better not hear anyone at Southwest ever say, "That's not my job." Indeed, for all of its warmth and fuzziness, Southwest sets exacting standards and practices tough love. The airline has strict attendance policies, for example, because absent or late workers can make planes late. People who are not team players or who don't treat others with respect don't last long, either. "We are as religious about firing as we are about hiring," Barrett said.

To build spirit and reward its people, Southwest stages what seems to be a never-ending parade of parties and ceremonies. Its annual awards banquet is a big event—hundreds of people are flown to Dallas for a black-tie dinner honoring employees who have been with the company for ten, twenty, twenty-five or thirty years. Southwest sponsors Founder's Awards and President's Awards and Heroes of the Heart Awards, along with departmental Employees of the Month, Quarter and Year Awards, Perfect Attendance Luncheons and Best of the Best contests where mechanics, inspectors and stock clerks compete for gold, silver and bronze medals. Its people organize holiday parties, picnics, barbecues, fishing trips, bowling nights and annual Valentine's Day and Halloween bashes with prizes for the most outrageous costume. "We celebrate everything," Barrett said. Kelleher and Barrett never miss an opportunity at such occasions to say how much they respect and appreciate and love the people of Southwest.

As Southwest spread beyond Texas to both coasts—its three

busiest airports are now Phoenix, Las Vegas and Baltimore/Washington—the company formed a Culture Committee that is explicitly responsible for keeping the spirit alive for people in the field who rarely get to headquarters in Dallas. Composed entirely of volunteers who give up their own time, the committee of more than a hundred people meets three times a year at headquarters and then fans out across the country to spend time with employees. "My purpose initially was for us to go out and spread the word," Barrett said. Gradually, the culture ambassadors became ad hoc troubleshooters as well. When a ramp agent from rainy Seattle complained that the company-issued foul-weather gear didn't do the job—there was apparently some talk about "those idiots in Dallas who don't understand rain"—a culture ambassador alerted headquarters, which fixed the problem. More often, the committee organizes celebrations in the field, promotes local community service projects, or seeks out unsung heroes whose contributions deserve recognition. Southwest executive vice president Donna Conover, who oversees the "people department," said it is this generosity of spirit that makes the company special—and more successful. "Once you stop thinking about yourself, what you can get done is incredible," she said. "That's what our employees have always been about."

No, Southwest is not a place for cynics. But even cynics have to admit that the Southwest culture works. Statistics show that its workers are among the most productive in the airline industry. Southwest has about eighty-five to ninety employees per aircraft, easily the lowest among the major airlines, and it flies about nineteen hundred passengers a year per employee. (By comparison, American and United fly fewer than a thousand passengers a year per employee.) "Our people work harder, and they take pride in their productivity," Barrett said.

The statistics don't capture the spirit of Southwest. Only stories do that. After our conversation, Barrett sent me a batch of mail from customers and employees, each with a story: An aircraft mechanic found a BlackBerry device, tracked down the owner's contact information and sent it back to him. A ticket agent fetched luggage for an elderly passenger and personally escorted him to a bus. A flight attendant led passengers in a spirited rendition of "Happy Birthday" for a seventy-year-old woman on board. A pilot took it upon himself to push a woman in a wheelchair onto a flight. (She wrote: "My ex-husband had been a fighter pilot, and he flew for Pan American and United. I KNOW that employees of those airlines would not do that for one of their passengers.") One ticket agent, after waiting on an elderly woman who spoke little English and paid for a ticket in small bills, gave her a free ticket—which the ticket agent had earned for her perfect attendance in the past year. The stories sound too good to be true, but they are. Here is my favorite, written by Southwest first officer Pat O'Brien, about a flight from Orange County, California, to Sacramento on November 18, 2002:

> I have read many Winning Spirit articles describing how one of our employees demonstrated some Positively Outrageous Service while showing their LUV, albeit to a customer, still a complete stranger. What happened on Flight 1512 was a nearly full airplane full of "strangers" giving aid and comfort to a fellow passenger. Flight attendants Merina Hampton, Keely Rogers and Terri George made a huge difference in one man's day.
>
> About ten minutes prior to push from Orange County, one of our passengers, Vince, became a bit frantic in search of his wallet. Merina and Keely helped him search the terminal area for his wallet, which turned up at the security checkpoint. Unfortunately, approximately $100 in cash had been removed. Vince was grateful to at least have his wallet with his personal belongings but Keely noticed he had other things on his mind. During the short walk back to the gate, Vince confided with Keely that he had just been fired from his job and was on his way home where he would have to tell his wife.
>
> After getting back to the aircraft, Merina, Keely and Terri decided they were going to try to take up a small collection for Vince

so he would at least be able to get home with some pride and a little bit of Southwest LUV.

This is where Merina, Keely and Terri's Positively Outrageous Service snowballed into something quite unbelievable. After getting airborne, Merina made a short PA describing Vince's plight, without actually pointing him out to the other passengers. Merina asked if anyone was willing to spare any loose change, it would truly help Vince out.

During the beverage and snack service, the flight attendants collected an amazing $466 as well as three potential job offers for Vince. This selfless act of kindness by a plane full of "strangers" needed to be acknowledged by the people of Southwest Airlines.

On our in range call to Sacramento operations, I relayed the story and asked if they could gather up some fellow station employees to thank our very giving passengers. The people in Sacramento gathered dozens of employees to thank each and every passenger with cheers of praise as they cleared the jet way.

The giving spirit of our Southwest employees has almost come to be expected. What is amazing is that in this case the spirit has showed to be contagious because of three dedicated employees' initiative to get the LUV rolling.

Interesting, isn't it, how one good deed leads to another? That's Southwest in a nutshell. (No pun intended.) Treat your people right. They'll treat customers right. They'll reward you with business— and you'll be able to reward your shareholders. It's a virtuous circle, and there's no reason why it can't work in most any business. Southwest proves that even a wildly successful, billion-dollar public company can have a heart.

Great companies like Southwest usually do many things well. They are good employers, they deliver good products or services and they are good citizens, too. But Southwest's commitment to its people is what sets the company apart. Every company shaped by spiritual values must treat its people well. That is the single most important indicator of a company's values, and the key to its long-term health. But treating people well does not require the antic spirit of Southwest. To look more closely at the question of what a company owes to its workers, we'll now visit United Parcel Service, which employs 360,000 people in two hundred countries, to see how UPS deals with the men and women who keep about thirteen million packages moving every day.

4

WHAT DOES A COMPANY OWE ITS WORKERS?

UPS

Unlike, say, *Dick Clark's Rockin' New Year's Eve,* some things in life are worth staying up late to see. One of them is the massive $1 billion hub of UPS's global air network, located in Louisville, Kentucky, and known as Worldport. That's why, on a muggy summer night at 2:25 A.M., I found myself standing on a platform in the middle of Worldport, surrounded by a vast network of conveyor belts that carried packages into distant reaches. Hundreds of thousands of packages arrive in Worldport every weekday night for a brief stopover—they're changing planes, essentially—before taking off for their next destination. The facility is so highly automated that many of the packages make their way through it untouched by human hands.

People at UPS are proud of Worldport, and for good reason. It is big—a total of 122 miles of conveyor belts crisscross a facility that is the size of eighty football fields. It is efficient—the facility can sort 304,000 packages in an hour, moving them along the belts at speeds of up to a thousand feet per minute. And it is intelligent—overhead cameras read "smart labels" on the packages and feed the information into a database, which then tells the sorting system how to steer the packages to the proper departure gates for their connecting flights. When the governor of Kentucky, the mayor of Louisville and top executives of UPS gathered for the grand opening of Worldport in 2002, John McDevitt, a UPS vice president, declared: "You are looking, ladies and gentlemen, at a one-of-a-kind structure—the Versailles of global commerce, the Biltmore of shipping technology, the St. Peter's of innovation."

I can't say that I thought about Versailles when I first saw Worldport. Instead, I felt like I had stepped into an immense, clattering, steel-and-rubber, nonstop version of the children's board game Chutes and Ladders. Package after package glided by, many imprinted with familiar brands: HP, Cisco Systems, Gateway, Amazon and Nike. (I saw one labeled "southern tropical fish." UPS moves lots of things, some of them alive.) The conveyor belts funneled packages together like cars merging onto an interstate, shunted them onto exit ramps, carried some to bridges taking them to greater heights and unceremoniously dumped others into waiting bins. Eventually, workers stacked the packages inside igloo-shaped shipping containers, big enough for four or five people to stand inside, that were then loaded into the bellies of waiting jets. All of this happens very quickly. On the night of my visit, nearly a hundred UPS planes had converged on Louisville from across the United States, landing between 11 P.M. and 2:41 A.M. They all departed by 5:28 A.M., for points as far away as Anchorage, Alaska, and Cologne, Germany. In those few hours, a total of 675,944 packages were sorted and sent on their way.

Two things struck me about Worldport: the way the facility appeared to run itself, and the fact that it did not. Stand in the middle of the place, and you see miles of conveyor belts, thousands of packages and very few people. As it happens, about 40 percent of the packages that wind their way through Worldport do so without human intervention. That's impressive. So is the fact that the system sorts packages with close to 100 percent accuracy. But every package must be unloaded off one plane and loaded onto another, and all the next-day envelopes have to be laid into trays with their bar codes face up, and a fair number of odd-shaped or heavy packages, which are known as "irregs," require special handling. Belts must be maintained and repaired. Computers require programmers. Flight crews need to be fed and shuttled to and from their aircraft—UPS runs the eleventh biggest airline in the world—and almost every night, because something usually goes awry, contingency plans must be implemented. The upshot is that five thousand people are needed to keep Worldport operating each night. Another eighteen thousand work for UPS in greater Louisville, operating the airline, delivering or sorting packages or working in a new business called "supply chain solutions," as part of which UPS stores and manages, as well as transports, goods for its customers. Worldwide, UPS employs 360,000 people, a number that is growing, not shrinking, even as the company deploys more advanced technology. Technology matters, but people are the heart of Worldport, and of UPS.

Every company, as we've noted, says that people are its most important asset. UPS acts that way. Few companies of this size, or any size, reward, engage and motivate their people better than UPS. In confidential surveys, most employees are generous with praise for their supervisors and for the company. About three in four say, "I am proud to work for UPS." This is remarkable for several reasons. First, much of the work at UPS is routine and repetitive. While the company has diversified lately, mostly it still moves things from place to place. There's nothing inherently exciting or glamorous about that. Second, UPS runs a highly engineered operation with rules that govern how each job should be done. Office workers, for example, are not allowed to eat or drink at their desks. Conventional wisdom says people resist that degree of control. Finally, UPS is heavily unionized, and most companies believe that unions bring conflict and tension to the workplace.

But when the Teamsters Union signed a six-year contract with UPS in 2002, its president, James P. Hoffa, said, "UPS is not our enemy. UPS is a company that employs more than 210,000 Teamster members. It is a company whose union employees are earning top dollar and top benefits. If there were more companies like UPS, America would be a better place." Even after concluding contract negotiations, not many union leaders talk that way about business. (Hoffa's comments reminded me of what the flight attendants' union leader said about Southwest.) Both UPS and the union say that the 1997 Teamsters strike was an aberration; at the time, the union president, Ron Carey, had become a target of a federal corruption investigation, and the strike provided a welcome distraction. The CEO of UPS, Mike Eskew, told me that he approaches labor negotiations with the idea of giving people as much as the company can afford. "It's not about maximizing profits," he said. "That's not it at all. It's how much can we share, and still compete and grow." Hourly workers at Worldport, most of whom are part-time, get above-market salaries, health care benefits, free college courses on site and opportunities to advance into management.

When I asked managers at Worldport what they liked about working for UPS, no one said a thing about the infrastructure or the technology that makes the hub so unusual. Instead, they talked about the camaraderie that UPS fosters and about the satisfaction they get from working together. "The one thing about this place is that nobody is going to succeed unless everybody succeeds," said Jerry Wassell, a twenty-year veteran of UPS who joined as a part-time package sorter and now oversees a thousand people at Worldport. Jeff Straub, another veteran manager who rose through the ranks, nodded in agreement. "The key to success in this organization is attitude," he said. "Believing you can do it. Working as part of a team. Partnership is our legacy." A former UPS executive later told me that soon after she joined the company, a colleague approached her with a big smile and an outstretched hand and said, "Welcome, partner!"

It sounds old-fashioned, and in some ways it is. UPS is the kind of company that was once common in America—a place where people are hired out of high school or college, work in a factory or climb the corporate ladder, and stick around for thirty or forty years until they retire with a pension and gold watch. Think of General Motors, or IBM in the 1950s, or General Electric before Jack Welch. It's a place where managers wear suits Monday through Thursday and where you will see six or eight men dressed in white shirts— white shirts!—seated around a table in the company cafeteria. While other businesses celebrate the new, UPS values its traditions. The company has policies, committees, rules and procedures, some of which have been preserved for decades. Sometimes it is rigid. To promote efficiency, for example, drivers are trained to follow "340 methods" outlined in a "standard practice manual." They are told to walk at a brisk pace but not to run, to secure their keys on their left pinky to avoid fumbling them and to buckle their seat belts with the left hand while inserting the ignition key with their right. Managers say that every rule has a purpose, but they concede that mavericks and free spirits probably will not feel comfortable at UPS.

Instead of excitement, UPS provides security; in place of freedom, it offers community. Many find that appealing at a time when other employers casually cast off workers and people are generally not as connected to their neighbors, towns, clubs or places of worship as their parents were. "Beginning, roughly speaking, in the late 1960s, Americans in massive numbers began to join less, trust less, give less, vote less and schmooze less," scholars Robert D. Putnam and Lewis M. Feldstein write in *Better Together,* a book about rebuilding community that includes a chapter about UPS. People at UPS do more than belong to a community. They own it, literally. Until it sold stock to the public in 1999, UPS was a private company that was 100 percent owned by its employees and retirees. Today, while anyone can buy UPS shares, about 55 percent of the stock and more than 90 percent of the voting shares are still held by employees and retirees. Lots of millionaires work at UPS.

More than the money, though, what binds people at UPS is their shared sense of purpose. People at the company work hard. Think about driving a van in city traffic, or loading and unloading packages in the middle of the night, or managing the world's most complex transportation network using planes, trains, intercity trucks and vans. The very difficulty of the work draws people together. Don Cohen, who wrote the chapter about UPS in *Better Together*, said, "Being able to 'hack it,' showing the strength and persistence the work demands day after day, defines what it means to be a real UPSer."

Yes, people who work at UPS call each other UPSers. Like most close-knit cultures, UPS has its own customs and language: its chocolate-brown vans are called "package cars," its planes are called "browntails," and drivers are called "service providers." Everyone at UPS speaks in acronyms: PCMs are prework communications meetings, ERI is the Employee Relations Index, and CERCs are the Co-chaired Employee Retention Committees. For years the company even had its own fight song, sung to the tune of the "Field Artillery March":

> *Over hill, over dale*
> *As they hit the concrete trail*
> > *Our brown wagons go rolling along.*
> *Shout it out, without doubt*
> *Service rides on every route*
> > *As our wagons go rolling along.*
> *Then it's hi hi hee*
> *In the brown-shirt cavalry*
> > *Shout out our message loud and strong*
> *Where'er you go*
> *You will always know*
> > *Our brown wagons go rolling along.*

To understand UPS, you need to know the man who used to lead his troops in a spirited rendition of that anthem—the founder of United Parcel Service, James E. Casey.

S TEP inside UPS's gleaming headquarters, which opened in 1994 in a parklike setting on the outskirts of Atlanta, and you can practically feel the presence of Jim Casey. A large portrait of Casey hangs in the lobby, just around a corner from one of the company's original package cars, a Model T Ford. UPS executives quote Casey all the time, saying things like "Service is the sum of many little things done well" or "Our horizon is as distant as our mind's eye wishes it to be." The company published a collection of Casey's speeches and writing, and a highlight of the annual conference where about 225 top managers from UPS get together is a "Jim Casey evening" where the company's CEO gives a talk inspired by Casey's ideas. Every year, the company gives a Jim Casey Community Service Award to the UPS employee, often a driver or part-time package sorter, who has made the greatest contribution as a volunteer in his or her community.

During my visit to Atlanta, I spent a couple of hours with Mike Eskew, who became CEO of UPS in 2002. He must have referred to Casey at least two dozen times. He explained that UPS's ultimate goal is to treat each customer and each package as if the company's future depended upon them, which, in a sense, it does. "Our vision is to be Jim Casey," Eskew said. "He knew every package and every customer. We want to come full circle." Later, Eskew told me about UPS's low-key but impressive commitment to philanthropy— the company and its employees gave $52 million one year to the United Way, more than any other company. Eskew mused that perhaps UPS ought to crow a bit more about its charitable giving, if only to inspire others to be more generous. Then he caught himself. "Jim Casey taught us not to crow. Jim Casey believed in quiet philanthropy," Eskew said. "I sure hate to disagree with Jim." He sounded as if Casey might walk into the room at any moment to chastise him.

There's no danger of that. Jim Casey died in 1983 at the age of ninety-five, just a month after he retired from the UPS board of directors. A high-school dropout who started a bicycle messenger service in Seattle in 1907, Casey lived long enough to see United Parcel Service become the world's premier delivery company, which it remains to this day. UPS serves customers in more than 200 countries using 1,750 operating centers, 2,000 daily airplane flights, 88,000 vehicles and those 360,000 people. It has gone beyond transportation to offer what it calls "supply chain solutions," a range of shipping-related businesses that include running a warehouse for Nike.com, repairing printers for Hewlett-Packard and storing and delivering spare computer parts for IBM. In 2003, UPS generated $33.5 billion in revenues and $2.9 billion in profits. The company is three times as profitable and far more efficient than archrival FedEx, which takes a different approach to business—it adamantly opposes unions, for example. Because UPS still "runs the tightest ship in the shipping business," it can offer a money-back guarantee on shipments to all addresses in the forty-eight contiguous U.S. states.

But, as Jim Casey liked to remind people, anybody can deliver packages. What sets UPS apart is the culture that he built with every bit as much care as he devoted to package delivery. UPS's work ethic, its sense of community, the fact that the people who work there own the place, its policy of promoting from within, even its obsession with neatness—all of these can be traced back to the founder. So can the company's unassuming mien. When a writer named Philip Hamburger was preparing a profile of Casey for the *New Yorker* in 1947, Casey sent him a long letter in which he said: "Remember that the story is to be about *us*—not about me. For, in simple fairness to the many capable people who . . . have been associated with the company, no single individual should be given a disproportionate share of credit for the development of the United Parcel Service you are writing about today."

More than half a century later, UPS executives mingle with drivers and sorters, office doors stay open and people answer their own phones. People call each other by their first names, no matter their rank or title. There's no "Mr. Eskew," just Mike. The company has no executive dining room, corporate jet or luxurious office suites for the brass. Eskew does not even have his own personal assistant; instead, the twelve members of the management committee share a pool of four secretaries. Like the other two thousand people who work at UPS headquarters, he eats lunch in the cafeteria. Jim Casey would approve. "There have been no supermen in our company— no star performers to hog the limelight," he once said. "There can be no glamour, no romance, no truly great success, unless shared in by all."

Casey was, by all accounts, a humble man. A lifelong bachelor, he lived for many years in simple hotel rooms and always wore a dark suit and tie. Neither money nor power interested him much. Over the years he and his brother, who also worked at UPS, gave the bulk of their money, $438 million in all, to the Annie E. Casey Foundation, named after their mother. (It grew to become the eleventh biggest foundation in the United States, with $2.7 billion in assets in 2003.) Two things excited Casey—the people of UPS and the packages they delivered. Casey understood that business was a collective enterprise and that UPS's success depended upon winning the commitment of its people. To that end, he began distributing shares in the company to its managers in the early 1920s. "The basic principle that I believe has contributed more than any other to the building of our business," he said in 1955, "is the ownership of our company by the people employed in it." Casey also paid attention to small things. He had a knack for remembering people's names and went out of his way to thank people for the work they did. He took to heart the task of ensuring that every package entrusted to UPS was handled with care. In the *New Yorker* profile, Casey could not contain his delight during a visit to a department store where shipping clerks were hard at work: "Deft fingers! Deft fingers wrapping thousands of bundles. Neatly tied! Neatly addressed! Stuffed with soft tissue paper! What a treat! Ah, packages!"

Mike Eskew does not get quite as ebullient about packages, but he, too, believes in the fundamental goodness of the work at UPS. On the wall of his office is the cover of the December 19, 1953, issue of the *New Yorker,* showing a gaggle of children who have gathered around a UPS delivery truck. We know how they feel—when the familiar brown van pulls up outside the door, it's hard not to experience a pleasant tingle of anticipation. "There's something good and honest, maybe even noble, about what we do," Eskew said. "That makes this a special place." Scoff if you wish, but UPS people like to think that they do more than deliver packages. They talk about "enabling the global economy," or, during the holiday season, getting gifts to children in time for Christmas. Good companies give their workers a sense of purpose.

Like most senior executives at UPS, Eskew, who is fifty-four, has spent his entire career at the company. He grew up in Vincennes, a farming town in southwestern Indiana, and worked in his father's surveying business for 50 cents an hour, from the time he was a small boy right through high school. He earned a degree in engineering from Purdue and went right to UPS, where his first task was to redesign a parking lot so that more cars could be squeezed in. "All I wanted to do was find a place where I could work hard," he said. Although he worked only briefly as a driver, Eskew rode around with them a lot to watch them work and see how they could become more efficient. "We like to think that we have measured the world," he said. ("In God we trust," goes one company saying. "Everything else, we measure") Eskew's career took him to Germany, UPS's first overseas market, in the mid-1970s, after which he did stints in Maryland, California, Connecticut, Kentucky (where he helped start the UPS airline), and New Jersey. He finally settled into the Atlanta headquarters in 1993.

By his own account, Eskew made his way to the top of the company almost by accident. "I never wanted a promotion. Never wanted to change jobs," he said. "I always liked what I was doing.

And I never had visions of running this place. Most days, even now, it's just another job." This stretches credulity, but Eskew's self-effacing personality is typical of the people I meet at UPS. When I asked Jim Kelly, Eskew's predecessor as CEO, to describe Eskew, he said: "Mike's a quick study. He's a down-to-earth guy. People respond to him very well." There is nothing charismatic about Eskew, nothing that screams CEO, but with a few exceptions—Herb Kelleher of Southwest and Howard Schultz of Starbucks come to mind—the leaders of successful companies with strong values tend to be low-key types who listen as well as they talk. That style certainly fits the culture of UPS. When *Fortune* went looking for *underpaid* CEOs in 2003—chief executives who delivered good returns for shareholders without grabbing too much for themselves—Eskew made the list. He earned $2.9 million in 2002, as UPS shares rose by 17 percent. "I think I'm well paid," he said. "Don't tell our board of directors, but I'd do this for nothing."

Broadly speaking, UPS's domestic workforce consists of three groups. Because of the nature of the shipping business, where bursts of activity alternate with slack time, UPS employs about 120,000 part-time workers. Most load, unload and sort packages, and most work at night. Nearly all are represented by the Teamsters. These are entry-level jobs, typically held by college students, immigrants and people just out of school. Some 80,000 UPSers work as drivers. They, too, are union members, and customarily they get their jobs after years of working part time as sorters or loaders and accumulating seniority. The average driver at the company has been on the job for fifteen years. Another 30,000 people are managers. Almost all of them also started at the bottom, as drivers or sorters. UPS will look outside the company when hiring for specific skills—computer programming, say, or flying a plane—but there's a strong bias in favor of promoting from within. "We're all just a bunch of ex–truck drivers," said Kurt Kuehn, who became UPS's first director of investor relations after the company's IPO. "There's almost an antielitism in the company. All of us worked our way up."

Let's consider one group at a time, beginning with managers, to see how UPS treats its workers. Few managers start out at UPS intending to spend their careers there. What usually happens is that after signing up for part-time work, often during college, some people find that they like the culture. Then they take full-time jobs, get promoted and start to accumulate stock. At that point, they're hooked. Kuehn, who grew up in a blue-collar family in Naples, Florida, began as a temp during the Christmas rush and subsequently went to work as a full-time driver and industrial engineer. He liked the people, and he was grateful when the company offered to put him through business school. "One of the paradigms at UPS is that you're here for the rest of your career," he said. "We tend to invest in people and take a very long view." The only blot on his record was that he'd gone to Yale. "Frankly, we don't hire a lot of Ivy League candidates," Kuehn said. "Guys who come in with inflated expectations or think they're smarter than everybody else don't do well." Kuehn's career has taken him from Naples to Miami, to Billings, Montana, to Greenwich, Connecticut, and then to Atlanta.

Executives at UPS move around a lot. Eskew said that's because the company wants to keep people challenged and expose them to a variety of jobs and settings. "If you're comfortable," he said, "we're going to give you something new to do." This can be tough on families, and UPS may have to rethink this practice in an era of two-career couples. But, like military officers, UPSers who jump from assignment to assignment are likely to feel more at home in the organization than they are in any particular place. Because UPS is not a company of specialists, people over time stop identifying themselves as engineers or accountants or lawyers and start thinking of themselves as UPSers. "You can see that needle moving more towards UPSer," Eskew said. UPS has an almost cultish feel, but you could have said that about many companies during the 1950s, the era of *The Organization Man* and *How to Succeed in Business Without Really Trying,* where people learned do to things "the company way." In some respects, UPS resembles the military or a police force or fire department. In all of those organizations, the needs of the individual take second place to the needs of the group. But the individual can count on support from the group, on and off the job. Patti Hobbs, a UPS manager in Louisville, told me that when she traveled to the Dominican Republic on a volunteer project, UPSers welcomed her to the island, took her around and invited her to their homes. "You take care of each other," she said. "That's just the way UPSers are."

While UPSers are bound to each other by their sense of community, their interests are aligned with the company itself because they own stock. Do companies "owe" workers a share of ownership? Arguably, they do. More important, there's probably no more effective way to win a worker's loyalty. Jim Kelly, Eskew's predecessor as CEO, said: "When you believe you are working for yourself, and your future depends on it, you're going to throw yourself into your work." Like Southwest, UPS has a culture of frugality; people don't like to see the company waste money because it's their money. An unexpected side benefit of employee stock ownership is that it forced UPS, as a company, to be financially conservative because it always needed a substantial cash reserve to buy back shares from retirees or employees who wanted to sell them. UPS remains one of fewer than a dozen companies with an AAA credit rating from Standard & Poor's.

Stock ownership also promotes long-term thinking. Even young UPS managers get a substantial portion of their compensation, perhaps 15 to 20 percent, in stock. Although they can sell at any time, there's a cultural expectation that they will hold their shares for many years and a reward for doing so: The company gives employee-owners a 1 to 3 percent annual stock dividend on top of the ordinary dividend and whatever capital appreciation the market provides. Most managers hold stock well into retirement. So, for example, if UPS has to decide whether to invest in new technology to make its vans more energy-efficient, the executives who decide to make the investment will probably reap the gains even if they don't materialize for many years. (Perhaps for this reason, UPS is a green company.

It has used electric-powered vans in New York City for decades, and it operates more than eighteen hundred vehicles that use alternative fuels rather than gasoline.) Long-term stock ownership is "a wonderful mechanism," Kuehn said. "Here you have guys who are fifty-five or sixty years old, with millions of dollars' worth of stock, worrying like crazy about the next decade. It's hugely different from what you see in the market, where guys are trying to get the stock to pop so they can cash in their options and get the heck out."

Employee ownership also keeps people on their toes. Being so insular, UPS runs the risk of becoming cautious or hidebound, but for the most part it has adapted quickly to changing markets or technology. Senior executives, who have their life savings in the firm, promote what they call "constructive dissatisfaction," urging one another to be honest about how the company can improve. Said Eskew: "We're never complacent. We're never stale. We're always our own biggest critics." Only once—when UPS allowed FedEx to grab a commanding lead in the overnight delivery market, because it did not believe there was sufficient demand for next-day package delivery—did the company suffer a big hit because it was caught napping. But UPS recovered to the point where it now has about a 45 percent share of air shipments.

More often, UPS has reinvented itself. It evolved from a bicycle messenger service to a delivery service for downtown department stores, the company that served every address in the United States, a global firm, and most recently a company that manages logistics and supply chains for others. The "What Can Brown Do for You?" advertising campaign is an attempt to communicate this expanded mission. UPS preserves its core beliefs but constantly reexamines its strategy and tactics. "The values are still the same," Eskew said. "That's the thread that leads from Jim Casey to today." But few managers get bored at UPS because the company is always doing something new.

Keeping UPS's 80,000 drivers and 120,000 part-time package loaders and sorters engaged and energized is not as easy. Like most employers, UPS provides a mix of psychic and tangible rewards. The ethic of partnership, by itself, goes some distance toward breaking down the "us-versus-them" mentality that divides management from the rank and file in many companies. Drivers, in particular, are held in high esteem. "Being a driver at UPS is an exalted position in the company," said one executive. Managers know that the men and women in brown are the face that UPS presents to its customers and therefore are vital to its success. In the old days, drivers were given small illustrated cards saying: "Check and double-check: Are your shoes shined? Is your hair cut? Are you clean-shaven? Are your hands clean? Is your uniform pressed?" Even today, drivers meet each morning with their supervisor, who checks to see whether they pass muster.

While the job of driving a package car might seem monotonous, UPSers told me that it is not. Drivers contend with a fresh set of variables every day—weather, traffic, new customers or old ones with changing needs—as they deliver an average of about three hundred packages to about a hundred different customers, with deadlines, depending on the package, of 8 or 8:30 A.M., 10:30 A.M. and 3 P.M. "It's a juggling act every day, of how do you manage all these demands," said an ex-driver. Pay significantly exceeds industry averages—about $23 an hour for an experienced driver—and benefits are generous. Since 1995, drivers have been eligible to buy company stock at a discount, and more than half are now owners. It's not uncommon for drivers to turn down the chance to become managers because they like the work they are doing.

Turnover among the package sorters and loaders is higher. What they are given is more basic—decent pay, good benefits and, for some, the opportunity to move up. Their work tends to be monotonous. At Worldport, I watched a woman whose job consists of taking envelopes out of mailbags and laying them with the bar code facing up on trays, all night long, and I saw many people who lift packages, one after another, from shipping containers to conveyor belts, or vice versa. More than half of UPS's part-time workers are college students, while others are immigrants or people who are entering the workforce for the first time. UPS has hired more than fifty-eight thousand people who were formerly on welfare, as part of the welfare-to-work initiative launched by the Clinton administration—a commitment that Eskew said has been good for the company as well as for the new employees, most of whom turn out to be committed workers. Some part-timers hope to accumulate union seniority to become drivers. Others become part-time supervisors, sometimes in a matter of weeks or months. But most come to work for UPS because the wages and benefits are better than average: pay starts at $8.50 an hour and averages $10.72 per hour, and workers get health insurance, dental and vision plans, paid holidays, vacations and tuition assistance.

The primary reason that these jobs differ from dead-end jobs like flipping burgers at McDonald's or running a cash register at Wal-Mart is that UPS helps part-timers to obtain new skills and better jobs. At fifty UPS hubs across the country, workers can enroll in a tuition-assistance program called Earn and Learn, where they get grants and loans to go to school. In Louisville, an important hub, UPS went further by helping to organize local colleges and universities into an institution called Metropolitan College. The college offers classes at Worldport during the evening, before the night shift begins. More than 80 percent of Fortune 500 companies offer tuition assistance, but few offer classes in the workplace and extend the benefit to part-timers.

Every UPS worker also gets heard. This matters. Unlike most companies, UPS doesn't just talk to people through newsletters and Web sites; it listens, too. People at UPS participate every day in a brief PCM—a prework communication meeting—during which a supervisor talks with people about their job or the company. Topics at the PCMs vary from the latest road closings to the company's quarterly earnings to the fact that Omaha Steaks is about to ship eighty thousand packages. "If our managers don't talk to mechanics and drivers and sorters every day, they're not going to be successful," Eskew said. "I don't care how smart you are. This is a company of people, and to be able to motivate and communicate and spend time with people is awfully important."

Once a year, UPS surveys its employees to find out how they are doing and how the company is doing. The Employee Relations Index (ERI) survey solicits responses to twenty-five statements, such as "In my day-to-day work, I can have direct impact on the success of my work group" (89 percent in the latest survey), "I know what I need to do in order to be considered for a promotion" (74 percent), "My management team treats employees with respect" (74 percent) and "My management team is sincere in its attempt to understand the employee's point of view" (66 percent), and analyzes the responses by region, division and smaller work groups. Some of the ratings could be better, of course, but the important thing is that they are taken seriously. Managers are evaluated, in part, on the feedback.

Not surprisingly, given the company's scale, the UPS workforce is racially and ethnically diverse. Minorities make up 52 percent of new hires at UPS, 35 percent of the overall workforce and 28 percent of managers. An African American executive named Calvin Darden, who is senior vice president for operations in the United States, has been mentioned as a possible successor to Eskew, and UPS has been ranked among the 50 Best Companies for Minorities by *Fortune* for five consecutive years. (The NAACP named UPS its Corporate Citizen of the Year in 2002, and the Urban League did the same in 2003.) Since 1968, UPS has run an unusual Community Internship Program (CIP) that places about fifty managers a year in four-week programs working for nonprofit organizations in New York; Chicago; Chattanooga, Tennessee and McAllen, Texas. These executives, who tend to be rising stars, are dispatched to poor communities, where they serve food to the homeless, counsel recovering drug addicts or help construct housing for migrant farmers. CIP was another one of Jim Casey's ideas—he wanted UPS's predominantly white managers to try to do something about the poverty and inequality that set the stage for the urban riots of the 1960s—and it has survived for thirty-five years because UPS leaders think it's a good way to build understanding and empathy in their senior managers. "I call it emotional capital," said Don Wofford, the UPS executive who runs the program. "People are put into environments where they have to learn to relate to people who do not look like them, who do not live like them, who have different experiences. They come back and they can better understand what some of our people are going through." Not many companies train their leaders to better relate to the poor. Then again, I can't think of a company that is more woven into the fabric of American life, for better or worse, than UPS. "We see every town, every village, every street, every day," Eskew noted. Because the company is so tied to the overall health of the economy, it has a business interest in seeing poor people, and everyone else, do better. "They are our next generation of people, our next generation of customers. If they do well, we do well," Eskew said.

The UPS way is not for everybody. I don't think that many people who work at Southwest Airlines would enjoy UPS—it's too straitlaced. My friends in journalism, who tend to rebel against structure, would not do well there either. But I think that Teamster chief James P. Hoffa was right when he said that America would be better off if there were more companies like UPS. This is a place where words like *loyalty* and *teamwork* and *community* still mean a lot. This is a place whose long-term health is tied to the health of the broader society, and so the company takes its social and environmental responsibilities seriously. This is a place where workers who give of themselves can expect much in return.

What does a company owe its workers? At UPS, they get decent wages, generous benefits, training, education, as much responsibility as they can handle and a piece of the action. Newcomers to the workplace, without money or skills but with a strong work ethic and a will to succeed, can achieve the American dream of providing a better life for their children than the one they have. Yes, anybody can deliver a package, as Jim Casey liked to say. But not many companies deliver the goods to their people as well as UPS.

5

CAN A COMPANY FIGHT THE MARKETPLACE?

STARBUCKS

Working out of a home office, I take a coffee break almost every afternoon. I spend about $15 a week at my neighborhood Starbucks. But I never really tasted coffee until I visited Starbucks' corporate headquarters in Seattle.

There, Willard "Dub" Hay, Starbucks' senior vice president of coffee, who oversees the purchasing, roasting and blending of coffee, and Peter Torrebiarte, a buyer of green, or unroasted, coffee, led me through my first formal coffee tasting.

We met in Starbucks' tasting room, which is equipped with several small coffee-bean roasters, an industrial stove, grinders and an espresso machine. The spacious room is used to sample coffee submitted to Starbucks and for coffee classes for the three thousand people who work in the home office. Two sets of seven nine-ounce glasses had been lined up along a table, one set for Dub and one for me. Fourteen grams—about three to four tablespoons—of freshly ground coffee, each from a different Starbucks product, filled the bottom of each glass, to make extra-strong coffee with lots of flavor and aroma. We strapped on aprons, and Peter poured boiling water into each glass. As we waited for the coffee to cool, Dub explained the process and told me a little about himself.

"This is called cupping," he said, "and it's the way you evaluate coffee, whether you are in Papua New Guinea or in Seattle." We would first smell each coffee, moving back and forth between brews to discern the differences. There's no school for this. "It's very much an apprenticeship," said Dub. "You sit at a cupping table with someone who's been doing it for twenty-five or thirty years, and start describing flavors. Some people are better tasters than others." Starbucks' tasters evaluate coffee before they decide to buy it, before it is shipped to the United States, after it arrives at the roasting plant and several times before it is bagged, sealed and shipped. Each time, a small amount is roasted and brewed for a tasting.

Dub, who is fifty-four, got into the coffee trade after flying U.S. Navy fighter jets in Vietnam. He bought coffee for Procter & Gamble, ran all the coffee-buying operations at Nestlé USA, and traded coffee, cocoa and sugar derivatives for Merrill Lynch and UBS (formerly Paine Webber) before joining Starbucks in 2002. Like most people at Starbucks, Dub takes his coffee very seriously, and although he left the military a long time ago, he maintains a commanding presence.

I gently dipped my spoon into a glass of Starbucks Breakfast Blend and sniffed it tentatively. He was unimpressed by my technique.

"Stir it real good and get your nose down into it," he ordered.

I did just that.

"It smells great," I said cheerfully, and immediately felt like a fool. Why didn't I say something intelligent about its body, roundness or earthy scent? We moved along the table—each coffee was richer and more complex than the last—and after smelling several glasses, I didn't think I could tell one from another. Peter told me that a Kenyan blend has a "citrusy aroma." All I smelled was coffee.

Then I bent over a steaming glass of a Starbucks offering called Ethiopia Sidamo. It is bold, rich and complicated, almost like a fine red wine, and as I inhaled deeply, I felt a tingle of lemon in my nose. I glanced at the label. "Lemony with floral aroma," it said. Maybe I was trainable after all.

Then it was tasting time. "We're going to look for body, acidity and flavor," Dub said. "Body is how it sits on your palate. Does it feel heavy? Is it light and tingly? Is it rounded? Does it have a syrupy feel? Acidity is not pH. It's an astringency. Some coffee has acidity. Some has none. Then flavor, which can be quite specific."

My mother would not like what came next. Dub dipped his spoon into a glass, raised it to his mouth and sucked it in with a slurping sound so loud that it would attract glares at any Starbucks. He swirled the brew around in his mouth and then spit it into a spittoon.

"You don't just want to taste it with the tip of your tongue?" I asked.

"Oh no," he said. "You pull it to the back. Up into your sinuses."

We spent fifteen or twenty minutes sucking, swirling and spitting. What a way to earn a living.

I could not help but be struck by the attention that Dub and Peter paid to what were, in the end, subtle variations in taste. You'd have thought we were at a château in the Loire Valley. The day before, I had toured Starbucks' roasting plant in Kent, Washington, a suburb of Seattle, where roasting coffee is treated as an art, to be learned during a long apprenticeship and then passed on to others. Dub and Peter and the roasters I met all shared a passion for coffee.

Much as I enjoyed my tasting, I wondered whether a cup of coffee merited all this fuss.

"Half your customers probably just want to pour something down their throat to wake up in the morning," I told Dub. "Maybe they go to Starbucks because it's more convenient than a gas station or the 7-Eleven."

"I don't think so," he replied. "People appreciate what we go through to deliver a fantastic cup of coffee. Otherwise, I don't think they'd be willing to pay the premium. As opposed to going to a 7-Eleven or gas station and getting something hot, black and wet."

I'm not sure he's right about most customers. But I have to admit that ever since my trip to Seattle, I drink my coffee black, pay closer attention to the taste and enjoy it more. And I do know this: Starbucks has somehow persuaded about twenty-five million people to visit its stores every week and pay $1.60 for a twelve-ounce cup of drip coffee, $3.10 for a grande latte and $4.30 for a venti mocha Valencia. Whether they are paying for a jolt of caffeine, for the taste and aroma or simply for the chance to unwind away from the demands of home or the office doesn't matter in the end. What matters is that consumers are willing to pay those premium prices, and to do so again and again. "Before Starbucks, it was unthinkable to imagine paying $3 for a cup of coffee," said Orin Smith, the company's president and CEO. "Today, it's commonplace."

This is the key to understanding Starbucks. Without the willingness of loyal customers to pay a premium for high-quality coffee, Starbucks could not have become one of the great growth companies of our time. Nor could Starbucks have changed the way millions of people start each day. Who knew the difference between a latte and a cappuccino before Starbucks came along? (Let alone a half-and-half, two-pump, grande vanilla skim latte, which someone ordered at my local Starbucks the other day. I kid you not.) Most important, Starbucks could not have sustained the values that make the company a good partner for its workers and for coffee growers in about twenty countries where the company buys its beans. Only because the coffee is good—and expensive—can Starbucks share its good fortune with its own employees and with the growers. So Dub has a point: It all does come back to the coffee.

—

WHEN I ask corporate executives why their companies don't make products of higher quality, or take better care of their workers, or do more to protect the environment, they often respond by talking about the market. Newspaper executives say there's not much of a market for thoughtful articles about complex public issues. Hollywood studio chiefs say the market prefers escapist action movies to adult fare. Some Detroit automakers say that they'd like to make cars that pollute less and consume less gasoline but that the market demands roomy, powerful SUVs. Other companies say they can't provide health insurance to their workers because doing so would price their products out of the market.

There's some truth to all that. Businesses need to serve markets to survive. They can't shove products down the throats of consumers, or charge too much for what they sell. But markets aren't static. And while customers shape markets, so do companies. That's what Starbucks has done, time and again. It transformed the market for selling coffee in the United States. It ignored the prevailing labor market and sought to become an employer of choice. And while cheap coffee beans are abundant because of a crisis in the world market, Starbucks pays higher prices because it wants to build sustainable relationships with coffee growers in the developing world. Great companies like to rattle existing markets or create new ones. As Howard Schultz, the creator of the modern Starbucks, once said: "You don't just give the customers what they ask for." Rather than be shaped by markets, Starbucks has been guided by values.

When Starbucks opened its first store in Seattle's Pike Place Market in 1971, there was no market to speak of for the dark-roasted, Italian-style coffee on its shelves. Three friends with a passion for gourmet coffee—Jerry Baldwin, an English teacher, Zev Siegl, a history teacher, and Gordon Bowker, a writer—started the company with an investment of $1,350 apiece. They named it Starbucks Coffee, Tea and Spice after the first mate in Herman Melville's *Moby-Dick,* and their modest hope was to bring good coffee to Seattle. Until the mid-1980s, they sold only coffee beans, tea and spices—no mocha coconut Frappuccino, no vanilla latte, no brewed coffee at all. Two things transformed Starbucks from a local retailer into a global juggernaut: the arrival of Howard Schultz and the invention of the FlavorLock bag.

Schultz, who joined as head of marketing in 1982, fell in love with the ritual and romance of the espresso bar during a business trip to Milan. He wanted Starbucks stores to reproduce the Italian coffeehouse experience. The original owners did not—they were unwilling to enter the restaurant business. Frustrated, Schultz quit to start his own chain of coffee bars, called Il Giornale and staffed by "baristas" who made the coffee. He then turned around and acquired Starbucks for about $4 million in 1987.

Even after the merger, Starbucks owned just eight stores in Seattle and one in Vancouver. It had little prospect of spreading further: shipping freshly roasted coffee long distances was impractical because, once it is roasted, coffee loses flavor after a week of exposure to air and light. It was the invention of the FlavorLock vacuum-sealed bag, which preserves freshness for months, that permitted Starbucks to expand to Chicago in 1987. Five years later, Schultz and his management team—a key hire was Orin Smith, who joined as chief financial officer in 1990 and eventually succeeded Schultz as CEO—took the company public, raising $28 million to help finance the rapid expansion that followed.

What Schultz, Smith, and their people accomplished as they built Starbucks is remarkable. Coffee consumption in the United States has declined since the 1960s, when about 75 percent of adults drank coffee every day; today about half of all adults are regular coffee drinkers. Coffee shops had been around forever, but most sold a weak, stale brew for 50 or 75 cents in two sizes, small or large, that were served two ways, black or regular. (A veteran Starbucks roaster, Tom Walters, told me: "My mother lived from the 1920s to the 1980s and no one ever served her a fresh cup of coffee. That's a travesty.") Early on, skeptics derided Starbucks as a West Coast yuppie fad that would never amount to anything. Instead, Starbucks has done for coffee what Nike did for sneakers: it turned a cheap

commodity into a premium brand, imbued with emotional qualities—romance or relaxation for Starbucks, athletic excitement for
Nike. What Starbucks is really selling, its executives will tell you, is
something they call "the Starbucks Experience." They say that customers come to Starbucks for a "taste of romance" to break up their
everyday routine, or to reward themselves with an "affordable luxury," or to find a "third place" where they can interact with friends,
other customers or the baristas. Some of this is hype—many customers just want coffee—but at least one sociologist has described
Starbucks as the American equivalent of English pubs, French cafés
and German beer gardens. Like UPS, Starbucks is tapping into the
desire for community—UPSers find community at work, while Starbucks creates places where people can connect with one another.
"We're not filling bellies," said one company executive. "We're filling souls."

Orin Smith understands the need Starbucks is trying to satisfy.
Smith is a modest, soft-spoken man who usually cedes the spotlight
to the brash, charismatic Schultz. But he has played an important
role in guiding the company's growth and promoting its values,
which were first written down after he joined the firm. Gray-haired
and grandfatherly, Smith, who is sixty-one, grew up in Chehalis,
Washington, a logging town of about eight thousand people south
of Seattle. "It's not a lot more than a wide spot in the road," he said.
One of five children of a plumber, Smith felt rooted there. "It was a
great place to grow up," he said. "You knew everybody in the community, and everybody cared. Today, there's less and less of that.
People don't know their neighbors. They don't have people over for
coffee. They don't talk to one another over the backyard fence. And
nobody builds a front porch today. We had all those things. It was
not a wealthy community, not then and not now, but that didn't
matter."

When I asked Smith whether his own values had come from his
family, his faith or his education, he replied, "Probably all of the
above." At the University of Washington in the early 1960s, he stud-

ied literature, history and politics. "It was a time when you were forced to think more deeply and question the conventional ways of being," he said. Later, after earning an MBA from Harvard Business School, he worked as an analyst for the Washington state government because he was interested in public service. He joined Starbucks because liked the stores and felt good about the people in charge. They talked explicitly about how they would try to build a better kind of company.

None of them expected to build such a big company. When Smith signed on in 1990, the business plan projected that Starbucks could open as many as five hundred stores in thirty cities. "All along the way, we underestimated what was possible," he said. By the end of 2003, Starbucks had more than seven thousand stores in all fifty U.S. states and more than thirty foreign countries. It sells coffee in supermarkets through an alliance with Kraft, helped to create bottled Frappuccino and canned DoubleShot beverages made by PepsiCo, and lent its name to what became the best-selling coffee ice cream, made by Dreyer's. In its 2002 fiscal year, Starbucks brought in revenues of $4.1 billion and net income of $268.3 million. A $100 investment in the company's stock at the initial public offering in 1992 had grown to nearly $3,000 by 2003. Even in a lukewarm economy, Starbucks has stayed hot.

Despite the company's scale, Starbucks thinks about its business as a network of relationships. This is a hallmark of firms guided by spiritual values. Smith, who became president and CEO in 2000, told me that he believes Starbucks has succeeded because it has built strong, durable relationships with customers, employees and suppliers. Because people visit Starbucks so often—the average customer stops in five times a month and many come more often—they feel an emotional connection to their neighborhood store. To be sure, coffee is the last socially acceptable addiction, but you can buy coffee in lots of places. "If it was a sterile, impersonal relationship," Smith said, "we would not have the brand strength and business strength that we have." Just as Southwest wants to build ties to its most frequent flyers and UPS drivers get to know people on their routes, Starbucks wants to make its best customers feel welcome. Regular customers like to be recognized, whether by the airline ticket agent, the UPSer in brown or their local barista.

The baristas are vital to the Starbucks experience. Finding and keeping good ones has become a challenge for the company as it has grown. (Starbucks employs nearly seventy-five thousand people, all but about six thousand in the stores.) From the beginning, Starbucks has tried to treat its baristas well—certainly better than most retailers or fast-food outlets treat entry-level workers. "It's an ironic fact," Schultz has said, "that while retail and restaurant businesses live or die on customer service, their employees have among the lowest pay and worst benefits of any industry." Schultz wanted to do better, not only because he felt it was good business but also because he had seen, up close, what can happen when people are cast off by their employers.

Fred Schultz, Howard's father, had held a succession of blue-collar jobs that wore him down. The family had little money; they lived in public housing in Brooklyn. When Howard was seven, his father broke his ankle while working as a truck driver. His mother was pregnant and the family had no income, no health insurance, and no safety net to fall back on. In his book *Pour Your Heart into It,* Schultz wrote:

> Years later, that image of my father—slumped on the family couch, his leg in a cast, unable to work or earn money, and ground down by the world—is still burned into my mind. . . .
>
> The day he died, of lung cancer, in January 1988, was the saddest day of my life. He had no savings, no pension. More important, he had never attained fulfillment and dignity from work he found meaningful.
>
> As a kid, I never had any idea that I would one day head a company. But I knew in my heart that if I were ever in a position where I could make a difference, I wouldn't leave people behind.

As CEO of Starbucks, a job he'd held for less than a year when his father died, Schultz found himself in a position where he could make a difference. Like most start-ups, Starbucks was not profitable. But Schultz managed to persuade its board of directors that none of its employees, not even part-timers, should go without health insurance. He argued that the additional costs would be offset, at least in part, because baristas would stay longer, reducing the costs of recruiting and training. (Typically, newcomers receive at least twenty-four hours of training to learn how to make all those espresso drinks.) Even though most baristas work part time, Schultz wanted to keep them happy and encourage them to sustain the connections that many had built with regular customers. "Treat people like family," Schultz has said, "and they will be loyal and give their all." Most family businesses ran that way, he thought, so why couldn't a big company do so as well? No one keeps track of this kind of thing, but Starbucks was one of the very first big companies to offer health benefits to part-time workers.

In 1991, Schultz and his board of directors decided to share ownership in Starbucks with the employees. This was so unusual at the time that the firm needed permission from the Securities and Exchange Commission to grant stock options to more than seven hundred employees and still remain a private company under the law. Once again, the decision was as much personal as it was business-driven. Schultz was inspired by his father's story, while Smith, who had worked as a management consultant, had seen enough downsizing and cost-cutting to last him a lifetime. "We were idealistic about what kind of company we wanted to create," Smith said. "We didn't want to be like some of the places we've all experienced." Starbucks granted the options, which were called Bean Stock, to all of its people, including eligible part-timers. Employees would hereafter be called partners. That first year, each partner was awarded options to buy stock worth 12 percent of his or her base pay, which came to $2,400 worth of stock for a barista who earned $20,000. An employee who held on to that first grant would have owned about 2,250 shares of stock, worth about $78,000, at the end of 2003. Bean Stock grants have been given out every year since 1991, and some years they have amounted to as much as 14 percent of base pay.

It's no exaggeration to say that values, not markets, shaped the employment practices at Starbucks. Instead of following McDonald's, say, or Wal-Mart, which pay low wages and expect high turnover, Starbucks opted to try to build stronger relationships with its partners. Even though the vast majority leaves for other jobs, the investment pays off, according to Smith. Starbucks has made *Fortune*'s list of the 100 Best Companies to Work For in five of the last six years. "Our recruiting is made easier because we're an employer of choice," Smith said. Turnover is well below industry averages. And, like UPS, Starbucks carefully tracks the satisfaction levels of its people. Several years ago, when the company pushed people too hard to save money, it heard complaints and pulled back. "We squeezed to get margins and it was a mistake," Smith said. "We've learned from it and we don't do it anymore." In its last survey, Starbucks found that about 82 percent of its workers were either satisfied or very satisfied, while 14 percent were neutral and only 5 percent were dissatisfied. (Gallup's national surveys, you may remember, found that 70 percent of all employees have either neutral or negative feelings about their work.) Of course, some Starbucks workers feel overworked and undervalued; several years ago, a group that sued over unpaid overtime won an $18 million settlement. But, Smith said, "there's no question that our people, for the most part, think this is a special place." Starbucks knows that the most important way the company communicates with its customers is through its employees. One reason Starbucks spends so little on advertising—about $30 million a year, a pittance for a big brand—is that the stores, and its people, provide all the advertising the company seems to need.

Like most high-growth companies, Starbucks has encountered setbacks. In an effort to generate evening traffic, the company experimented with full-service restaurants, called Café Starbucks, which served hot meals, beer and wine. The concept did not pan out. A grandiose plan to turn the Starbucks Web site into a "lifestyle portal" by developing partnerships with gourmet food and home furnishings stores proved to be an expensive distraction. And while Starbucks has become a big hit in Asia—a five-story Starbucks in the premier shopping district of Seoul, Korea, is one of the world's busiest—its growth has been sluggish in Europe, the birthplace of espresso. Because executives in Seattle have been reluctant to delegate authority to global licensees, for fear of ceding control over the brand, some joint-venture partners overseas feel like they are micro-managed. "It's a big job to control people," Smith said wryly. "We have to trust our partners. We have to learn how to get out of their way and recognize that once in a while they will make mistakes." When a company has been as successful as Starbucks, top managers sometimes think they have all the answers.

Success itself has become a problem for Starbucks. The company is approaching ubiquity, expanding into the suburbs and even small towns. (Six stores are located within a ten-minute drive of my home in Bethesda.) Its omnipresence has become fodder for comedians. "A New Starbucks Opens in Restroom of Existing Starbucks," read a headline in the satirical newspaper *The Onion.* Starbucks products are available on United Airlines, in Starwood, Hyatt and Marriott hotels, in Barnes & Noble bookstores and in about nineteen thousand supermarkets—even, if you include the bottled drinks, at highway rest stops and in 7-Eleven stores. Not surprisingly, many people regard Starbucks as just another soulless big chain. They say no company so vast can provide a special experience, let alone build relationships with customers that are more than transactional.

More worrisome are the risks posed to the Starbucks brand by a ragtag army of critics. Campus activists, neighborhood preservationists and antiglobalization protestors have all gone after the company. (I once saw a bumper sticker in San Francisco that said

"Friends Don't Let Friends Go to Starbucks.") Much of the criticism is ill-founded. In Manhattan, a character known as Rev. Billy of the Church of Stop Shopping has invaded stores and dumped trash on the tables, accusing Starbucks of "corporate ruthlessness" and destroying "the mom & pop greasy spoons and bohemian coffee bars that make our neighborhoods unique." This is false, as it happens: while Starbucks has grown rapidly, the number of coffee bars operated by local owners and rival chains has grown even faster, according to the Specialty Coffee Association of America, an industry group. A group called the Organic Consumers Association, meanwhile, has called for a boycott of Starbucks because it serves milk from dairies using the genetically engineered bovine growth hormone called rBST. But less than 5 percent of the nation's milk supply can be certified as hormone-free, and Starbucks customers who ask for it can get hormone-free milk or, for that matter, soy milk. During the World Trade Organization meetings in Seattle in 1999, the antipathy toward Starbucks hit home when black-masked anarchists smashed windows in three downtown stores.

The Starbucks backlash distresses company executives. They have tried to build a better kind of company, and now they are being lumped in with all of big business. But they cannot claim that they didn't see it coming: their own market research found nearly a decade ago that the biggest threat to the Starbucks brand was a growing belief among customers that the company was becoming corporate and predictable. Schultz has long feared that rapid growth would make it difficult to sustain the company's values. "How do we grow big but maintain intimacy with our people?" he has said. "This is the toughest dilemma I face as the leader of Starbucks."

Its coffee-buying practices in particular have been brewing as an issue for a long time. In 1994, Chicago labor activists picketed stores, accusing the company of exploiting coffee growers in Guatemala. Perhaps because the charges were off the mark—Starbucks did not then and does not now own coffee farms, grow its own coffee or employ growers—the company dismissed them. The idea that a company could be held responsible for actions taken far up its supply chain was novel in the mid-1990s.

Besides, its executives said, Starbucks did care about coffee growers. The company demonstrated its concern by supporting educational, health and social service projects in origin countries. Starbucks launched a partnership with CARE, for example, in 1991, and became one of the nonprofit's biggest corporate donors. Since 1998, Starbucks has worked closely with the nonprofit Conservation International to help preserve a "biodiversity hot spot" in Chiapas, Mexico. The company pays farmers there a premium for "shade-grown" coffee, which is cultivated by a traditional method that preserves tropical forests. (Otherwise, under economic pressures, some growers cut down trees to boost production.) Most important, Starbucks has always paid top prices for coffee, often twice as much as other buyers, so that it can obtain the highest-quality beans. The specialty coffee business has been a boon to growers. "Philanthropy is important, but it's a drop in the bucket compared to the impact of the higher prices we pay," Smith told me. "Almost nobody else was paying those prices." The Starbucks people saw themselves as part of the solution, not part of the problem. "When we get labeled, it's pretty painful and it can pretty quickly make you angry," Smith said. They felt maligned.

When the world coffee market collapsed in 1999, Starbucks became an even more inviting target for activists—although the company had nothing to do with the precipitous drop in coffee prices. Grown in about seventy tropical countries, coffee is the world's second most traded commodity, after oil, with a global export value of more than $5 billion a year. Until 1989, coffee prices were set by an OPEC-like mechanism called the International Coffee Agreement, which was intended to stabilize third-world economies and minimize discontent that could be exploited by leftists. When the cold war ended, the United States withdrew its support for the cartel. After an oversupply of low-grade coffee from Vietnam flooded the market in the late 1990s, there was nothing to keep prices up. Many of the world's twenty-five million growers were devastated as the price per pound for commodity-grade coffee fell below 50 cents, from a peak of nearly $2. "Farmers who can't make a living are abandoning their farms," Peter Torrebiarte, Starbucks' green-coffee manager and a native of Guatemala, told me.

The Fair Trade movement—which would soon pose a problem for Starbucks—arrived in the United States in 1999, just as the coffee crisis hit. The concept of Fair Trade requires a brief explanation: Beginning in the 1940s, churches in North America and Europe sought to provide relief to poor people in the so-called third world by buying handicrafts and, later, commodities directly from the producers. To ensure that products carrying the Fair Trade label do, in fact, benefit the poor, a global alliance of nonprofit groups established a system of independent, third-party certification. To use the Fair Trade label—think of it as the politically correct equivalent of the Good Housekeeping Seal—companies must contract with one of the nonprofits, which will then monitor its practices. (Currently, there are Fair Trade systems in place for tea, chocolate and bananas as well as coffee.) Coffee sold with the Fair Trade label in the United States must be purchased from democratic, worker-owned cooperatives at a price set by TransFair USA, the nonprofit certifying agency in this country. In 2003, the price was set at $1.26 per pound for regular coffee and $1.41 per pound for organic coffee—more than twice the price of commodity-grade coffee.

The Fair Trade movement and its allies immediately targeted Starbucks. This had more to do with the company's visibility than with its coffee-buying practices. Starbucks buys only high-quality arabica coffee and pays prices that are near the Fair Trade minimums. (In 2002, the company paid an average price of $1.20 per pound.) Its purchases represent only about 1 percent of the world's beans—most coffee is still sold in supermarkets, fast-food outlets, or gas stations—so a change in its practices would have only a limited impact on growers. By contrast, the coffee divisions of four big multinational corporations—Nestlé, Kraft, Procter & Gamble and

Sara Lee—buy about half of the world's coffee and pay far less per pound, probably an amount close to the commodity-grade price of about 40 to 50 cents a pound. (They don't disclose their costs.) But how do you go after companies that don't have stores and sell coffee under many different brands—Chock full o' Nuts, Folger's, Maxwell House, Nescafé and Yuban? Starbucks is not just a convenient target but also a tempting one because of the contrast that can be drawn between $3 lattes and impoverished farm workers. It's a false contrast, of course—in theory, at least, higher prices for coffee make possible higher prices for the growers. In any event, a vocal group of activists organized by a human rights group called Global Exchange showed up at Starbucks' annual shareholders meeting in March 2000, demanding that the company sell Fair Trade coffee. Protests were planned. Campuses were mobilized. An open letter to Schultz accused Starbucks of exploiting growers. "The farmers who make you rich earn poverty wages," it said. "Sweatshops occur not only in the factory but in the field."

Surprisingly, Starbucks was unprepared for the onslaught. "We got blindsided," Smith said. Starbucks executives naively felt that their good intentions and track record would shield them from attack. "The advocacy groups, quite frankly, they either didn't get or didn't want to get the model," Smith said. "They wanted somebody they could bang on." The activists saw Starbucks as just another big business. "They have a basic distrust, or cynicism," Smith said. Nevertheless, Starbucks chose to make peace rather than resist the Fair Trade pressures. The people at Starbucks say they share the goal of the Fair Trade movement—they, too, want to enable coffee growers to make a living and stay in business—and so they hastily negotiated a licensing agreement with TransFair USA. Days before the protests were to begin, Starbucks announced its plans to launch a line of Fair Trade–certified coffee.

Officially, Starbucks endorses the concept of Fair Trade. In its 2002 corporate social responsibility report, Starbucks said that it bought 1.1 million pounds of Fair Trade–certified coffee, representing about 1 percent of its total purchases. That was nearly twice what it bought in fiscal year 2001. Privately, though, Starbucks executives have mixed feelings about Fair Trade. They did not like being put on the defensive. "The emphasis that the Fair Trade people have placed on specialty coffee is, by and large, misdirected," Smith said. The global coffee giants buy far more commodity coffee, and at cheaper prices, he noted. Starbucks also says that Fair Trade is a limited response to the coffee crisis, in part because only coffee from worker-owned cooperatives can be certified as Fair Trade. Most coffee, including most of the high-quality coffee Starbucks needs, comes from plantations, wholesalers or small farmers. Besides that, the very idea of Fair Trade poses a threat to Starbucks: the company does not want to promote the "brand" of Fair Trade, if only because it implies that the rest of Starbucks' coffee is somehow tainted. It's not hard to imagine how Starbucks executives feel when they see Medea Benjamin, the executive director of Global Exchange, quoted in a *Time* magazine article about Starbucks saying: "Coffee without the Fair Trade seal is very likely sweatshop coffee." She's right about most coffee sold in the United States, but not about the coffee sold at Starbucks.

Global Exchange wants Starbucks to do more to promote Fair Trade. It is asking the company to buy, brew and sell more Fair Trade coffee and to offer a decaf Fair Trade blend. By contrast, Paul Rice, director of TransFair USA, the certifying organization, told the *National Catholic Reporter:* "I think Starbucks gets a bad rap. It's a mistake to target Starbucks because they are not doing enough, and not target Kraft or Nestlé or Procter & Gamble who aren't doing anything and won't even return my calls." Recently, P&G, through its Millstone brand, and Kraft, whose coffee brands include Maxwell House and Jacobs, made major commitments to buy Fair Trade coffee and support sustainable coffee production—a big breakthrough for the activists and socially responsible investors who brought pressure to bear on Kraft and P&G.

So how will Starbucks deal with the coffee crisis—and with its critics? It will not embrace the Fair Trade model. Nor will it seek to exploit the depressed coffee market. Instead, true to form, Starbucks has set out to create a market of its own. In 2001, Starbucks announced a set of coffee-sourcing guidelines, developed with the help of Conservation International, that will revamp the way the company buys coffee. Under the guidelines, Starbucks will pay higher prices to farmers who meet a long list of social, environmental, economic and quality standards. The guidelines are complicated, but their purpose is simple: to enable growers to earn a decent living, to conserve the tropical environment and to provide Starbucks with a reliable supply of quality coffee.

This is not the approach most companies take when the price for a commodity they need begins to fall. As Smith said: "We could take a short-term view and say, OK, this year we're going to jump right in. There are low prices out there. Let's optimize. Then, the next thing you know, I'm going to lose a bunch of my farms. . . . If we allow that to happen, it will threaten, on a long-term basis, our supply." Starbucks expects to need lots more coffee in the years ahead. "We're at seven thousand stores now," Smith said. "We're talking about a minimum of twenty-five thousand on a global scale." Coffee czar Dub Hay put it simply: "The growers are our future."

Many coffee growers have embraced the guidelines, according to the company. Two years after they were introduced, Starbucks had received more than 160 applications from suppliers in fourteen countries in Latin America, Asia and Africa. (Some came from big groups of farmers.) Those growers who earn the maximum rating under the guidelines will be paid 10 cents extra per pound for their coffee and be given "preferred supplier" status, meaning that they will be first in line to sell more coffee to Starbucks when it is needed. "When we're growing at 30 percent a year, they stand to gain," Hay said. In return, the growers will have to obey local labor laws and international conventions governing workers' wages, human rights, health and safety. They will have to employ growing and processing methods that help conserve soil, water and biological diversity. They will also have to produce high-quality coffee, of course. "They're graded on a point system," Hay said, "and they are going to be audited and verified." I asked him if farmers in the program might feel micromanaged by Starbucks. "This was built with grower input," he replied. "We're all in this together." Most growers welcome the arrival of Starbucks, according to the company and its nonprofit partners. Said Dub: "This is the only place in my buying career when I've looked someone in the eye and said, 'Are we paying you enough?'"

Convincing the activists that Starbucks is doing the right thing will be difficult. Starbucks says that its practices are more comprehensive than the Fair Trade standards and that third parties will audit them. But it also concedes that the vast majority of the coffee it sells will not carry the Fair Trade brand. Today, that's a nonissue with most consumers. But if Fair Trade wins a bigger following, Starbucks' go-it-alone approach will appear suspect. "The question they have to ask is, 'Will consumers accept corporations who audit themselves?'" said Haven Bourke of TransFair USA. "In these days of post-Enron and post-WorldCom, we think the independent third-party guarantee of credibility is very important." Smith acknowledges the risk. "From a brand standpoint, Fair Trade is a great name," he said. "I give them a lot of credit for it, and I don't disagree with what they are trying to do." But, he said, the company's standards are superior, and they make more sense for Starbucks and for the growers. Whether Starbucks can sell its story in the marketplace of ideas is an open question.

I'm going to keep on drinking Starbucks. Yes, Starbucks is a sprawling multinational corporation, intent on spreading its brand to every corner of the world. That's what big companies do. (Recently, the company opened stores in Vienna, Madrid, Paris and Mexico City.) But big does not necessarily equal bad. Although people at Starbucks do not talk about religion or faith or soul or heart—except in the title of Schultz's book, *Pour Your Heart into It*—the company's practices are rooted in spiritual values. Starbucks practices the Golden Rule with its workers and the coffee growers, treating them with respect and care. Its success is driven by these

long-term relationships. Sustaining those relationships will be difficult as the company grows to ten thousand, fifteen thousand or
twenty-five thousand stores. But I believe that Howard Schultz,
Orin Smith and their partners around the world will do their utmost
to try.

6

A PRIEST,
A MINISTER AND
A RABBI

The Mendoza School of Business at Notre Dame is no ordinary business school. Faculty meetings begin with a prayer. Not far from the dean's office is a small chapel. And long before the teaching of business ethics came back into vogue, Notre Dame had integrated ethics, values and faith into its curriculum.

So it came as no surprise when graduate students in a class called Religion, Spirituality and Work turned their attention to a question that probably would not occur to most future MBAs: can marketing Coke or Pepsi be a way to serve the common good?

"If you're a great marketer," C. P. Thompson asked, "do you want to spend your time trying to sell Coke instead of Pepsi? Is Coke that much different from Pepsi? It's colored sugar water." Thompson, thirty-four, an engineer in Silicon Valley for ten years, has come to Notre Dame to pursue an MBA in finance.

"Coke isn't evil," replied twenty-eight-year-old Wyatt Shiflett, who made a good living as a stockbroker at Morgan Stanley before returning to school. "By creating market share, they create jobs. They create wealth for the shareholders, and their employees."

"But they just take jobs away from Pepsi," said Thompson. "It's a mature market. It's a zero-sum game." He went on to say that he couldn't see himself marketing Advil, say, as opposed to generic ibuprofen, or selling gas-guzzling SUVs. But it's Coke—he called it sugar water—that really got under his skin.

For Father Oliver Williams, who taught the class, the argument hit close to home. Donald Keough, Coke's former chief operating officer and a Notre Dame trustee, is an acquaintance. "Great benefactor, very dedicated Christian, put several of his children through here," Williams said. A campus dormitory, Keough Hall, was named after his wife. But does a life spent selling Coke align with Catholic social teaching, which says people and institutions should promote the common good? More broadly, what guidance does Catholicism offer business leaders?

I had come to Notre Dame to explore that question with Father Williams, a pioneer in the spirituality-at-work movement who has taught at the university for thirty years. By then, I had spent lots of time with CEOs discussing faith, values and business. Some were overtly religious or spiritual, but even those who were not, I felt certain, had been influenced by the great religious traditions and their moral and ethical teachings. I also felt sure that religion has useful things to say to businesspeople. After all, most big companies disappear or die within a span of forty or fifty years, according to *The Living Company,* by Arie de Geus. By contrast, Christianity has endured for two thousand years, and Judaism has been around for even longer. They have proven that they can adapt to changing markets. I decided to seek out a priest, a minister and a rabbi who had thought about business. If nothing else, they would know something about sustainability, I figured.

Father Williams has studied the interplay between business and religion since 1980, when he organized a conference at Notre Dame called "The Judeo-Christian Vision and the Modern Corporation." Back in his office after class, he told me that Catholicism does not offer hard-and-fast rules about what kinds of work to do or which companies make acceptable employers. What's key is to ask the difficult questions, as his students are doing.

Williams personally has no quarrel with Coke. "It isn't harmful, obviously," he said, "and people do find joy in it." What about critics who say that companies like Coke contribute to the epidemic of obesity? Williams says the company should do more to discourage overuse: "Responsible drinking can apply to sugared sodas as well as alcohol." But, he said, "the company has created an awful lot of jobs." Williams also has seen first-hand Coca-Cola's impact on South Africa, where he has taught and worked for many years. In 1986, he wrote a book, *The Apartheid Crisis,* arguing that U.S. companies could play a constructive role in ending apartheid. Coca-Cola has been and remains a leader when it comes to hiring and promoting black workers, he said. And its trucks, which reach even the smallest villages, deliver not just soft drinks but health information, medical supplies and even condoms to help control the spread of AIDS. "They've done a wonderful job there," Williams said. The point is, he said, a business executive can do God's work most anywhere.

That Williams is more of a pragmatist than a purist is no surprise when you know his history. One of six children of a gas station owner and entrepreneur, Ollie grew up in suburban New Jersey and worked summers on Wall Street, where he became fascinated by the stock market. After earning an undergraduate degree in chemical engineering from Notre Dame, he enlisted in the U.S. Navy, expecting that a business career would follow. But, while stationed aboard a ship in the Mediterranean, the ship's commander told him to fill in as the Catholic chaplain. "I don't know anything about theology," he protested. Replied the officer: "I don't recall asking you about that." Williams found the work of a chaplain so rewarding that after his discharge he returned to Notre Dame to study for the priesthood.

He went on to earn a Ph.D. in theology from Vanderbilt and, after being ordained in 1970, he returned once more to South Bend as a faculty member in theology. His interest in business never waned, though, and in 1980 he received a fellowship at Stanford Business School to study ethics. He has focused on religion, ethics and business ever since.

I began our conversation with a simple question: what, according to Catholic social teaching, is the purpose of a business? "The purpose of a business is to enable human flourishing," Williams replied. That may sound simple, but it's not. At the most prosaic level, he explained, business exists to generate the material wealth needed to live a virtuous life—that is, business enables us to acquire the food, clothing and shelter without which neither the mind nor the spirit can be developed. Only after our basic needs are met can there "be a moral or intellectual life," Williams said. "We're creatures of flesh and blood. We're not just cerebral." A second purpose of business is to provide opportunities for us to develop character and virtues, as well as talents and skills. "An array of virtues are required in business," Williams said. "Industriousness, frugality, honesty." We can choose to cultivate other virtues, too—borrowing from Aristotle, Williams named the classic virtues of wisdom, justice, temperance and fortitude, all of which can be developed in the business world. A third purpose of business, at its best, is to enable us to join with others and become God's partners as we transform the world from what it is into what it ought to be. "It goes back to Genesis," Williams said. "When we are called to be the masters of the fish and the birds, and the stewards of God's world, the vision is that God has created the world and our role is to be cocreators. To take the givens, and to shape them so the world is more human. Obviously, we're not on the level of God. We can't make something out of nothing. But I sometimes ask my students, what has created more jobs than anything else in the last fifteen years in the United States? It is human imagination and sand. Silicon. That's an example of our role as cocreators." Next time you visit Silicon Valley, think about that.

I'm reminded that we can bring our own sense of purpose to work that might otherwise seem mundane. Workers at Southwest Airlines don't just transport people from place to place—they serve them, and ideally leave them smiling. UPS drivers do more than deliver packages—they make commerce possible. In a book about faith and work called *Being God's Partner,* Rabbi Jeffrey Salkin tells the story of a mover who with evident joy helped Salkin's family move to a new home, and explained why he felt he was doing God's work:

> "Moving is hard for most people," the man said. "It's a very vulnerable time. People are nervous about going to a new community, and having strangers pack their most precious possessions. So, I think God wants me to treat my customers with love and to make them feel like I care about their things and their life. God wants me to help make their changes go smoothly. If I can be happy about it, maybe they can be, too."

Father Williams, too, said that by reframing our approach to business and seeking out the holy in what we do, many of us can discover a greater sense of purpose in our work.

That Catholicism would develop a fundamentally favorable view of business represents a "sea change, a paradigm shift" from the medieval belief that commerce was at best tolerable and at worst pernicious, Williams explained. Catholicism's monastic tradition long held that God was to be found in solitude and contemplation, not at work; Church thinkers taught that commerce would lead to acquisitiveness. "Their fear was that the world would give honor to the ones who had the most money, rather than the one who had the noblest virtue," Williams said. These were not groundless worries—business magazines publish lists of the world's richest men, not its most generous. Even now, some church people argue that Christianity and capitalism are incompatible, citing as evidence the biblical passage where Jesus tells his followers: "No man can serve two masters: ye cannot serve God and Mammon." The Harvard theologian

Paul Tillich once wrote that "any serious Christian must be a social-ist," and Monsignor John A. Ryan, a prominent twentieth-century Catholic moralist, once asserted that there was an "unbridgeable gulf between the Catholic and capitalistic conceptions of life." Williams disagrees. The way for Catholics to avoid serving Mammon at the expense of God is to strive to make sure that their pursuit of self-interest is tempered by moral virtues. Put another way, Catholic social teaching tells us that business and the economy should always serve humanity, not the other way around.

Two influential Catholic documents flesh out this argument. In 1986, the U.S. Catholic Bishops published a pastoral letter, called *Economic Justice for All: Catholic Social Teaching and the U.S. Economy,* which attracted widespread attention. Five years later, Pope John Paul II issued a sweeping social encyclical called *Centesimus Annus.* Both documents reject socialism and accept the likelihood that capitalism will be the basis of future economic life. But the capitalism they prescribe differs radically from the way most business is conducted today in the United States. The Catholic leaders write that every person should have the right to participate in the economy and to shape his or her own work. They say that wealth, income and power should not be concentrated among the few. They warn of the dangers of greed, consumerism, militarism and ecological decay. And they argue in no uncertain terms that labor should have priority over capital and that a concern for the poor should be at the heart of decisions shaping economic life. As Pope John Paul II once put it: "The needs of the poor take priority over the desires of the rich; the rights of workers over the maximization of profits; the preservation of the environment over uncontrolled industrial expansion; production to meet social needs over production for military purposes."

How, then, should businesspeople translate those principles into action? That's often unclear, Williams said. It's likely to require a willingness to experiment, a "process that involves trial and error, a matter of seeing what works in the marketplace." This does not mean that the underlying principles are negotiable. "I'm going to go to the wall over saying that the priority of labor over capital is a good principle, and is rock bottom, and is never going to change," he says.

Certainly Catholics should oppose excessive compensation for CEOs, though precisely what is excessive and how salary scales should be structured are matters for debate. "We all don't need to be paid the same," Williams said, "but the incongruity we've seen between the low and high end of the spectrum is outrageous. There's no way it can be justified." So, for example, prominent Catholics who served on the board of directors of the Walt Disney Co., among them Father Leo O'Donohue, the former president of Georgetown University, should have spoken out against the big grants of stock options for Michael Eisner, the company's chairman and CEO. (In the late 1990s, Eisner cashed in accumulated options worth $570 million.) Few directors, though, see executive compensation as a moral issue. "Boards weren't doing their jobs," Williams said.

But Williams takes issue with Catholic ethicists who argue that, as a matter of principle, all corporations should offer employee stock ownership plans so that workers can share ownership of their companies. That's not practical, he said, or even desirable if it means that workers are forced to take lower salaries today in order to get stock that may or may not be valuable in the future. "You may need the money now," Williams said. "And you may not be so well off in thirty years if the business doesn't work." Workers should, however, have a voice in deciding how they will be compensated.

Even on the question of what constitutes a just wage, Williams gives business executives some wiggle room. While all workers are entitled to a living wage, safe working conditions, health care and paid vacations, competitive pressures can make it difficult for even conscientious business owners to provide all those benefits. "No one should go without health care," Williams said, "but if Burger King wants to give full health benefits to all its workers, they're going to price themselves out of the market." That puts the most generous employers at a competitive disadvantage. "My advice there is that you should lobby the government," Williams said. "That's the only way to level the playing field." It's an unorthodox notion—not many businesspeople are likely to ask the government to force them to raise wages, offer health insurance or pay higher taxes so that the government can offer universal health care—but Catholic social teaching demands no less. Williams said: "Men and women who are moral and have real character and get into positions of power can really change things."

I asked Father Williams where he's seen that happen. He told me about Caltex, a unit of Chevron Texaco that operates an oil refinery in Cape Town, South Africa. Williams had a friend, Paul Bulley, who became a top Caltex executive and wanted to help build the new South Africa. Bulley helped the groundskeepers at the company start their own small firm, giving them the tools they needed and teaching them about business. The groundskeepers learned how to keep the books, attract new customers and manage their workload, and then they went out on their own. "These were basically people with no marketable skills," Williams said. "That's the way people with power and money can use it to help the poor."

ENRON was still making headlines when I went to see Max Stackhouse, a professor of ethics at Princeton Theological Seminary who has taught, studied and written about religion and business for thirty years. Predictably, he's disturbed by the accusations against former CEOs Ken Lay, Jeff Skilling and others, some of whom were active in their churches. Unexpectedly, he's got a beef with their pastors, too. "I'm really angry at the pastors of those people—because many of them were churchy types—and at the stream of piety that developed in that network, which did not raise questions, internal questions, structural questions, psychological questions about what was going on," Stackhouse said. But how were the pastors supposed to have known what was going on, when regulators, industry analysts and the press did not? Well, in Stackhouse's view, religious leaders who watch as their parishioners accumulate and spend vast fortunes with dizzying speed should ask some friendly but pointed questions. He explained: "First of all, you say, 'Let's go play golf, or tennis.' And then you sit around on the porch afterward, and have a beer, and say, 'Have you thought about the relationship of your faith to all of this? I don't know how it looks to God, but maybe you should think it through. It doesn't look too good to me, and I'd like to talk with you and your wife about it a little more.' " Such conversations between pastors and businesspeople don't happen nearly as often as they should. "It's a legitimate role for the church," he said. "But I think the clergy are basically incompetent when it comes to dealing with money, and moneyed people. They haven't been trained."

Stackhouse has been doing his part to help clergy develop an effective pastoral stance toward business. As the Stephen Colwell Professor of Christian Ethics at Princeton Theological Seminary, he urges divinity students to learn business and economics. He helped to edit *On Moral Business,* a 980-page anthology of classical and contemporary writings on ethics and economic life. He also writes for scholarly and popular journals about such topics as globalization, arguing that multinational corporations have the potential to help unify the world and to lift millions of poor people into the middle class. That's not a popular position in the mainline Protestant circles where Stackhouse, an ordained minister of the liberal United Church of Christ, often finds himself. But he is a firm believer in the potential of business, which he calls "indispensable to the well-being of the common life."

He didn't always feel that way. The son and grandson of Methodist clergymen, Stackhouse studied philosophy at DePauw University, where he became both a political activist and "the raving campus atheist, mostly for adolescent reasons," he told me. As an idealistic young professor, he joined the Democratic Socialist Organizing Committee, a group led by the writer and activist Michael

Harrington that favored both socialism and democracy. But Stackhouse resigned after spending a year in East Germany, where his students persuaded him that socialism and freedom were incompatible. "From then on, I began to explore alternative theories of capitalism," he says. This became the focus of our conversation, which unfolded in his book-lined study in Princeton.

Unfettered capitalism has not worked, Stackhouse believes. It generates too much inequality and "an economic egocentricity with little place for generosity, compassion and social justice," he has written. In its place, Stackhouse favors a reformed capitalism that is judiciously regulated by the government, committed to producing quality goods and services, and shaped by business leaders who embrace their moral obligations to serve others. Coming to grips with those obligations is a challenge for executives because "modern business is largely without a nuanced vocabulary to deal with its own moral potential and limitations," he said. "Economics and law alone cannot generate business morality." Something else is needed—and that something is a theologically grounded morality.

By this, Stackhouse means a set of beliefs and principles that cross religious lines. These are what I have called spiritual values. "All profound religion," Stackhouse has written, "has at its depths a celebration of giving and not getting, of sharing and not possessing, of sacrificing and not only accumulating." But how can a business career be built around giving, sharing and sacrificing?

One place to begin is by rethinking the very idea of career. The English word *career* comes from the French *carrière,* which means "racecourse"; used as a verb, *career* also means "to move headlong at full speed," which, unfortunately, is the way many businesspeople approach work. Instead of thinking of business as a career, Stackhouse suggests that we reenvision it as a calling, vocation, or profession. Those concepts come out of the biblical traditions, and they were first applied to rabbis and priests. Religious leaders were believed to be called by God—*vocation* comes from the Latin word for call—and they responded with a profession, which was both an avowal of faith and a promise to cultivate one's talents and use them for the common good. Over time, pursuing a profession came to mean doing work that required specialized training and carried with it an obligation to serve. Medicine, law and education were all seen as professions.

Business was not, even after graduate schools of business were created to train corporate managers. Most corporate jobs don't require advanced degrees or special training. Nor are there professional codes of conduct for business, as there are for medicine or law. Stackhouse would like businesspeople, with the encouragement of educators and clergy, to think of their work as a profession or calling. Pastors could, for example, take a moment in church to single out an executive who has been given expanded responsibilities and say, "We're proud of you. We're going to pray for you and bless you. And we'd like you to think about excellence not only for yourself but for everyone involved."

"The idea is to connect what you're doing—daily, mechanically, nose to the grindstone—to some larger purpose," Stackhouse told me. "To put it in the old-fashioned terms, you're doing your job because you have a sense that it has to ultimately serve God and serve your neighbor. And in the global environment, when you talk about your neighbor, that's a big bunch of people."

OK, then, but how are businesspeople to serve their global neighbors? Or, as the British economic historian R. H. Tawney asked:

> Granted that I should love my neighbor as myself, the questions which, under modern conditions of large-scale organization, remain for solution are: Who precisely *is* my neighbor? And how exactly am I to make my love for him effective in practice?

Stackhouse has lots of ideas—businesspeople can build factories in underdeveloped countries, offer job training to unskilled workers, wisely give away their wealth and so forth. But, like Ollie Williams, he is reluctant to get specific. Biblical messages are powerful, he says, but they lay out broad obligations—the obligation to work hard and well for the greater good, the need to care for the poor and oppressed, the importance of exercising stewardly responsibility for God's creation. "In the final analysis," he said, "the church has nothing to offer the world of economic life but words and examples—words about how things ought to be, and examples of how to live together."

One powerful word is *stewardship*. "Stewardship is a very broad and deep and profound resource," Stackhouse said. "It really cuts through the whole notion of property as possession." The concept can be traced to the way Christians read Genesis, he explained, and particularly to the idea that "ye shall have dominion" over God's creation. Dominion isn't domination, but a "kind of custodial responsibility," Stackhouse said. One of the most famous sermons in the history of Protestantism—John Wesley's "The Use of Money," in which he counsels his followers to "gain all you can . . . save all you can . . . and give all you can"—is all about stewardship. "God placed you here not as a proprietor but a steward," Wesley wrote. "As such he entrusted you, for a season, with goods of various kinds; but the sole property of these goods still rests in Him, nor can ever be alienated from Him."

While this may seem far removed from twenty-first-century business, stewardship is at the heart of one of today's big issues: corporate governance. CEOs of many companies—Enron, Tyco and WorldCom were only the most notorious—lost sight of the fact that they were stewards of other people's money. So did their boards of directors. So, for that matter, does every businessperson who fudges on an expense account with the rationale that he or she is only taking from "the company." (You don't need to think of the money as God's, but at a public company, it helps to remember that millions of investors have trusted the company to spend their money wisely.) "If you're a manager in a large firm," Stackhouse said, "you're a steward of other people's resources—in a moral and spiritual as well as a legal sense." This is another argument against bloated CEO pay.

The biblical idea of covenant is another powerful concept that the Church offers businesspeople. In the Bible, the word *covenant* describes the eternal bond between God and humanity; in business, Stackhouse told me, relationships that today are governed by legal contracts can be redefined as covenantal. He explained: "For the most part, a contract is, 'I will do this for you, and you'll benefit, and you will do that for me, and I'll benefit.' I deliver the three thousand bucks to you. You deliver the used car to me. If it doesn't fall apart when I'm driving home, we're done." By contrast, a covenant binds people into forms of solidarity and shared responsibility that are deeper and more durable, more akin to a long-term partnership than a short-term transaction. (It's what businesspeople call a "win-win," a deal that provides real and lasting benefits for both parties.) Like a contract, a covenant requires fairness and openness, but it also relies on trust and a measure of faith. A marriage is a familiar example of a covenant.

In business, covenants can define the relationships between a company and its workers, a company and its suppliers, or even a company and its hometown. "When a town depends on the well-being of a corporation, and the corporation depends on the well-being of the town, one can really talk about building a deeper level of trust, and appreciation, and mutual generosity and support that's quite constructive," Stackhouse said. He cites a prosaic example—a hardware store decides to sponsor a Little League team. This is partly about branding and generating goodwill, maybe even selling screws and nails. But it can also be a spiritual act, a gesture on behalf of community, teamwork, keeping kids off the streets and getting fathers and mothers involved in their lives. At its best, it affirms the covenant between the business and the community.

More often, the notion of covenant is applied to relations between owners and workers. Greyston Bakery, Tom's of Maine, Southwest Airlines, UPS and Starbucks all value workers for who they are, encourage them to develop their potential, and invite them into the decision-making process. Often, workers share ownership. Max DePree, the former CEO of Herman Miller, whom we'll meet in the next chapter, actually used the word *covenant* to describe the relationship between the company and its workers. But he and Stackhouse both make clear that much is expected from both parties in a covenant. Everyone needs to perform, or no one's job is secure.

Many businesspeople will find these ideas appealing. Who would not want to discover a larger purpose in work, or build relationships that are deep and long-lasting? But many will ask if this view from the pulpit can guide businesspeople of faith. I later asked Stackhouse, by e-mail, whether a capitalism shaped by spiritual values is a realistic possibility.

His vision, he replied, is only partially realistic. "But life is altered by a combination of the realistic and the idealistic," he wrote. "If we lose the latter, we are less than the angels, and merely beasts. If we lose the former, we are more than the animals, but more angelic than is believable. But perhaps it is possible to 'do well' by consciously also 'doing good' and 'doing what is right.' Now that would be the great hope of a profoundly serious business leader."

I T WAS a bitterly cold winter day, but I was only mildly surprised to see a yellow Cannondale road bicycle standing by the entrance to Adat Shalom Reconstructionist Congregation when I arrived for a meeting with the rabbi, Fred Scherlinder Dobb. Rabbi Dobb, who is passionately committed to the environment, rides his bike just about everywhere—even when temperatures dip into the mid-teens.

"It's exhilarating in its own way," he said cheerfully as we settled onto a couch in his study. "But, obviously, it's not just about the pleasure or the exercise. It comes from the idea that values must trump convenience or aesthetics." About the only time he leaves the bike at his home in Washington, D.C., about six miles away from the Bethesda synagogue, is when he's going to preside over a ceremony where appearances are important—that is, when he feels an immediate obligation greater than the constant one he feels to the earth. "If you'll pardon the expression, I'm not orthodox about it," he said. "But I'm not liberal about it, either."

Rabbi Fred, as he's known, is my rabbi. I've known him for a couple of years, and I've decided to interview him because I admire the way he lives his values. When Adat Shalom, a congregation formed in 1988 with nineteen families, decided to build its first synagogue, Dobb and the congregants—an opinionated, engaged, theologically and politically liberal group, now numbering about 450 families—hired architects and contractors who were committed to green construction practices. Much of the wood for the building was harvested in a sustainable manner, carpets were made with recycled content, the landscaping favors native plants and the interiors are lit by sunlight or by energy-efficient fluorescent bulbs. (The *ner tamid,* or eternal light, in the sanctuary is a low-watt bulb powered by a photovoltaic panel on the roof.) When Adat Shalom hired a janitorial service, the congregation agreed to add $8,000 a year to the low bid for the contract, with the proviso that the extra money be passed through to the workers so they can earn a living wage. At home, Fred and his wife, Minna Scherlinder, buy electricity generated by wind and turn their thermostat down to 59 degrees at night to conserve energy. He explained: "Lived spirituality and religion, as I understand them as a Reconstructionist rabbi, mean taking real actions to uphold our values, to protect creation and to honor the image of God in all aspects of our lives." Lest he be seen as ecologically pure, Dobb pointed out that his share of the pollution generated by the airplanes that he periodically flies puts him above the allowable per-person limit for greenhouse gas emissions, at least according to a set of calculations published in a magazine called *Yes! A Journal of Positive Futures.* "I am keenly aware that I am taking baby steps toward sustainability," he said. Still, he is also the only person I know who monitors his own contribution to global warming.

Dobb was raised by his mother in a middle-class neighborhood of Toledo, Ohio. They didn't have much money, a fact he could not ignore because they were surrounded by families with more. "Socially, I was upper-middle-class," he said. "But I grew up with a firsthand understanding of food stamps and reduced-price lunches at school." Midway through his junior year at Brandeis University, Dobb set off on a 3,300-mile walk from Los Angeles to New York as part of a project called the Global Walk for a Livable World. By then, he was both a fervent environmentalist, with a love for the outdoors, and a committed Jew; he gave more than 250 talks along the way at synagogues, churches and schools. After study in Israel and at the Reconstructionist Rabbinical College, he became the first full-time rabbi at Adat Shalom in 1997, at age twenty-seven.

Ever since, Dobb has had to strike a balance between expressing his strong political and environmental views—which are well to the left of the mainstream—and ministering to relatively affluent congregants, including businesspeople, who might be put off by his opinions. "There's that great line that clergy are supposed to 'comfort the afflicted and afflict the comfortable.' I need to be able to do both," he said. "So for my SUV-owner congregant whose mother just died, her choice of vehicle is irrelevant at that point. But at the Kol Nidre service, if I have chosen a so-called prophetic topic, the fact that even the president of the synagogue drives an SUV should not dissuade me." There are also tactical questions he ponders. "How strident should I be in order to create the greatest net impact? Sometimes that's by telling it like it is. And sometimes that's by a quiet modeling of a more sustainable approach."

His Jewish environmental values are rooted in Torah, the first five books of the Bible. The creation story in Genesis, he explained, clearly places humans in the context of a natural world populated by other, sacred creatures. "Humans are not created until the sixth day," he said, "and we don't even get that day to ourselves." After humans are created, when the reader might expect to find the common refrain that God looked at the Divine handiwork and saw that it was good, God says nothing. Not until several verses later does God behold *all* of creation and call it very good. "Humans on their own don't even merit a 'good,' much less a 'very good.' It's the interconnected whole where humans take their place with all the rest of it that is 'very good,'" Dobb said. "So God looks at a complex interconnected ecosystem like a wetland and says, 'Very good.' We look at it and say, 'Wal-Mart, or interstate or golf course,' and there's something wrong with that. So just at a basic level, this text critiques much of modern economic and social practice."

Like Max Stackhouse, Rabbi Dobb believes that the biblical verse giving humans dominion over the earth does not give us the right to dominate, as some have argued; instead, it requires us to exercise careful stewardship of the planet. So-called deep ecologists critique even the idea of stewardship, he reminded me. "Who are we to say we're on top?" he said. The verses about dominion are followed by the revelation that Adam and Eve, the archetypal humans, were vegetarians. "I happen to be a vegetarian," Dobb said, "and I feel strongly about the excesses of the modern meat industry. But, setting that aside, in this context dominion does not even include killing one animal for food. Thus how can we possibly understand dominion as giving us the right to make a species extinct or make a human footprint on the globe that doesn't leave room for everything and everyone else?" What's more, Adam and Eve in the Garden of Eden are told that their job is to *l'ovdah ul'shomrah,* which is understood to mean "serve the land, work the land and guard the land." "Right there," Dobb said, "is a phenomenal biblical litmus test for the ethical, spiritual and environmental health of any proposed course of action. Does it serve the land? Does it guard the land?"

The creation story also introduces the practice of Shabbat, a vital and powerful Jewish idea. Preserving one day each week for worship, study and family forces us to slow down, and reminds us that life is about more than production and consumption. As the scholar Abraham Joshua Heschel wrote in *The Sabbath:*

To set apart one day a week for freedom . . . a day for being with ourselves, a day of detachment from the vulgar, of independence of external obligations, a day on which we stop worshipping the idols of technical civilization, a day of armistice in the economic struggle with our fellow men and the forces of nature—is there any institution that holds out a greater hope for man's progress than the Sabbath?

Or, as Dobb put it: "Shabbat is a time of being, not of doing. It's a reminder that the most important and the most holy realm is not the workaday world. Our salvation does not lie in larger homes, more expensive jewelry or fancier cars, but the opposite. It lies in those moments of rest and renewal."

Living Sabbath values means accumulating less and giving more—an approach to life that's not only good for the earth, but for the spirit. "Despite Madison Avenue's protestations to the contrary, we live in a world of material scarcity. Everything that is produced or consumed—even a hybrid automobile, even Ben & Jerry's ice cream—comes at a social and environmental cost. We must do what we can to minimize those costs, but remember that they are always there," Dobb said. "In contrast, we live in a world of spiritual abundance. We have infinite resources to devote to learning, to friendship, to self-discovery and to community building. Shabbat is about that realm, and it suggests that one-seventh of our lives—and hopefully, from there, more—be focused on these inexhaustible worlds of meaning rather than the exhaustible world of things. So it challenges our entire social and economic order." Taking Shabbat seriously means closing businesses, even retail businesses, for at least one day a week. Bill Child, the Mormon founder and former CEO of a retail furniture chain called R. C. Willey & Co., shut his stores on Sundays, and insisted on doing so even after he sold his company to investor Warren Buffett. Buffett agreed, reluctantly, and the stores continue to thrive. The Atlanta-based Chick-fil-A fast-food chain also closes on Sundays at the insistence of its founder, Truett Cathy.

Before we leave the Torah, Dobb pointed me to what is perhaps the most frequently cited verse of *halacha,* or law, about the environment, which is found in Deuteronomy 20:19:

> When in your war against a city you have to besiege it a long time in order to capture it, you must not destroy its trees, wielding the ax against them. You may eat of them, but you must not cut them down. . . . Only trees which you know do not yield food may be destroyed; you may cut them down for constructing siegeworks against the city that is waging war on you, until it has been reduced.

While open to many interpretations, this passage has become the basis for a mainstream Jewish doctrine known as *bal tashchit,* which means, loosely, "do not waste." "It's the number one eco-Jewish commandment," Dobb said. Jewish environmentalists argue that a law that protects trees even in wartime reflects a strong bias in favor of preserving the natural order. At the very minimum, Dobb said, the principle of *bal tashchit* requires us to weigh short-term economic gains against long-term environmental values. He asked: "What about that one tree's marginal contribution to regulating the global climate? Toward providing habitat for native and perhaps endangered species? For anchoring the soil and preventing erosion, given that two-thirds of fertile American topsoil has already been washed away? For shade? For enjoyment of humans at a spiritual and aesthetic level?" Then again, what is deemed wasteful depends on one's hierarchy of values. To a housing developer, it may be wasteful to allow a grove of trees to stand in the way of new homes that provide shelter for families and construction jobs.

I asked Dobb about this. His environmental values may promote spiritual growth, but they do not seem to allow much room for economic growth, the pursuit of which drives so much in business. He responds that economic growth, by itself, is neither a worthy long-term goal nor a sustainable one. Religion teaches us to think about future impacts, even many generations out. "How do you extrapolate even modest economic growth into the one-thousandth generation?" he asked. "We cannot grow in GNP and population infinitely." Business, he said, should pursue sustainable growth—that is, growth that not only avoids harming the earth but also promotes social justice, because global companies cannot thrive for long in a world where billions are desperately poor. Dobb said: "Are we just meeting the ever-expanding needs of the hungriest, most affluent people on earth? Or are we meeting basic needs of all's God children and all of God's creation?"

Not far from Adat Shalom are new homes that sell for $750,000 to $1.5 million and feature soaring atriums, spacious gourmet kitchens and master bedroom suites with walk-in closets. What kinds of homes we build or buy, what materials go into them, what kinds of cars we make and drive, what kind of coffee we drink—all these are issues of faith, for businesspeople and consumers alike. "I want affluent Washington suburbanites, including members of my congregation, to realize that since the world cannot afford a six-bedroom home for every family, their decision to take up more space and more resources means that somewhere along the line others are forced to take up less," Dobb said. This isn't a matter of cause and effect—the owner of a $1 million home has not directly hurt the poor—but ultimately there are limits to what the planet can produce, consume and throw away. The more each of us takes, the less there is for others, Dobb said.

Often, though, the calculus of values can get pretty complicated. What if Habitat for Humanity wants to chop down trees to build a house for the homeless? What if a developer who builds apartments for the poor can't afford to hire union workers? Like Williams and Stackhouse, Dobb is not a purist. "Those are sacred questions, and they may be necessary trade-offs to make," he said. He applauds corporations that promise to offset their greenhouse gas emissions by planting trees, and those who lobby for stricter emissions controls or universal health care. "We need the most honorable businesspeople in each sector not only to stay in business but to flourish, so that these models are vindicated," he said.

Still, the thrust of his message is clear—that the way most business in America is conducted today violates the Jewish values of preserving the earth and promoting social justice. "We are already, quite likely, past the carrying capacity of the globe," he said. "If every one of today's 6.1 billion people lived at the upper-middle-class American standard, we would need five earths to support them. We need a radical slowing down if humanity is to survive and if the spirit is to triumph."

Ollie Williams, Max Stackhouse and Fred Dobb are atypical. They have embraced their responsibilities to help businesspeople integrate their faith and their work. More often, religious leaders have contributed to the Sunday-Monday gap. Few take a nuanced view of business, with its potential to do good as well as harm. As Williams put it: "Most pastors don't understand the economic system. They approach every successful businessman in one of two ways—either with open hostility, as if they were robber barons, or with undue deference, because they are potentially rich benefactors." Neither view is helpful to businesspeople who are seeking understanding, guidance or support. But thoughtful religious leaders have a lot to teach those of us in business about how to reconnect our faith and work.

7

HOW DO YOU MEASURE SUCCESS?

TIMBERLAND

Like most public schools in New York City, P.S. 19 in Queens is overcrowded and poor. Some twenty-two hundred pupils, who speak about fifty different languages, attend classes, some of which are held in the cafeteria because there aren't enough classrooms. Until recently, the schoolyard was nothing but crumbling blacktop.

On April 22, 2003, which was Earth Day, I joined about a hundred volunteers to try to do something about that dreary yard. The day before we arrived, a volunteer crew had torn up the blacktop, carted most of it away, laid out gravel pathways and spread topsoil across the open areas. Our job was to plant trees, bushes, ground covers and flowering plants—thousands of them—alongside the paths, to create what would be called a Learning Garden. It was a gray, misty morning as we got started, but everyone approached the task with enthusiasm. We split up into work crews and dug holes for the trees, trucked plants around on wheelbarrows and laid down logs for seating.

My crew, which was led by a spirited young volunteer from a

nonprofit group called City Year, included two volunteers from the Student Conservation Association, another from the Robin Hood Foundation, a man who works for the Porter Novelli public relations firm, a woman who produces special sections for *GQ* magazine and two twentysomething sales people who worked for Timberland— the company that helped to organize the volunteer project. And not just this project: for Earth Day, Timberland organized nature-oriented service projects at more than a hundred other sites in the United States, Europe and Asia. On Mount Agamenticus in York, Maine, Timberland volunteers cleared trails, erected signs and carted away debris. In Toronto, they cleared the land around a pond. In London, they cleaned up a stretch of the Thames River waterfront. All in all, it was an ambitious undertaking. Of Timberland's fifty-one hundred employees worldwide, nearly two thousand did community service on Earth Day.

This is business as usual at Timberland, although few of its customers are aware of the firm's commitment to voluntarism. The $1.2-billion-a-year company, which is headquartered in Stratham, New Hampshire, is better known as a designer, producer and marketer of boots, casual shoes, clothes and accessories. Until its best-selling product, a clunky yellow boot that's been around for decades, unexpectedly became a status symbol among black teenagers, Timberland projected a WASPy image and sold most of its shoes and clothes to suburbanites who think of themselves as outdoorsy. These days, the Timberland brand has cachet on Harlem's 125th Street as well. The company also sells more than $400 million of product overseas.

But Timberland is more than boots and clothes and a global brand. This company is explicitly committed to being a force for positive change in the world. Timberland tries to create social as well as economic value—by protecting the rights of workers at factories in China and Bangladesh where its products are made, by trying to minimize its environmental footprint, by sharing its profits and its marketing savvy with nonprofit groups and, most of all, by aggressively promoting community service. Timberland organizes global service events like the Earth Day celebration a couple of times a year; every company employee gets paid time off to do service; major sales meetings include service elements; and suppliers, partners, distributors and customers are encouraged to join in. That's why I found myself working at P.S. 19 with people from Porter Novelli, which does PR for Timberland, and *GQ,* in which the company advertises.

For Timberland, service is more than a way to give back to society—it is at the heart of the company's identity, at least according to Jeffrey Swartz, Timberland's president and CEO. Taking a break from digging and planting, Swartz and I spent some time talking about Timberland and its social impact, as well as his own values and how they have shaped the firm. Events like the Earth Day celebration, he told me, are more than a break from office routine. They are designed to define Timberland—its culture, its relationships and its mission as a company, which is "to equip people to make their difference in the world."

"Boots, brand and belief. That's what I'm selling, always," said Swartz, a midsized man with dark curly hair who exudes good cheer. Words spill rapidly out of the hyperactive executive, who, at forty-three, has become an evangelist for the idea of corporate social responsibility. He loves to talk about how business and values are—or should be—intertwined. Whether he's honing in on you in a one-on-one conversation or pacing in front of a crowd, his passion is contagious. "It's not that you first do well, you take care of yourself, and then you do good," he explained. That's the old model of making a lot of money, by whatever means necessary, and then giving it away. Instead, he said: "You must do well and do good simultaneously. That's the challenge."

He embraces this challenge with gusto. As the CEO of a public company who is answerable to investors, Swartz has to be tough-minded. When Timberland hit a rough patch in the mid-1990s, the company reluctantly closed factories in Mountain City, Tennessee, and Boone, North Carolina, and shifted production overseas. But when he gets up in the morning—at 4 A.M. most days, to say his prayers as an Orthodox Jew and then spend an hour studying Torah—what fuels Swartz is a desire to make the world a better place. His challenge, as he defines it, is to marry profit and purpose, to be both a businessman and an idealist and thereby show that shareholder and social value are not only aligned but also complementary.

To do that, he needs to rally his employees, partners, and shareholders to the cause. He needs to persuade consumers to buy Timberland products because of the company's values. And he needs to win over Wall Street. These are daunting tasks. But if Swartz can show that Timberland can do well by doing good, then other companies will follow. This is how he measures his company's success, and his own.

To that end, Timberland reports on its social as well as financial progress. In 2000, along with the standard annual report to shareholders, Timberland published its first corporate social responsibility report. In the sixteen-page report, the company described its community service efforts, charitable giving, environmental impact and global labor practices. More than fifty U.S. companies had issued social, environmental or sustainability reports along with their annual financial reports by 2003, acknowledging their responsibility to report on the full impact of their activities.

Business has never been more powerful, Swartz explained in his introduction, and so the time has come for companies to measure their success in ways that go beyond the bottom line. "It is no longer enough to measure business only by standards of profit, efficiency and market share," he wrote. "We must also ask how business contributes to social justice, environmental sustainability and the values by which we choose to live."

But how do you measure what happened at P.S. 19 on Earth Day? By the end of the afternoon, the sun was shining and the crumbled blacktop had been replaced by a lush, verdant and inviting garden. The school principal and some parents who came by to help seemed delighted by the transformation. And who knows? Maybe a few of us urban gardeners had been transformed a bit, too.

THE Timberland Co. has always practiced what is now called corporate social responsibility, although Nathan Swartz would never have used those words to describe the family business. A Russian immigrant who began making shoes as an apprentice stitcher in a small Boston factory in 1918, Nathan Swartz was a man of strong principles but few words. So, at least, says Jeff Swartz, who remembers taking long, mostly silent walks on the boardwalk with his grandfather, whom he called Papa Nathan, after Nathan Swartz retired to Miami Beach in the 1960s. But when Papa Nathan did speak, the man's words carried weight. "You got to do for others," he would say abruptly to his grandson, as they walked. "You got to take what you got and share it."

Jeff was just a boy at the time, but he still remembers one story that Papa Nathan told him, using the blunt language of his generation. It seems that when Nathan worked as a stitching room foreman before he started his own company, one of his men came to him with a problem:

"My son's a cripple," the man said.

"OK," Nathan replied.

"He's a cripple in his head," the man said.

"What are you talking about?" asked Nathan.

"I'm going to die soon," said the man.

"Could be," replied Nathan.

"I can't die," the man said. "Because when I die, there's no one to look after my kid and they'll put him away."

Nathan said nothing.

"You're the best stitcher I know," the man said. "Teach my kid to stitch."

Nathan replied, "So I got nothing better to do than to teach some schlepper's kid to stitch?"

Here Nathan paused. Puzzled, Jeff asked his grandfather what happened next. "What are you, an idiot?" Papa Nathan said. "I taught him how to stitch." Later, the man came back to him, thanked him and said, "Now I can die." This time Nathan replied: "Not yet. Get back to work."

When Jeff told me the story, we both laughed out loud at the image of this gruff old Jew passing his wisdom down to a kid in Miami Beach. But it's clear that Nathan Swartz had a lot of influence on his grandson. (Jeff studied Russian at Phillips Academy, in part so he could talk to his grandfather in his native language.) Nathan Swartz had worked very hard all his life and literally gave up a part of himself for his family: a few days before his son's wedding, he had sliced off part of his finger because he was rushing through piecework to make extra money to pay for the big event. After he acquired a small firm called the Abington Shoe Co. in 1955, Nathan brought his sons, Sidney and Herman, into the business. He wanted his grandson Jeff to do better. "I did not come to this country and endure what I've endured to have you end up in the shoe business," Papa Nathan would tell Jeff. "You're going to go to college and you're going to get a profession. You're going to be a doctor or a lawyer or an accountant. My grandson is not going to be a schlepper."

But Jeff had grown up in the factory, working there every summer, sweeping floors and painting walls. He watched the way that his grandfather and his own father, Sidney Swartz, ran the place. One day, Jeff saw his father reach into his pocket, pull out a wad of bills and count out some cash for a factory worker who needed help with a family problem. Jeff asked his father how he knew about the man's troubles. "I know everybody in this mill," Sidney Swartz told him. Then he added: "If I don't take care of Freddy, who is going to take care of us?" In small, family-run companies, everyone knows that it's good business to take care of your people.

The summer after Jeff finished high school, Papa Nathan died— killed by a drunk driver—and Jeff cut short a trip to Israel to be with his father. It was then that he felt the business tug at him. "There's a sound and a rhythm to a factory," he said. "It is alive. It is where human beings transform raw materials into someone's dream."

Before leaving for college, Jeff told his father, with some trepidation, that he wanted to work at Timberland. "I don't know anything about business. I don't know if I'm any good at it," Jeff remembered saying. "But I am sure of this. We're family. So I want you to think about whether it is okay if I come to work with you." Until then, Sidney, out of deference to Papa Nathan, had never pushed his son to join the business. This time, he said: "I've waited my whole life to hear you say that."

Two decades later, Timberland remains a family firm. Jeff Swartz, who studied comparative literature at Brown and earned an MBA from the Tuck School at Dartmouth, joined the company for good in 1986, became chief operating officer in 1991 and took over as president and CEO in 1998, when Sidney Swartz retired and became chairman of the board. This transfer of power—call it nepotism if you like—was made possible because Timberland created two classes of shares when it went public in 1987. The Swartz family today owns 46 percent of the stock in the firm and 82 percent of the voting shares, which elect the board of directors. To some degree, family control shields Timberland from the short-term pressures from Wall Street to show earnings each and every quarter. (Jeff Swartz does not project quarter-by-quarter earnings for financial analysts.) Still, the family retains a fiduciary duty to operate the firm for the benefit of all of its shareholders, an obligation it takes seriously, as we'll see.

The company that Jeff Swartz runs today still bears the imprint of Nathan Swartz. Papa Nathan laid out the pattern, cut the leather and stitched the prototype for its original six-inch waterproof boot, which was called the Timberland boot. By using new technology that fused the soles of the boots to the uppers, the company produced a truly waterproof boot that was also lightweight and flexible. It proved so popular that Abingdon changed its name in 1973 to the Timberland Co. Since then, Timberland has expanded dramatically—it began making men's casual and boat shoes in the late 1970s, added lines of women's shoes and clothing in 1983, began selling in Europe in the 1980s, and took the brand to Asia in the 1990s. The company calls itself a global lifestyle brand—that sounds a lot glitzier than a shoe company—and, in fact, more than half of its 205 retail stores are located in Europe and Asia. But Timberland's core business remains shoes, and especially boots. Footwear generates about 75 percent of the company's revenues, and Nathan Swartz's waterproof boot, which is sold in such hues as aluminum, blue and chili, along with the original yellow, now called wheat, remains Timberland's signature offering.

How Timberland—a brand created by immigrant Jews and imbued with an outdoorsy New England feel—became the favorite boot maker of the hip-hop generation is something of a mystery. The Timberland boot, which was originally sold to blue-collar workers as a functional work boot, became popular with suburbanites and college kids who found it a practical fall and winter shoe. In the early 1990s, sales spiked in African American neighborhoods. Curious about what was happening, Bruce Todtfeld, the firm's global director of boots, visited stores, talked to buyers and learned that black teenagers had adopted the boot as their own. "They called it rough, rugged and raw, and that's how they characterize the urban lifestyle," Todtfeld said. "They felt like they owned the boot." Black teens had their own way of wearing the boots—always with the laces untied, and ideally in pristine condition, because brand-new Timberlands are a status symbol. (One reason sales were so high was because some kids discarded the boots when they got scuffed.) Timberland responded by bringing out new styles and colors, some of which got their own street names: a brown-and-green hiking boot was known as "beef and broccoli," and the classic yellow boot was called simply "butter." The company then gave away boots and clothes to selected musicians, designers and fashion editors of urban-oriented magazines. When musicians Will Smith and Sean Paul wore Timberlands in their videos, the boots grew in popularity not just among black kids but also among the millions of white teenagers whose tastes are shaped by hip-hop culture.

The growing strength of Timberland's brand, which is rooted in boots, has driven the company's financial success. Revenues have grown from $862 million in 1998, the year that Jeff Swartz became CEO, to $1.342 billion in 2002. Net profits have grown from $59 million to $118 million. Despite a falloff in both revenues and profits in recent years as the economy slowed, long-term investors in Timberland have done very well. During the ten years ending in 2002, Timberland shareholders enjoyed a 22 percent annual return, a performance that ranked the company number one out of the twelve apparel companies in the Fortune 1000, a group that includes Nike, Polo and Liz Claiborne.

All of that matters to Jeff Swartz. Although he tends to leave the details of finances and operations to others, Swartz needs Timberland to produce steady growth in revenues and profits to keep investors happy. This is a challenge because the company operates in mature and competitive markets in the United States. "To me, it's about slow growth, it's about careful growth," Swartz said. "But it is about growth." While Timberland is already the number one seller of shoes and boots in North America, the company has plenty of room to grow in its domestic apparel business and in all of its businesses outside of the United States. This won't be easy because of the challenge of customizing the product and message for each market. "If you're at Sears and looking at Timberland PRO [a work boot] we tend to talk more about functionality," Swartz said. "If you're in Tokyo, we talk about the heritage of the brand. And if you're in London, we talk about the moment—because it's more of a fashion-forward brand." Did I mention that Timberland also replaces about 50 percent of its product line every year with new designs, to stay current, and that it licenses its brand for use on sunglasses, wallets, backpacks and watches as well? The point is, what was once a New England shoe company has become a global business with a multiplicity of moving parts, and so it tells you something that Swartz has decided to add another layer of complexity to the enterprise. He wants to recast the Timberland brand so that it stands for strong values. "I want to have a conversation with consumers about values, shared value—about what we make, how we make it and why we make it," he said. As much as he cares about financial performance, Swartz is most passionate about generating social value at Timberland.

Swartz's desire to give back is Papa Nathan's legacy as well as a reflection of his own religious faith. His commitment to community service arose after he met a man named Alan Khazei and got involved with City Year, a nonprofit that Khazei and Michael Brown, his roommate from Harvard and Harvard Law School, started after they graduated in 1988. Khazei and Brown created City Year to convince people in their late teens and early twenties, from diverse racial, economic and educational backgrounds, to take a year off from school to do community service. In 1989, they asked Timberland for fifty pairs of boots for City Year's first group of volunteers in Boston. After Swartz sent the boots, and then sent another batch the following year, Khazei came to see him. The two men, who were about the same age, hit it off right away, and at one point Swartz said wistfully that he'd love to do the kind of work Khazei did. "You can," replied Khazei. "You think your job is to build a business and mine is to change the world. We can do both, together." On the spot, Swartz committed $50,000 to sponsor a City Year team and agreed to join the organization in a day of service at a drug treatment center near Timberland's New Hampshire factory. The event touched Swartz in a way he hadn't expected. "I painted some walls and felt the world shaking under my feet," he said. Poor kids on drugs? In a time of plenty? This, he thought, was not the vision of America that had drawn Papa Nathan to this country so many years ago.

Swartz threw himself into helping City Year. When the nonprofit expanded beyond Boston in the early 1990s, Timberland became its first national sponsor and Swartz, at thirty-three, became chairman of the City Year board, a position he held for nine years. The partnership had a profound effect on Timberland and on Swartz. It gave him the courage to get beyond the analytical methods he'd been taught in business school and live his values at work, as he explained in 1996 to a researcher from the Harvard Business School:

> My grandfather [lived] his convictions. He just knew that you make a good boot and treat people with integrity. He didn't bounce it up against analytical models from business school. . . . My father is the same way. The best year Timberland had as a private label manufacturer was the year he decided we couldn't continue as a private label manufacturer. The idea was informed by all of his experience and knowledge. It was a conviction. . . . I spent most of my life learning how to avoid having convictions and being embarrassed about convictions. I thought: "Convictions are like your religious beliefs which you certainly didn't bring to work. I belong to the legal fiction called a corporation. I don't have a point-of-view, a personality or any convictions. And while I am a moral persona, I am just a corporate executive; my job is to come up with strategies." Now I am relearning the notion that you work from convictions. I can't articulate it in a more real way. I just knew Timberland needed to be part of its community. It's in my heart, it's in my being.

In the last decade, Timberland has equipped thousands of City Year volunteers, donated more than $10 million and shared its marketing and fund-raising expertise with the organization. "I've met with tons of business leaders and lots are wonderful," Alan Khazei told me, "but I've never had the response that we got from Jeff. It was like pushing on an open door."

Swartz was so taken with the power of community service that he instituted a program called the Path of Service at Timberland. Employees were given sixteen hours of paid leave a year (since expanded to forty hours) to do community service. Timberland later created what it calls Serv-a-Palooza, an annual day of service; all of its worldwide offices are shut down so employees can volunteer in their communities. ("How's that for an alternative definition of globalization?" Swartz asks.) The company says community service costs Timberland about $2 million a year, but the money is well spent because it helps attract, retain and engage employees. When I spent a day at company headquarters in Stratham, several workers told me that the community service commitment had sparked their interest in Timberland. "Your private and corporate life are seamless," said Danette Wineberg, a corporate lawyer who uprooted herself from Michigan to join Timberland, in part because of its values.

Community service has also become a way of building teamwork and breaking down hierarchies inside Timberland. "This is work today," Swartz told me during our break from digging and planting at P.S. 19. "We put a cross-functional team together, with different skills, with a clear problem that needs to be solved, limited resources, a fixed deadline and, by the way, there's no one to solve it but us. So what are we going to do? We figure it out. When we go back to the office and talk about the democratization of decision making, and I say to you, it's not the CEO who should lead, it's you who should lead? Now you've seen what I'm talking about." Doing service builds a sense of community at Timberland. "Many companies pay thousands upon thousands of dollars for the type of team-building skills we learn through giving together," Swartz said. "This is not philanthropy. We are making an investment in our infrastructure that will pay off [in terms of] productivity and effectiveness."

Community service has even been incorporated into Timberland's sales tactics. Several years ago, for example, the company wanted to convince Macy's to carry a new line of shoes for women. While planning its sales pitch, Timberland learned that Macy's had been a long-time donor to Inwood House, a home for teenage mothers in New York. So a Timberland account executive invited the Macy's people to join in a women-only day of service at Inwood House. The Macy's buyers were hard-nosed, well-dressed professional women, no more inclined to paint a house than they are to paint their own nails. But they agreed to go, and Timberland arranged to have them paint the shelter, using the color palette of its shoes for some of the rooms.

Afterward, Timberland invited the women to dinner at Tabla, a restaurant owned by celebrity chef Danny Meyer. Swartz and Meyer had worked together on a charity, Share Our Strength, run by Bill Shore, a member of Timberland's board. Meyer agreed to appear at the dinner and donate his profits to Share Our Strength. As Swartz worked the crowd, he swears he saw a new attitude on the part of the Macy's buyers: "The look on their faces said, 'I am powerful.' Not 'I am powerful as a buyer,' but 'I am powerful because I changed some girl's life today. I got to learn about Timberland's corporate philosophy. I got to know the people who sell to me as human beings. I'm having this wonderful dinner at this fancy restaurant and you're telling me that by eating the food, I'm feeding the hungry of New York. I get to meet a celebrity like Danny Meyer. And the shoes, by the way, are great-looking.'"

Near the end of the evening, a Macy's buyer asked Swartz: "Was this all about selling us shoes?" "Sort of," he replied, trying to duck the question. When she persisted, he said: "Absolutely it's about selling shoes. But it's also about making a connection." In that sense, Timberland's approach is no more than a new twist on the old practice of a salesperson entertaining a client. As Swartz put it to me: "Instead of going to a Yankees game, let's go save the world." But it's different, too. When it works—and not all clients respond to the invitation to serve—Timberland sells product, builds relationships and pushes the cause of community service. As much as selling shoes, Swartz wants to sell people on the idea of helping others. "I'm trying to build a world that I want my kids to grow up in," he said.

Tikkum olam—"healing the world"—is the Hebrew phrase for what Swartz is trying to do. He rediscovered Judaism at about the time he found City Year, and that, too, changed the way he does business. His wife, Debbie, provided the spark. Swartz had just run the 1991 New York City Marathon, which, she knew, meant he would need another goal right away. Swartz had always been driven—too much so, in her eyes; rarely did he stop to appreciate his accomplishments. "Seen it, done it, good-bye" was the way he thought about knocking down goals, by his own account. This time, before he'd even had the chance to shower, Debbie gave him a gift, a few books of commentary about the Bible, which he had been reading, albeit not in a systematic way.

Swartz had been raised as a Reform Jew, but he had not studied his tradition. "Our religion was Israel and bagels," he said. "Three times a year, we'd go to synagogue and there was a Passover Seder." About all he remembers from his bar mitzvah ceremony was wearing his first, oversized suit and getting stuck in traffic on the way to synagogue—he said this with a grin because he no longer drives on the Sabbath. "It was a joyous family experience," he said, "but I didn't have a clue." The biblical commentaries that Debbie gave him took hold of him, and they wouldn't let go. "It is a bottomless pit," Swartz said. "That was, in itself, an extraordinary gift. Because it did change my view of life. From transactions—from A to B and on to C—to missions." It also gave him a longer-term view. "The work that needs to be done was here before I was born and it'll be here long after I'm gone," he said. "So this life is not about solutions. This is about mission."

With his customary focus, Swartz studied the Bible, learned Hebrew and became an Orthodox Jew. He committed himself to such traditional practices as eating only kosher food and doing no work of any kind on the Sabbath, which extends from an hour before sundown on Friday to sundown on Saturday. "Everyone knows that for twenty-five hours I'm shut down. No phone, no e-mail, nothing," Swartz said. Passover Seder at the Swartzes' is a big event—one year, Jeff invited about thirty people, including some non-Jews, and decided to provide them with a "short letter of introduction" to the liturgy. It grew to seventy-eight single-spaced typewritten pages.

As important as his Jewish practices, though, are the principles that Swartz relies upon to guide his business behavior. He once got into a battle with a departing employee and found he could not withhold the man's salary because the Bible says every worker must be paid at the end of each day. And when it comes to Timberland's use of contract labor overseas—an enormously controversial issue for the clothing and footwear industries—Swartz tries to live up to the biblical admonition to "turn from evil and pursue good." That obliges him to do what he can to protect the human rights and improve the lives of the workers, most employed by suppliers in Asia, who make boots, shoes and clothes for Timberland.

This gets complicated, of course. While Swartz does not use religious language to talk about global labor practices at the office, he tells his people that they can and should think about the issue in moral terms. "The first moral question is, do you belong in China at all?" he said. "You pay business tax to a totalitarian regime that oppresses people. How does that feel? Not good." But if Timberland wants to stay in business and keep its costs competitive, it has little choice but to seek out cheap labor. That's partly because very few customers are willing to pay a premium for products made in the United States. "If we tried to make all our products in New England," Swartz said, "we'd be out of business. Close the doors and shut the place down." Today, nearly 90 percent of Timberland's footwear and much of its apparel is made in Asia; the company buys products from about 160 vendors who employ about thirty-three thousand people. That raises questions about how you do business with contractors in developing nations. Pay, it turns out, is not the big issue, at least not for Swartz. By and large, jobs working for contractors who supply Timberland are desirable because they pay above-average wages; factory jobs in China's Guangdong Province, for example, pay about $55 a month, and workers who put in overtime earn $80 to $120 a month. That is more than enough to attract migrant workers from the countryside. The tougher issue, especially in China, is the government's failure to protect workers' rights, limit their hours, enforce their right to overtime pay and guard against child labor. "The Chinese labor law is not worth the paper it's printed on," Swartz said. Contractors routinely exploit workers, so it is up to Timberland to intervene on their behalf. "It takes much more effort—an order of magnitude, twice—not to exploit people," said Swartz.

To that end, Timberland has adopted a code of conduct that its vendors are supposed to follow and to post in a place visible to their workers. (It has been translated into twenty languages by Timberland.) The code of conduct says what you would expect such a document to say—that each employee's labor must be voluntary, that no child under sixteen should be employed, that employees should have the right to associate freely and bargain collectively, that regular hours are limited to forty-eight hours over each six-day period, that workers should get at least one day off after working six consecutive days and that all overtime must be voluntary and paid at a premium rate.

The important question is how the code is enforced. When I met Cheryl Marihugh, Timberland's director of global business alliances, she told me straightaway that her number one job is to make sure that the code is more than words on a piece of paper. "I feel like I work as a workers' advocate," said Marihugh, a former Peace Corps volunteer. "We have the ability to make their lives fair, and to make their lives better. That is what motivates me." Marihugh personally spends about 25 percent of her time visiting vendors and factories overseas that supply Timberland, and she manages a staff of six internal auditors who visit each factory every three to five months. Since 1998, Timberland also has contracted with Verité, a nonprofit group based in Amherst, Massachusetts, which has a global network of independent, trained auditors who monitor factories in an effort to protect workers' rights to safe, fair and legal working conditions. The auditors interview workers, often away from the workplace, and report back to Timberland on any abuses. Verité works with about fifteen companies, including such respected corporate citizens as Reebok and Eileen Fisher. Mil Niepold, the director of policy at Verité, says Timberland is among the best. "Timberland puts its values into action on the ground," she said. "They take their responsibilities seriously." This does not make the system anywhere near perfect, Marihugh told me. Timberland has discovered vendors who insist on excessive work hours, refuse to pay overtime or require workers to take pregnancy tests before being hired. It pushes those factory owners to change and has severed relations with at least two dozen who after repeated prodding failed to live up to the code.

Beyond monitoring its workplaces, Timberland supports after-work programs designed to enhance the lives of people employed by its contractors. With Verité, it offers life skills training so that workers in China can take classes in English or learn budgeting or computer skills; they are also taught about labor law, wage calculation and Timberland's code of conduct. In Vietnam, Timberland and CARE have formed a partnership to improve the quality of life for workers by providing basic education about topics ranging from job safety and managing money to HIV/AIDS. "This is not just a Timberland problem," says Marihugh. "The question is, how can we work with management, workers, trade unions and NGOs to improve standards for all?"

Timberland measures its social value in other ways, too. As a company that designs products for the outdoors, Timberland strives to limit its impact on the natural environment. In the Netherlands, Timberland uses steam from a nearby power plant that would otherwise go to waste to heat its biggest European distribution facility; it also buys all of its energy for that facility from utilities that employ wind and water power. Newer retail stores are built with recycled or renewable materials, including bamboo floors. And, with a group of companies including Nike and Patagonia, Timberland helped start a nonprofit called the Organic Cotton Exchange that promotes the use of organic cotton. Growing cotton by conventional means requires intensive use of pesticides, which affect the health of workers and damage the ecosystem. The trouble is, organic cotton costs more. In all of its stores, Timberland offers a stack or two of organic cotton T-shirts—although there's not much evidence yet that consumers will pay more for organic products except when it comes to the food they eat.

This points to what may be the most important question now facing Swartz and the company: Can consumers be persuaded to buy Timberland products because of the company's social mission? Timberland's values clearly pay off with employees, and they can appeal to partners and distributors, too, as the story about Macy's shows. But the degree to which consumers are attracted to socially responsible companies or products remains limited, notwithstanding the success of Ben & Jerry's and Newman's Own. Surveys show that most people expect companies to be good citizens. And consumers say that they would prefer to do business with companies that are associated with good causes, all other things being equal. But all other things are rarely equal, and surveys about people's intentions don't prove much. More telling is the reality that Wal-Mart, a company known for low prices but not for strong values, continues to crush every competitor in sight. "When push comes to shove, people find it difficult even to name socially responsible companies," said Chris Coulter, an executive with Environics International, a Toronto-based consultancy on corporate social responsibility.

Marketing values is especially difficult because consumers are understandably skeptical, if not cynical, about companies that claim to be doing good. (This is the problem Starbucks faces as it tries to explain its coffee-buying practices to the public.) For Timberland, the challenge is formidable because the company's values, which are expressed through community service, global labor standards and a love for the outdoors, cannot be reduced to a simple phrase. The company has tried such themes as "For the journey," "Seek out" and "Don't wear it, use it," but they don't get the message across. The company mission statement—"We equip people to make their difference in the world"—does not appear on its marketing materials, annual reports or even on its Web site, at least not prominently.

Late in 2003, the company launched a new marketing campaign to identify Timberland as a "values" brand. As usual, Swartz was brimming with ideas and enthusiasm. He rang the bell on the New York Stock Exchange, led a day of community service on Ellis Island

and hosted a gala dinner at Chelsea Pier in Manhattan. The company began a Community Builders Tour that mixes service with promotions for Timberland products. There was talk about turning Serv-a-Palooza into a day of service for all Americans. Said Swartz: "I want the consumer to take away an invitation: get off the couch, pull on your boots and go make your difference in the world."

Packaging was also on his mind. Right now, he noted, consumers don't have to think about what goes into the products they buy, who made them, or how much those workers were paid. "What if we put it on our shoebox?" he asked. "What if, just like an FDA ingredients label, we listed our practices? Environmental impact. Toxins utilized. Trees cut down. Labor practices used. Global labor standards. What if that kind of transparency wound up on a shoebox at the point of sale? How would you like to be one of my competitors when that lands on the shelf?" The goal would be to make business more transparent and to persuade consumers to think about purchasing decisions as expressions of their own values. "It's an efficient-market theory," Swartz said. "If you understood what goes into making a pair of shoes, you'd value it differently."

These are big ideas, with implications that go well beyond Timberland and the shoe business. They are about using the power of business to get people to think about their responsibility to make the world a better place, whether by buying products made under fair labor standards or patronizing companies that do the right thing or taking time from their own lives for community service. Ancient wisdom comes in a variety of forms. As Papa Nathan used to say, "You got to do for others." That's as good a way as any to strive for success.

8

WHEN BAD THINGS HAPPEN TO GOOD COMPANIES

HERMAN MILLER

"What do you do?" When people ask me that question, I ordinarily say that I work as a writer for *Fortune* magazine. What I literally do, most of the time, like many of us, is sit and type words into a computer. Or I sit and read. Or I sit and talk on the phone. The point is, I do a lot of sitting, and I do it in an Aeron chair made by a company called Herman Miller. For that I am grateful.

A chair's a chair, you say? Not after you have spent some time in an Aeron. The Aeron performs—and, yes, that's the word for it—like no other chair. It adjusts to my body. It provides lumbar support when I sit up straight, and tilts back when I put my feet on my desk. Because the seat and back of the chair are made of a meshlike fabric called Pellicle, you can sit in an Aeron for hours and not feel any the worse for wear. What's more, the Aeron is one very cool-looking chair—it's sleek and curvy, so striking that it was named to the permanent design collection of the Museum of Modern Art even before it went on sale.

There's another thing about the Aeron that set it apart when it was introduced in 1994: it is a democratic chair. Until then, office chairs came in two classes. Most were produced for rank-and-file workers—they are known in the trade as "task seating"—and a few were made for executives. Plush, oversized, ostentatious thrones of dark wood and tufted leather, executive chairs were designed to confer status on their occupants. Mine's bigger than yours—that sort of thing.

By contrast, the Aeron—despite a retail price of $849—was designed as a chair for everyone, or at least everyone whose company could afford them. The Aeron did emerge as a status symbol during the Internet boom, but the chairs conferred cachet not on Silicon Valley CEOs but on their companies. It became a sign of cool to buy Aerons for everyone, especially the software programmers who stayed up all night writing code and needed a comfortable chair. An icon of the dot-com era, the Aeron signified that a company cared enough to give its people the best.

So it's fitting that the Aeron came from Herman Miller, a company that is infused with an egalitarian spirit, a belief that every person has special gifts and a tradition of innovative, practical design. Herman Miller's values were shaped by its founder, D.J. DePree, and his sons Hugh and Max, who ran the firm for seven decades. The company is grounded, literally and spiritually, in western Michigan, a region dominated by the conservative, church-going descendants of nineteenth-century Dutch and German immigrants. Improbably, the stodgy DePrees forged lasting partnerships with a succession of gifted, high-strung and eccentric designers—people like Charles and Ray Eames, George Nelson, Gilbert Rohde and Bob Probst—who helped Herman Miller become one of the top design-driven firms in the world. The Aeron was created by such a partnership between independent designers Don Chadwick and Bill Stumpf, who work out of their studios in Santa Monica, California, and Minneapolis, and a crew of Herman Miller researchers, engineers and production people in Michigan. Don Goeman, who is vice president in charge of research and development at Herman Miller, describes the process of creating the Aeron as "a blend of the science of seating with the art of growing a chair."

Goeman and I enjoyed a sumptuous dinner at a Holland, Michigan, lakeside retreat called Marigold that is owned by Herman Miller, whose corporate headquarters are nearby in Zeeland. He explained to me that the concept for the Aeron emerged from a Herman Miller research project called MetaForm, which was intended to design furniture for elderly people. Researchers found that the discomfort that older people feel after sitting for a long time is caused by the buildup of heat, as well as by the lack of flexibility in the chair. Although the MetaForm project was dropped, "the vision of an elastic, breathable chair stuck with us for Aeron," Goeman said.

Herman Miller knows what people want and need in an office chair because it funds lots of research into how people work. Hundreds of studies have been published on office furniture, analyzing such questions as whether a chair should seek to enforce correct posture or, alternatively, support or encourage motion. (A sample title: "Office Seating Behaviors: An Investigation of Posture, Task and Job Type.") Some office workers spend more than 90 percent of their time in their chairs, the company found. Herman Miller shared its research with Chadwick and Stumpf, who set out to create a chair that was both comfortable and attractive. Their black, machinelike design was unusual, and the early reaction from consumers was negative. Although Herman Miller executives know from experience that breakthrough ideas are off-putting at first, they had doubts about the Aeron. "We were launching a chair that stuck out like a sore thumb," recalled Goeman. "We thought it was cool, but were we drinking our own Kool-Aid?"

The worries proved unfounded. The Aeron was the right product at the right time, debuting as the business and technology boom of the late 1990s got rolling. The company, at the peak of the bubble, sold roughly fifteen thousand to eighteen thousand Aerons a week, and buyers ordered truckloads of desks, files and office systems from Herman Miller as well. The company itself got swept up in the technology boom, investing a fortune in software so that it could sell customized office systems over the Internet, just the way Dell sold computers. Sales rocketed from $984 million in 1994 to $2.2 billion in 2001. Who could have predicted that the new economy would lift a seventy-seven-year-old furniture company in Michigan to such dizzying heights?

What came next was sobering. When Internet stock prices fell, so did sales of Herman Miller furniture, including the Aeron. Failed dot-coms had thousands of practically new Aerons to sell; you could buy one on eBay for $400. (My brand-new one, purchased from an Internet discounter, cost just $599.) As the broader economy slowed, Herman Miller's sales plummeted by more than a third and the company reported its first loss in a decade. Herman Miller's values were about to be tested as never before.

It fell to Michael J. Volkema, the chairman and CEO, to steer the company through the downturn while simultaneously trying to preserve the caring, close-knit culture for which Herman Miller is known. Preserving what's good about the company in such bad times was a daunting challenge for the young chief executive.

Eventually, Herman Miller closed three plants and laid off 30 percent of its workforce. None of it was easy, Volkema said, and the CEO sometimes felt like he'd been buffeted by forces beyond his control. When Herman Miller put together its 2002 annual report, the company attached a low-cost plastic rain slicker to the cover; the report was titled, perhaps optimistically, "Coming Through the Storm Stronger for the Future." Inside, Volkema wrote: "This past year presented the worst business environment the contract furniture industry has experienced in decades, perhaps since the early 1930s." During our dinner, Don Goeman put it more bluntly. "It seemed like we were in free fall," he said, "and we didn't know when it was going to end."

—

MIKE Volkema, who is forty-eight, tries to take the long view of business at Herman Miller. That perspective, he told me, helped him and the company work their way through the slump, which began at the end of 2000 and stretched well into 2003. "Any company that lasts for eighty-five years is going to go through good and bad times," Volkema said. Herman Miller barely survived the Great Depression, and the company hit another bad patch in the early 1990s. It was a comfort to know that the firm had endured those difficulties with its values intact.

The primary value that has guided Herman Miller since the 1920s—the idea that each individual is unique, special and deserving of respect—goes back to the company's earliest days. D. J. DePree founded the company in 1923 with a loan from his father-in-law, Herman Miller, who gave the firm its name. D. J. would lead Herman Miller for the next thirty-nine years, to be followed by his sons Hugh, who ran the place from 1962 to 1980, and Max, who took charge from 1980 to 1988. The DePrees were all churchgoers and devout men who instinctively wanted to live their faith at work. But it took the death of a man named Herman Rummelt, who worked as a millwright at the company, to crystallize for D. J. what it meant to run a business in a way that was pleasing to his God. D. J. often told the story of the millwright, as did Hugh and Max. In a 1986 book called *Business as Unusual,* Hugh recalled hearing the story from his father this way:

> I visited [Herman's] wife that morning. The first thing she did was take me around the house and show me the handcrafted things Herman had made. They were all nicely designed and very wonderfully executed.
>
> Then she came in with a sheaf of papers, and this was the poetry that he had written. Then she told me about the night watchman we had who was in Rummelt's department. He had been a

machine gunner in World War I and had killed a lot of Germans. He thought he was a murderer and was going to Hell. She told me her husband spent hours between the watchman's rounds sitting with him with the Bible to show him there was reconciliation and forgiveness of sins.

I walked away from that house that morning rather shaken up.

Later, I attended the funeral, and the pastor read some poetry. Well, walking home from there, God was dealing with me about this whole thing, the attitude toward working people. I began to realize that we were either all ordinary or all extraordinary. And, by the time I reached the front porch of our house, I had concluded that we are all extraordinary. My whole attitude had changed.

In a book of his own called *Leadership Is an Art,* Max DePree tells the story and ends by asking: "It is nearly 60 years since the millwright died, and my father and many of us at Herman Miller continue to wonder: Was he a poet who did millwright's work, or was he a millwright who wrote poetry?" Mike Volkema, meanwhile, made sure that I knew the story and then said: "Our fundamental value is that people are special and important. They are uniquely created. They deserve the dignity that ought to be shown to each and every human being."

Those values are the wellspring of all that has followed at Herman Miller. The company's approach to design, its relations with its workforce, even its deep commitment to the environment—all of these can be traced back to D. J. DePree and his belief that all people are extraordinary. Herman Miller's first breakthrough came in 1929 when D. J. met a designer named Gilbert Rohde, who showed him a design for a simple chest of drawers and persuaded him to produce modern furniture that fit the needs and lifestyles of Americans. The company until then had produced furniture inspired by ornate eighteenth- and nineteenth-century European designs, a business it happily abandoned as soon as it found a market for modern pieces. Morally, D. J. was pleased to stop making copies of antiques, which to him verged on stealing; he preferred to create original furniture, despite the risks that come with innovation. More fundamentally, Rohde changed the way Herman Miller thought about furniture— he persuaded D. J. that furniture should not call attention to itself, as European antiques did, but instead should be useful. By the end of the Depression, Herman Miller had embraced the Bauhaus tradition of problem-solving design; it became the first U.S. company to mass-produce a broad range of modern furniture. "Gilbert Rohde elevated our thinking from selling merely furniture to selling a way of life," wrote Hugh DePree. Or as Volkema put it, referring to office environments: "We're not just about furniture. We're about the bigger idea of creating great places to work."

D. J. decided after working with Rohde that designers, like the millwright-poet, had special gifts that needed to be honored. The DePrees entrusted the future of their business to people with artistic temperaments and lifestyles who were a world apart from the stolid Dutch Reformed burghers of western Michigan. The renowned designer George Nelson told a story about meeting D. J., a Baptist with stern views about the evils of liquor, at a Detroit hotel in the 1940s. When Nelson ordered two very cold, very dry martinis, D. J. must have been pained, but he said nothing. Nelson enjoyed the martinis. More important, he enjoyed a fertile forty-year relationship with Herman Miller, and had this to say about D. J. many years later:

> What D. J. did to his designers was instill in them his belief that what they were doing was important. Because it was important, he trusted them without reservations of any kind. I remember a scrap of conversation with Charles Eames at his then-new house in Pacific Palisades.
>
> "Sometimes I wake up in the middle of the night in a panic," he remarked, "because I am suddenly wondering if that last stuff we sent to Zeeland was good enough. I don't think I could take it if we failed D. J.'s trust, and let him down. Does it ever worry you?"

Yes, it worried me. How could it not? Total trust is a rare privilege, but also a heavy burden. One's integrity is at stake.

Together, Herman Miller and its designers created such icons of twentieth-century American design as Eames' molded plywood chair and sling seating, Nelson's platform bench and bubble lamps and Isamu Noguchi's glass-topped coffee table. You can't walk into a contemporary furniture store without seeing the influence of Herman Miller. Since the company shifted its focus to office furniture in the 1960s its impact on workplaces has also become unmistakable. Herman Miller introduced the first modern ergonomic chair. And a product called Action Office, the first modular system of panels and components, gave us the office cubicle—for better or worse.

Herman Miller's partnership with its workforce also began with the DePrees. In 1950, the company adopted the Scanlon Plan, a boldly cooperative approach to labor relations named after Joseph Scanlon, a professional boxer, steelworker and labor leader who became a lecturer at the Massachusetts Institute of Technology. The plan called for the company to share power, profits and knowledge with workers. (Herman Miller is not unionized except at one plant, which had a union when the company acquired it.) The philosophy behind the Scanlon Plan was simple, Hugh DePree has written: "People need to be needed, need to be responsible, have the right to know, need and want to own the problem."

Making the plan work was more complicated. It called for open-book management, employee participation in decision making, an extensive network of committees and revenue sharing with workers based on complex formulas that measured profits, productivity and customer satisfaction. Specific practices have evolved over the years, but the spirit of the Scanlon Plan continues to guide Herman Miller. Like Southwest Airlines and UPS, the company thinks of its workers as partners and wants them to act as if they own the place. Using explicitly religious language, Max DePree described the relationships between managers and employees as "covenantal," as opposed to "contractual." Noting that the best workers are, essentially, volunteers—meaning that they will leave if they are unhappy—DePree wrote that the quid pro quo of a legal contract is an insufficient and limiting framework for a relationship between a company and its workers. More, he said, is needed:

> Covenantal relationships induce freedom, not paralysis. A covenantal relationship rests on shared commitment to ideas, to issues, to values, to goals and to management processes. Words such as love, warmth, personal chemistry are certainly pertinent. Covenantal relationships are open to influence. They fill deep needs and they enable work to have meaning and be fulfilling. Covenantal relationships reflect unity and grace and poise. They are an expression of the sacred nature of relationships.

This talk is translated into action in a variety of ways. Mike Volkema and other executives at Herman Miller are open about the problems facing the company, and they enlist help in solving them. When employees at all levels are evaluated, they are ranked in such categories as "integrity and trust," "business knowledge," "continuous learning," and "relationship building." Everyone is also graded on such behaviors as "honors each individual with honesty, dignity and respect," "chooses the path of highest standards when faced with conflicting priorities" and "listens intently and checks for understanding." Linda Milanowski, the company's director of people services, told me: "How you go about doing your job is a make-or-break issue here."

Since introducing Scanlon in 1950, Herman Miller has shared profits with its full-time employees. It introduced a stock ownership plan in 1983. Today, all workers get company shares in their 401(k) as well as a traditional defined-benefit pension plan. All full-time Herman Miller employees own stock, and together they own about 15 percent of the equity in the company. This, of course, doesn't protect them against losing their jobs in hard times, as we'll see.

Herman Miller's commitment to the environment is also extraordinary. That, too, goes back to D. J. DePree. Legend has it that he was staring out the window when he first saw Nellie Miller, the woman he later married; he subsequently decided that everyone at Herman Miller should be able to see the outdoors. He also decreed that half of the land owned by the company be kept green. Modern environmentalism at Herman Miller began about twenty years ago when the company built an energy center that generated steam and electricity by burning scrap wood from its own plant and from others, saving money on energy and waste disposal costs. Today, the company practices what's called "design for the environment," which is aimed, ultimately, at eliminating waste altogether. Herman Miller designs furniture that can be easily disassembled and recycled, so that when it is no longer needed it can be remade into something else instead of being thrown away. This has been called cradle-to-cradle design.

In the design of its buildings, too, the company has been a pioneer. A manufacturing facility called the GreenHouse, designed by green architect William McDonough, cost more to build than a typical factory when it opened in 1994, but it is less expensive to heat and cool, per square foot, than any other company building. The U.S. Green Building Council, a industry coalition, has given only fourteen buildings in the United States its gold rating for leadership in environmental design: two are Herman Miller buildings, and most of the rest were built for the government or nonprofit groups. About three hundred Herman Miller people currently work on environmental teams assigned to such areas as product design, green building, energy reduction, and transportation. These teams are places where the values of environmentalism and participatory management converge.

Environmentalism is good business, Volkema told me: "We have consciously decided that we are only going to the level where we can demonstrate to any businessperson—to the toughest CFO who walks through the door—that the things that we did got a return on investment they would be thrilled with." But it's more than business.

It's a bedrock value for the company, and a topic that Volkema, who is ordinarily low-key, engages with passion. "It's not sustainable to continue to denigrate the biosphere in the way that we do," he said. He's been to China and seen the explosion in consumption there, and he says there simply aren't enough resources to support a middle-class standard of living for everyone on the planet if we continue to produce and consume the way we do now. "Someone has to begin to lead in understanding how we can take the state of the art and knowledge that exists today and move it to a radically new level. It's a logical, right thing to do," Volkema said. "We often will ask ourselves, if not us, then who? We're not alone, but I know that when I get in a group of one hundred businesspeople, when the environmental issue comes up, you've got ninety-plus on the other side of the room wondering how they can escape the new regulation."

A company with such lofty goals—designing great workplaces, developing the gifts of its workforce, saving the biosphere—runs the risk of overlooking the mundane work of generating returns for shareholders. For the most part, Herman Miller has done well for its investors, too. Those who knew him say D. J. DePree did not focus much on profits and did not have to because the company was private and family-owned; even so, sales at Herman Miller grew robustly during his tenure. Since the company sold shares to the public in 1970—Charles Eames designed the stock certificates—it has delivered returns that far outpaced those of most big companies. A $1,000 investment in Herman Miller at the time of its initial public offering would be worth nearly $78,000 at today's share price; by comparison, an investment of $1,000 in the Standard & Poor's 500 Index would be worth about $12,400. More recently, during the boom-and-bust decade from 1992 to 2002, Herman Miller ranked number one of the eight furniture companies in the Fortune 1000 in total returns to shareholders, delivering an average annual rate of 16 percent a year. (The median annual return of Fortune 500 companies for the decade was 9 percent.) A big part of Volkema's job is to keep all of the company's obligations in balance. "Herman Miller has always had this triangle that put customers, employees and shareholders in a state of equilibrium," he said. "Whenever you get those out of equilibrium—we call it equity—if it becomes inequitable, eventually, the system will begin to break."

Things fell out of balance for Herman Miller in the early 1990s. After Max DePree stepped down as CEO in 1988, his successors, understandably, wanted to preserve the company's values and stellar reputation. But they seemed reluctant to make any changes at all, and the company grew insular. Some employees who were attracted to Herman Miller because they cared about the earth or wanted to work in a congenial place did not focus sufficiently on the business. Manufacturing processes grew inefficient. Bonuses became expected rather than performance-driven. A knowledgeable outsider told me: "It had become a think tank of enlightened business practices funded through the sale of office furniture." Volkema all but conceded this point. "Every company runs the risk of its strength becoming its weakness," he said. In 1995 Herman Miller booked more than $1 billion in revenues for the first time but recorded less than $5 million in profits, its worst showing in years.

The board of directors asked Volkema to take over as CEO. It was a job he had never intended to seek. A lawyer by training and an entrepreneur at heart, Volkema had joined Herman Miller in 1990 when it acquired Meridian, a maker of metal case goods that he had run for seven years. He liked working in start-ups and small companies. "I had this fundamental belief that I didn't want to climb the corporate ladder," Volkema said. "I had a bias against large organizations that were slow-moving, bureaucratic and political—everything that I thought took the fun out of life and work."

A lanky, soft-spoken and modest man, Volkema grew up in Columbus, Ohio, where his father was a lawyer. He met his wife, Valerie, when they were undergraduates at Calvin College, a Christian liberal arts college in Grand Rapids. Like many people who grow up in the small towns of western Michigan, she had no desire to leave. As Volkema recalled it: "She got out one of those little kid's compasses, and drew about a sixty-mile radius around Grand

Rapids, and said, 'You can live and work anywhere inside that circle that you want.' Twenty-seven years later, I'm still here." After earning a law degree, he joined Meridian, one of many furniture companies in western Michigan. (Steelcase and Haworth, two of Herman Miller's big competitors, are headquartered there, and Knoll has plants nearby. This is the legacy of the Dutch and German immigrants with woodworking skills who were drawn to the area because of its forests.) Meridian was a small company, so Volkema got involved in everything—product development, manufacturing, sales, hiring and firing. Sales grew from about $5 million to $100 million under his leadership. Still, running Herman Miller was a formidable challenge for the young executive. "It was really a little nutty that the board took a chance on me," Volkema said.

Volkema did have one advantage over his predecessors: he was unafraid of change. He believed in Herman Miller's values—like the DePrees, he is a religious man and a product of the Dutch Reformed Church—but he could see that the company's strategies and practices had to adapt to the marketplace. Volkema and his executive team cut staff, modestly, and set out to improve efficiency on the factory floor, making small, continuous improvements, inspired by Toyota's production system. They invested heavily in technology, spending nearly $500 million in the late 1990s to move sales, order taking, manufacturing and purchasing onto the Internet. They encouraged the growth of a new division called SQA, which stands for "simple, quick, affordable," and then used it as a model to simplify and speed up all of Herman Miller. Finally, to better align the company's operations with the interests of shareholders, Volkema and his management team deployed a metric called EVA, or economic value added, which captures a company's economic success better than conventional accounting measures. Herman Miller uses EVA to evaluate business decisions and calculate incentive pay—it's much simpler than the old Scanlon Plan—and everyone, including rank-and-file workers, is taught how it works.

Some of the changes provoked resistance. At one of his regular meetings with employees, Volkema was taken aback when a veteran plant worker complained loudly about the focus on efficiency and asked him, in effect, whether there was any limit to what the company would ask a human being to do. "It blew my hair back a little bit," he recalled, largely because Herman Miller pays a lot of attention to the conditions on the shop floor. (The GreenHouse factory I visited has a gym, a cafeteria, and plenty of color and natural light.) Volkema arranged to work next to the woman for a day and see if he could do the job. He concluded that, in this case, the efficiency expert had gone too far. The plant managers adjusted the production process and recommitted themselves to keeping the workers involved. "It can't be done to them. It has to be done with them," Volkema said. At the same time, he said, Herman Miller has to always "find better ways of doing things or all of that work will go offshore." This is the level at which it becomes challenging to integrate a company's core values with the realities of a competitive marketplace where labor costs matter.

Volkema's first five years as CEO produced great results, although he takes pains not to claim the credit. "When we had the Aeron chair in the middle of the dot-com boom, we looked like the smartest people in the world," he said. Early in 2001, that changed. Steep declines in the Internet, technology and telecom sectors, followed by the September 11 terrorist attacks and the war in Iraq, stalled the economy and eroded business confidence. As a business-to-business company selling high-quality products at premium prices, Herman Miller was hit hard. "We are sometimes like the BMW, caught in a cost-conscious market, where everybody is looking for Chevys," Volkema said. Sales dropped from $2.2 billion in FY 2001 to $1.5 billion in FY 2002 and $1.3 billion in FY 2003. Its stock price fell by nearly 60 percent from its peak. "We've seen unprecedented declines, not just for our company, but for our industry," Volkema said.

The company had to scale back. "We had to position the business so it could be profitable at a lower level," Volkema said, at least until he could see signs of a recovery. With that in mind, he and his team laid out what they called "nonnegotiable objectives" to guide their response. Their actions should not negatively impact customer service, their ability to sell or their long-term strategy of making cutting-edge furniture. Any changes should provide a sustainable economic benefit, not a short-term fix, and they should simplify the business where possible. And they should honor the corporate values.

Volkema thought about the future as well as the past as he looked for ways to curb spending. He decided that it would be shortsighted to reduce the budget for Herman Miller's Creative Office, which is its research and development arm. "That's not an easy thing to do as you're having to tell four thousand people that you don't have enough work for them to do," Volkema said. Spending money on research did not win the company points on Wall Street, where the investment horizons are short-term, and the research may not do much for Volkema's career. "I may never be able to see the full fruits of those investments, especially with the life expectancy of CEOs nowadays," he said. "But I have to think about our long-term legacy. The question is, do you want to be here in fifty years?" One measure of a company with strong values is its willingness to invest in a future that goes beyond the tenure of the current CEO.

Once Volkema had made up his mind about all the things he would not do, he was left to focus on the costs of manufacturing and distribution. The company worked harder to drive efficiency in its factories, outsourced its fleet of trucks and reduced the space it needed by more than 20 percent, in part by closing plants in Holland, Michigan; Rocklin, California; and Canton, Georgia. (The $20 million Canton plant had only opened in 2000.) Hoping at first to avoid or limit layoffs, Volkema and his executive team cut discretionary expenses, froze pay and eliminated bonuses, asked workers to take buyouts or retire early and eliminated temporary jobs.

The senior executives thought about reducing everyone's hours and pay, as a way to share the pain. They ruled out that option because it was neither sustainable nor fair to those who could not absorb a pay cut with no end in sight. As Linda Milanowski, the human resources executive, put it: "If you take production people down to four-day weeks, they're going to start struggling to buy gas and groceries." The company also worried about losing executives. "To retain the people we've got to retain," she said, "we've got to take care of them."

Facing the inevitability of mass layoffs, Volkema then needed to figure out which jobs to eliminate and how to take care of those who would be let go. Some decisions were relatively straightforward. When the Rocklin plant was closed, for example, nearly all the workers lost their jobs. Harder was deciding whom to let go after a manager was told to cut his or her budget by 10 or 20 percent. In each case, the manager—who is called a leader at Herman Miller— had to justify the decision, in writing, based on the employee's years of service, performance ratings and potential. Milanowski explained: "That's the delicate balance—some people would like it to be all about years of service, others only about performance." Initially, executives wrestled with such questions as to whether to spare people whose husbands or wives worked for the company. But as the number of layoffs grew, they decided that it was impractical to take each worker's personal circumstances into account.

Once the decisions about layoffs were made, the company did what it could to cushion the blow. Laid-off workers were given notice one at a time and face-to-face by their supervisor and by someone from human resources. (Unfortunately, this is by no means a common practice for assembly-line work.) That first meeting with the worker was designed to address bread-and-butter questions about severance pay and health insurance. Workers typically got two weeks' pay for each year of service, up to twenty-six weeks. Each worker then met with a counselor, either from Herman Miller or an outplacement firm, who tried to help with the emotional issues—for example, how do you talk to your family, friends or coworkers about losing your job? The counselor then arranged to call the worker at home that first evening to check in.

Outplacement services were made available to everyone, not just the managers who customarily get them. Laid-off employees could attend workshops to help them figure out what they would like to do next, and they were offered advice on writing resumes and handling job interviews. They also got access to computers and printers at a career services center in a building leased by Herman Miller. This is atypical, experts say. "I'd like to get other companies to do things as thoughtfully and compassionately as Herman Miller," said Scott Anderson, who runs the Grand Rapids office of OI Partners, an out-placement firm that works with many clients, including Herman Miller. "They set the standard."

This all costs money, of course. The company spent $30.5 million on severance and outplacement services in FY 2002—in effect, spending money to assist the laid-off workers that would otherwise have gone to shareholders. Some investors questioned the charges. "They wanted to know why our one-time charges were twice as high as a competitor's were," said Beth Nickels, Herman Miller's CFO. "Our response was that we feel strongly about how we're going to treat people. We want to bridge them to their next opportunity. We think it's the right thing to do. If you don't like that, you can go invest somewhere else." Self-interest comes into play as well. "Every employee who gets to stay sees how you treat everyone who has to leave," Volkema said. Or as Scott Anderson put it: "Every company, when they're hiring, wants to portray itself as a caring employer. Why any company would want to have the last chapter close on a completely different note is a mystery to me."

Whenever a company lays off workers, the question of how it compensates its top executives becomes relevant. Herman Miller's history is interesting in this regard. The company once limited the cash compensation of top executives to twenty times the pay of an average worker; this was intended to cap the CEO's salary and create an incentive for them to increase the wages of others, although it didn't work as planned because it didn't cover nonsalary compensation. Herman Miller's board of directors dropped the limit in 1995, but executive pay at the company remains lower than at comparable firms. Volkema's current contract gives him a base salary of $500,000. His bonus has ranged from zero to $374,000, depending on whether EVA targets were met. He also got grants of options and restricted stock that, when combined with the stock he bought himself, will give him ownership of one million shares of Herman Miller stock, which traded for about $23 per share at the end of 2003. He voluntarily gave up his bonus and 20 percent of his base pay in 2003 and 2004 in exchange for stock options, which are designed to align his interests with those of shareholders.

While Volkema doesn't have to worry about money, the long downturn has taken a toll on him. Worst of all was ordering layoffs. "It kills him," Linda Milanowski told me. "He hates it." The only good thing he can say about the slump is that adversity forced Herman Miller to reexamine itself and that the company has emerged smarter, stronger and more efficient. "We'd never wish this period on ourselves or anyone else, but real learning took place," Volkema said. "If it hadn't been for the crisis, we probably never would have had to go through the creative and hard work we did. There's no question that this has been a growing experience for us, in a strange and perverted way." The company now intends to be disciplined about hiring and spending in good times as well as bad. In a letter to shareholders, Volkema praised Herman Miller workers for their spirit, determination and willingness to sacrifice, and said they reminded him of the old saying that "tough times never last, but tough people do."

Near the end of 2003, Volkema saw indications of a turnaround. "Not all of the uncertainty has gone away," he said, "but I truly believe that Herman Miller is on the way back up." He told the investors the company is still brimming with ideas about the future.

I got a peek into the future during my visit to Zeeland when I stopped by Volkema's office. I had expected to find him in an Aeron chair, and he was. But I was surprised to see that he works in what is, by executive standards, a tiny office, with about 125 square feet of space. It's got eight sides, and it's covered by a canopy, made out of a translucent fabric, that points to the sky, calling to mind a sail or perhaps a church steeple. It was the first CEO cubicle I'd ever seen.

When it came time to meet with Volkema and Nickels, the CFO, we sat around a big table in a conference room and dining area next to his office that was far more spacious—flooded with natural light, stylishly furnished, open and airy. There were lots of spaces like that all around Herman Miller, public places where workers gather. This, I learned, was the office of the future, at least as Herman Miller envisions it: small private spaces and lots of inviting shared space, to promote collaboration, learning and casual interaction. Herman Miller has been doing lots of R&D lately—remember, Volkema did not cut research during the downturn—and it has learned, to no one's surprise, that people are happiest when they find community at work. What's more, many companies strive to be "learning organizations" that tap the collective knowledge of their people. The office as a "new urbanism" village, with its own green space and coffee bars, promotes all that. These possibilities, which tap into Herman Miller's legacy as an innovator, are what keep Volkema excited.

"People can never predict our future by looking in the rearview mirror," Volkema said. "We're hard at work right now trying to invent something that changes the game, and enlarges our market opportunity, and explodes our potential." This potential can't be recorded on a quarterly earnings statement, but it is nevertheless part of the fabric of Herman Miller. "Our creativity is a huge asset," said Volkema. "So is our culture of engaged people." Those intangibles have endured, and so will Herman Miller.

9

CAN ONE PERSON
CHANGE A COMPANY?

BARBARA WAUGH AT
HEWLETT-PACKARD

Barbara Waugh has been a radical all her life. She worked at a "freedom school" for African American kids in segregated Tallahassee, Florida, in the 1960s. She did feminist street theater in Madison, Wisconsin, in the 1970s. She ran a women's center for nine theological schools in Berkeley in the 1980s. And then she went into business.

These days, Waugh calls herself a corporate revolutionary. Mind you, she is not leading a charge against corporations. To the contrary, she believes that corporations have the potential to lead a revolution that will change the world for the better by serving the poor, promoting human rights and generating economic activity in the places where it is most needed. "After working to change the world through politics, education, government and the churches," Waugh says, "I believe I can have more impact through the corporate sector because more than any other sector, it will determine the future of the world." This is an unorthodox idea, but Waugh has put it into practice with great effect during nearly twenty years as a midlevel manager at Hewlett-Packard, the technology firm that helped to create Silicon Valley.

More than anyone I know, Waugh has found a way to change corporate America from within. This is why I'm telling her story in a book that to this point has focused on the accomplishments of company founders and CEOs. Certainly, the most straightforward way to build a great company guided by spiritual values is to start from scratch—as Bernie Glassman and Tom Chappell, Herb Kelleher, Jim Casey, Howard Schultz and the DePrees all did. But Barb Waugh's story demonstrates (as Kenny Moore's did) that you do not have to start your own company or become a CEO to make a difference in business—although it helps to work at a place like Hewlett-Packard, a company with a proud tradition of valuing its people and promoting innovation.

Probably the most important thing to know about Waugh, who is in her late fifties, is that she has accomplished almost nothing on her own. Her e-mail signature ends with the quote "Each of us is an idiot. Together we're a genius," which has been attributed to the Hollywood director Billy Wilder. Businesspeople would say that Waugh is the consummate networker, but her networking is not about building her career. It's about building community and agitating for change. Operating more like a community organizer than a middle manager, she shares knowledge, links people to one another, expands her circles of allies—she calls them coconspirators—and constructs ad hoc coalitions around one issue after another. Waugh's most valuable skill may be her ability to connect, energize and inspire people. (I know that because she has connected me to her network and energized me as I've worked on this book.) "Her style is the antithesis of top-down hierarchical management," says her former boss, Joel Birnbaum, who used to run HP's research laboratories. "Instead, she leverages grassroots beliefs and talents to produce dramatic results." Lynelle Preston, a young MBA at HP, says of Waugh: "She's the hub of incredible networks. I can go to her with any idea, and she knows exactly who should hear about it and how to make it happen."

Here are a few of the things that Waugh and her allies have accomplished:

• They mobilized gay and lesbian workers, who created a theatrical presentation to tell their stories to top executives of HP. As a direct result, HP became the first Fortune 50 company to offer domestic-partner benefits.

• They redefined the mission of HP's research labs, which employ about nine hundred scientists and engineers worldwide, to focus R&D on projects that are most likely to make a contribution to society.

• They helped create an HP project called eInclusion, which aims to deliver computer and Internet technology to the world's four billion poor people through sustainable microenterprises. In a *Fortune* column, my colleague David Kirkpatrick called eInclusion "the most visionary step I've ever seen a large tech company take."

It's no accident that Waugh was able to achieve all this at Hewlett-Packard, the legendary technology firm. HP generated $73 billion in revenues—making it, by far, the biggest company in this book in terms of sales—and it employed 140,000 people in 2003. Even at that scale, and even after the controversial merger with Compaq Computer that threatens to undermine the very idea of a corporate culture, HP remains a special place. Values and principles still matter at HP, as they have since William Hewlett and David Packard, two self-effacing engineers, created the company in a rented garage in Palo Alto, California, in 1938.

It's significant that HP began with a relationship. Close friends who met as Stanford undergraduates, Bill Hewlett and Dave Packard believed strongly in innovation, technical excellence, fiscal prudence and service to the community. But they were best known for the way they related to their people: they hired the best engineers they could find and then set high standards, trusted their employees, listened to them and treated them almost like family. "Bill and Dave had an essential faith in people," Steve Jobs, the founder of Apple Computer, who as a teenage geek was given a summer job by Hewlett, once said. "They believed people were noble." Their company's values, which became known as the HP Way, were a big reason why HP thrived for half a century, becoming one of the most admired firms in America. The HP culture has also been blamed for some of the company's troubles—critics say that HP lost its edge in the 1990s and suffered from "terminal niceness." The task of revitalizing HP while preserving its core values now belongs to Carly Fiorina, the dynamic CEO who arrived in 1999. How the HP Way will evolve—if, in fact, it endures—under Fiorina is an open question, and one about which Waugh and her colleagues care very much.

HP's culture is passed down through storytelling, and most people who work at the company have heard a story or two about the founders. There's the story about the engineer who arrived at work one morning to find his prototype of a new oscilloscope, made of thin-gauge aluminum, mangled out of shape on his desk. Beside it was a note: "You can do better than this—Dave Packard." That story showed how tough Packard could be, and how deeply he cared about the quality of HP's products. But Bill and Dave, as they were known, could be humble, too. In a book called *The HP Way,* published in 1995, Packard tells the oft-told tale of an HP researcher named Chuck House who refused to stop working on a display monitor after Packard and others ordered him to drop the idea. Without telling his bosses, House got some friends in manufacturing to produce the monitors, and he found a market for them; they went on to generate $35 million in sales. Packard subsequently presented him with a medal for "extraordinary contempt and defiance beyond the normal call of engineering duty." HP tolerated—and even rewarded—mavericks.

Relationships were the glue that held HP together. Bill and Dave loved the outdoors so much that they bought land in California redwood country, in the Colorado Rockies and on the Massachusetts seashore where HP workers and their families were invited to hike and go camping. Old-timers recall the annual company picnics, where the founders grilled the steaks, and they point to the more concrete ways that the company showed it cared: HP provided catastrophic health insurance for its workers in the 1940s, created a profit-sharing plan in the 1950s, and initiated flexible working hours in the 1960s. These were all pioneering practices.

One of the best-known HP innovations is a technique called "management by walking around," or MBWA. Executives are supposed to spend unstructured time on the shop floor, in research labs or wandering around cubicles, so as not to lose touch with the real work being done. The practice is not quite as simple as it sounds, as Packard explained. "It needs to be frequent, friendly, unfocused and unscheduled—but far from pointless," he wrote. "And since its principal aim is to seek out people's thoughts and opinions, it requires good *listening*." MBWA came naturally to Bill and Dave. They were unpretentious, approachable and genuinely interested in what their people had to say. "We were very close to our employees," Packard wrote. "We understood their jobs and shared much of their lives with them."

Both founders believed firmly that HP was about more than making technology and making money. It was about making a contribution to society. Packard explained it this way:

I think many people assume, wrongly, that a company exists simply to make money. While this is an important result of a company's existence, we have to go deeper and find the real reasons for our being. As we investigate this, we inevitably come to the conclusion that a group of people get together and exist as an institution that we call a company so that they are able to accomplish something collectively that they could not accomplish separately—they make a contribution to society, a phrase which sounds trite but is fundamental.

Shaped by the Great Depression and World War II, Hewlett and Packard were driven by an ethic of service more than selfishness. "I think of the old HP as a benevolent patriarchy," Waugh said. "Bill and Dave made all the decisions and, as good fathers do, they cared about us and shared their wealth. Not only in the form of profit sharing and generous benefits, but in the form of giving back to our communities."

Still, when Bill and Dave decided to write down HP's corporate objectives during the company's first executive retreat, held in Sonoma, California, in 1957, they put profit at the top of the list. "Profit is the best single measure of our contribution to society," they wrote, "and the ultimate source of our company strength. We should attempt to achieve the maximum profit possible consistent with our other objectives." Those other objectives were important, too: they included creating quality products, providing opportunity and satisfaction to employees, preserving an open and entrepreneurial culture and making a contribution to the community. But the way that the founders talked about profit—both as the company's lifeblood and as the best gauge of its success, a revealing metaphor in a firm that made high-quality measuring instruments—made clear that they never lost their focus on the bottom line. During the thirty-nine years when first Packard and then Hewlett ran HP, the company grew from a two-man operation to a global enterprise with forty-two thousand employees, $1.9 billion in sales and $158 million in profits.

When HP ran into trouble years later, some people blamed the HP Way. Packard himself had feared complacency; he had once printed up T-shirts saying, "We don't pay you to be comfortable at HP." Inevitably, though, the company attracted people who were attuned to the HP culture—they liked the company orchestra or the profit-sharing plan—but lacked killer business instincts. (This was akin to what happened at Herman Miller after the DePrees stepped down.) Lewis Platt, HP's CEO from 1992 to 1999, was an intelligent and exceedingly decent man, but his critics felt he lacked toughness. His first wife had died of a brain tumor when he was young, and the experience of caring for their children taught him the difficulties of juggling work and family. He made it his business to make HP a family-friendly place. But, as author George Anders writes in *Perfect Enough,* a book about HP, the company was losing its competitive edge. Ambitious and gifted executives, frustrated by the slow pace of decision making, fled HP. Somehow, Anders writes, the HP Way had been turned on its head:

> Explicit financial success had been shunted to the back of the pack. Much of the company's energy was going into the softer values: community service, respect for the individual, and the creation of a great workplace. There wasn't anything wrong with these values; in the right setting, they were enormously admirable. But they couldn't single-handedly guide a company for long.

During the Internet boom of the late 1990s, HP came to be seen as a sluggish giant, admired for its values but no longer ahead of the technology curve. The HP board brought in the hard-charging Fiorina from Lucent Technologies to get the company moving again.

When Barbara Waugh heard about the new CEO, her first reaction was: "Carly who?" HP had never hired a top executive from the outside. But Waugh was thrilled that Lew Platt and HP director Dick Hackborn, who led the search, had embraced the idea that a woman could run the company. No U.S. corporation as big as HP had ever hired a female CEO. Part of the reason HP was willing to do so was that Waugh and others had organized the firm's female engineers, bringing them together for annual conferences at which they got to know one another and lobbied top managers on women's issues. Platt and Hackborn were as close to being feminists as white male sixtysomething executives could be. "It was fabulous from that perspective," said Waugh.

That Waugh herself had been hired by HP was testimony to the firm's willingness to take chances on people. Her technology experience was limited to a six-month stint as an administrator of a struggling electronics college. She had a doctorate in psychology, a master's in theology and work experience as an actress, car mechanic, machinist, newspaper columnist, civil rights investigator and teacher. Maybe because she'd held so many jobs, someone figured she belonged in personnel. Whatever the explanation, Waugh became staffing manager of a division in Santa Clara. One reason she liked the job was that the toilets were clean; her duties at the electronics college had included maintaining the office bathroom.

A lifelong rabble-rouser with roots in the church world, Waugh is a small, intense and energetic woman with spiky white hair and a quick smile. We met for the first time in Palo Alto, over a long lunch in the HP cafeteria, and since then we've met several times and spoken often. I feel as if we're kindred spirits—products of the 1960s who decades later are immersed in corporate America. "Business in my mind was the enemy and the bad guy and not to be trusted," she told me, and I remembered feeling the same way years ago. Waugh's thinking shifted during the early 1980s when she ran the women's center at the Graduate Theological Union in Berkeley and realized that their good works were supported by businesspeople. "I decided," she recalled, "that I'd rather be on the inside, deciding where the money goes, than on the outside."

Waugh traces her activism back to her family. Her parents, devout Presbyterians, were elders at their church in Miami who worked with a Christian anticommunist group called Moral Rearmament. "My folks were activists at the neighborhood level," she said. "If something was wrong, they fixed it." As an undergraduate at Florida State, Waugh tutored black kids at a church-supported "freedom school" and joined an interracial dating group designed to build ties between the campuses of FSU and nearby Florida A&M, a historically black college. While attending the University of Chicago divinity school, she threw herself into anti–Vietnam War organizing and the women's movement. There she underwent a crisis of faith. Seeing, among other things, how women were mistreated at the divinity school, she pulled away from institutional religion. "I lost all notion of God at divinity school," Waugh said. "Since faith, for me, had been so closely identified with religion, I lost my faith, too." She married, briefly and unhappily, and struggled for a time. "I went into a deep depression," she said. "I could not see the purpose of life."

Through sheer force of will—mostly because she was tired of feeling bad all the time—Waugh made up her mind after a few years that she would again commit herself to making the world a better place, however she could, with or without God's help. "I really went about it very pragmatically," she said. "I decided that I was going to find a dream so big that interesting things would show up in my life." When people occasionally tell her that they aren't as altruistic as she is, Waugh has to laugh. "There is not a shred of altruism in my so-called altruism," she said. "I do this for me because I cannot stand my life when I am living at the scale of me, me, me, mine, mine, mine, more, more, more. When I get down to that level, I can actually lose my mind over the dust balls in the corner of the room or the fact that the kids' socks don't match. Who wants to live like that? And who wants to walk around depressed?"

Over time, Waugh and her partner of the last twenty-five years, an activist, consultant and former United Church of Christ minister named Anastasia Cusulos, have returned to the church, albeit in their own way. Sometimes they worship at a Unitarian Universalist church in Palo Alto because they like the Unitarians' commitment to social action; they also attend Glide Memorial United Methodist Church, an interracial church in San Francisco known for its musical, emotion-packed services. Waugh also swears by a daily spiritual practice that she adopted in the mid-1990s: most mornings, she writes several pages in a journal, as a way to discover what's on her mind and what intentions she'd like to carry through the day. This practice is a way to combat her natural inclination to depression and negativity, she said, and it seems to work, because Waugh comes across as upbeat and optimistic. "But I have to consciously force that," she told me. "It's not like I'm a Pollyanna who wakes up in the morning, happy to be alive in this wonderful world. It's Barbara, who slogs up out of a deep sleep after she wrestles all night with demons." Still, she has been surprised by how frequently her optimism turns out to be warranted.

Faith, for Waugh, encompasses faith in God, faith in people, even faith in corporate America's ability to do good. All of this shapes her work at HP. She reminds herself, for example, to assume the best about people, both allies and adversaries, whom she tries to envision as potential allies. "The '60s way of doing things," she has said, "was to identify a very complicated organization, pick out its worst elements, and go after them. You'd attack them." This approach—of dividing the world into good people (us) and bad people (them)—had a couple of serious drawbacks, she now believes. "First, we miss the bad in the 'good' guys, most importantly in ourselves," she said. "And, second, we miss the good in the 'bad' guys, which is where the real possibility for change lies." Identifying someone as an enemy, she thinks, cements them as an enemy, while speaking to the better part of their nature opens them to change.

Today, rather than spotlight the negative, she does just the opposite: "You seek out the positive deviants and support them. You feed them; you give them resources and visibility." She calls this "amplifying positive deviance," and although that's a mouthful, it turns out to be an effective way to promote change. (It's what I'm trying to do in this book.) Why expend precious energy trying to stamp out the negative, which ends up creating enemies, Waugh asks, when the alternative—ignoring the negative and celebrating the positive—works just as well, if not better?

Waugh's HP work is also informed by her belief that we all share responsibility for repairing the world. Remember whom you work for, she said: "I feel that our real boss has to be whatever we think the Higher Power is—whether it's God or nature or the Great Spirit or some vision of a world that works for everyone." This gives her a mandate, as she sees it, to speak up when she senses an opportunity to remedy an injustice or make a contribution. "I don't let anyone else define what my business is," Waugh told me. "I have defined it as bringing the corporate sector into full stewardship for the planet. So everything, by definition, is my business and everyone reports to me." I'm taken aback by this, but she means it. "I basically do performance evaluations up and down the ladder," Waugh tells me. Of course, she is careful about how she delivers them.

These, then, are Waugh's principles for living spiritual values in corporate America: Remember whom you work for. Recruit co-conspirators. Amplify positive deviance. And try to turn "enemies" into allies. (She has written a book, called *Soul in the Computer: The Story of a Corporate Revolutionary,* about her work at HP and her tools for change.) In practice, Waugh simply goes to work every day and tries to figure out how she can most usefully spend her time and energy. (What her precise job duties are, if any, are not clear to me. As best as I can tell, HP recognizes the value of having someone around who spreads knowledge and goodness and connects people to one another. So she is permitted to do pretty much what she pleases.) In her early days in personnel, for example, Waugh was an advocate for diversity, helping to persuade white male engineers to hire and promote more women and minorities. It wasn't always easy, but she discovered that, at least at HP, "there is a foundation of decency you can rely on." This gave her hope when the diversity issue turned personal in the mid-1990s: Waugh learned that HP's senior executives, after studying the question, had decided not to offer domestic partner benefits to the families of its gay and lesbian employees.

She was deeply upset. Apple Computer, headquartered in nearby Cupertino, had become one of the first companies to offer domestic partner benefits in 1994. She'd assumed HP would follow suit, even though at the time only a handful of Fortune 500 companies provided gay and lesbian couples with the benefits made available to married people. Still, HP acted like HP—even as they said no to the proposal, senior executives invited leaders of a fledgling network of gay and lesbian workers to a meeting to discuss the issue. That was all Waugh needed to hear. Drawing on her experience doing feminist street theater, Waugh saw an opportunity to transform the "issue" of domestic partner benefits into the personal stories of HP employees. She sent out a questionnaire to gay and lesbian workers, asking two questions: "How has homophobia affected your productivity?" and "What business issue would you rather be discussing with the CEO and his staff than homophobia?" Working with a growing number of allies, she used the answers to create what was called a Reader's Theater—a dramatic presentation of stories that personalized the issue. Employees who didn't want to go public could ask to have their stories told by others.

About a dozen employees read the stories to CEO Lew Platt and his senior staff. One woman who lived in a conservative town had written about how a lesbian couple living nearby had been burned to death in their home. Another said she would be leaving HP so that she could get health insurance for her partner and their baby. A general manager, who came out of the closet to perform in the play, talked about his partner's death from AIDS and the support they had received from his vice president at HP. When the play ended, there was silence. One executive said simply: "I had no idea." Said another: "Discriminating against employees for any reason is not the HP Way." A few executives remained opposed to domestic partner benefits, but they were eventually persuaded that providing equal benefits for equal work did not mean that they were endorsing the gay lifestyle.

Platt and his staff eventually asked the group to perform the Reader's Theater around the company, as did friends of those in the gay and lesbian network. The play was performed more than sixty times during the next six months. The company reversed its decision and made domestic partner benefits available in 1997. IBM followed just a few months later, notes Emily Duncan, a vice president for diversity at HP. "We really made a difference in the industry," she said. Today, more than two hundred of the Fortune 500 companies provide domestic partner benefits. Waugh points out that this is an arena where big business is leading, not following, the rest of the world. "HP is providing its people a community of a much higher quality than the towns—or countries—in which many of us live," she said. Some HP country managers overseas told headquarters that it was against the law where they lived to recognize homosexual relationships. They were told that inside HP, things would be different.

Waugh's biggest tangible accomplishment to date—the eInclusion initiative—grew out of her work redefining the scope of HP Labs. I'll describe how this happened because the process is as important as the end result. In 1993, Joel Birnbaum, who then ran HP Labs, asked Waugh to find out how to promote cooperation within HP Labs and make the unit the best industrial research lab in the world. They surveyed their employees and got so many provocative answers back—eight hundred single-spaced pages in all—that Waugh edited them into a Reader's Theater so that they could be widely shared. That, in turn, got more discussions going, which fostered the creation of informal groups, which stimulated more ideas, which were brought back to top managers. Out of this messy process grew several concrete initiatives, including the creation of a grassroots research program, run entirely by rank-and-file engineers, which funds about half a dozen "out-of-the-box" projects each year. One goal was to change the culture of HP Labs, making it more bottom-up and less top-down, to draw on everyone's ideas and energy.

Around this time, an engineer named Laurie Mittelstadt dropped by Waugh's office and made a seemingly casual remark. "Being the best industrial research lab *in* the world doesn't do it for me," Mittelstadt said. "It's presumptuous. But I'd get up in the morning to be the best *for* the world." They both saw right away what a big difference this little tweak would make. "HP for the world" became a way to sum up not just the mission of HP Labs but also the overarching idea behind all of HP. A graphic designer created a logo and poster with the slogan "HP for the world" above a picture of Bill Hewlett and Dave Packard, their original garage and the globe as seen from space. Bill and Dave, by then retired, signed the original poster, and eventually the image adorned T-shirts, mouse pads and mugs, even the Visa cards issued by the HP credit union. The original poster hangs by the entrance to HP Labs.

But what did "HP for the world" mean in practice? That would take years of brainstorming, networking and experimentation to discover. Waugh got an inkling when she read a book called *Give Us Credit,* about the Grameen Bank and the microlending revolution it created in Bangladesh. Dr. Muhammad Yunus, a U.S.-educated economist, created the Grameen Bank in 1976 to make small loans to the poorest of the poor; it has since made loans to millions of borrowers who use the money to start microbusinesses such as raising livestock, food processing or tailoring. More recently, a Grameen-related enterprise in Bangladesh loaned more than thirty thousand people money to buy cell phones, which become the village equivalents of pay telephones in places where no phone service is available. Waugh got so excited by the Grameen model that she bought twenty-five copies of the book for HP colleagues.

Meanwhile, sustainability expert Stuart Hart had visited HP Labs to speak about how companies can profit by attacking environmental problems or trying to alleviate poverty, especially in the developing world. Hart, who teaches at the Kenan-Flagler Business School at the University of North Carolina, has made it his business to encourage companies to find innovative ways to serve the world's four billion poorest people. He works with HP, Ford, Johnson & Johnson and DuPont, among others, in a consortium called the Base of the Pyramid Learning Laboratory. "I look at this as a huge opportunity for those companies that have the moxie, the creativity and the execution ability to really pull this off," Hart says. "There are only going to be a few that figure it out, and they're going to profit."

Finally, as part of the grassroots research initiative, an HP Labs engineer named Jim Sheats had begun working with the MIT Media Lab and with José María Figueres, a former president of Costa Rica, to produce "cyberkiosks" to bring technology to the developing world. The kiosks, made from recycled shipping containers, included computers, printers and Internet connections designed to provide rural villages with information about weather, health care, farming techniques, crop prices and the like. Connecting the dots, Waugh arranged for Sheats to go to Bangladesh and meet with Muhammad Yunus, who, it turned out, wanted kiosks for his country. All of this unfolded quietly and on a small scale. "We had a VP who, under the radar screen, was slipping us money, like the $50,000 it took to equip one of these shipping containers," Waugh said.

Then came a stroke of luck. Early in 2000, a friend in corporate communications asked Waugh if she had any stories to illustrate the inventiveness and spirit of HP that Fiorina could use in a speech. Waugh told her about the cyberkiosks and Grameen, and the PR woman took the stories to Fiorina. Fiorina loved the projects. Within weeks, an HP executive was assigned full time to see whether it would be possible to scale up the idea of delivering computer and Internet technology to the developing world. That became eInclusion. "It was Carly partnering with a skunkworks," Waugh said. This story illustrates how Waugh promotes change at HP—she finds ways to create and energize informal, grassroots networks and then connects them with people who have the power to provide resources and scale. "It turns out," Waugh said, "that the hierarchical leaders benefit every bit as much as the grassroots when the grassroots are empowered." Bringing formal and informal leaders together, she argues, enables even a big company like HP to be speedy and agile.

"HP for the world" was becoming real. HP's philanthropy programs were recast to promote eInclusion: in East Palo Alto, Baltimore and San Diego County, the company helped to design and build "digital villages" that brought the benefits of technology to poor people. These philanthropic efforts helped HP learn how to deliver products or services to people who had little or no experience using technology. The San Diego project, for example, connected eighteen Indian reservations to each other and to the Internet; the Native Americans, trained by HP volunteers, built parts of the Internet backbone themselves because neither cable operators nor phone companies offer broadband access in the area.

More ambitious are HP's efforts to create what the company calls iCommunities in Dikhatole, a town outside Johannesburg, South Africa, and in Kuppam, a rural community of 320,000 people in the state of Andhra Pradesh in southern India. Living conditions are primitive in Dikhatole—there's no running water or electricity—and the unemployment rate is more than 30 percent. But HP, working with local nonprofits, a South African steel company and Microsoft, has built a training facility with ninety Internet-enabled workstations. There young people have the opportunity to acquire literacy, computer and business skills that will improve their chances of finding work. In Kuppam, HP has begun to provide the rural poor with online access to government records, schools, health information and agricultural data. One hope is to stimulate small tech-based businesses: village photographers, armed with solar-powered digital cameras and printers, now take ID photos for documents and portraits of weddings or family gatherings. "Most of us design products for the Western world, not knowing what the needs are in the rest of the world," said Srinivas Sukumar, a twenty-five-year veteran of HP and friend of Waugh's who helped set up both the South Africa and India projects. They required a new approach to technology development, he said: "First, you have to learn what problem the community want to solve. Then you try to solve it. Then you apply some creativity or research to make it cost effective or adaptable to a new business model." At a minimum, the iCommunities will build goodwill and promote the HP brand in

India and South Africa; at best, they will help the company to invent new and profitable lines of business.

Fiorina has become a strong supporter of the eInclusion project, which, she hopes, can help make HP a technology leader in the developing world. A year she spent in Ghana as a teenager left a strong impression, and she has visited Africa a couple of times since becoming HP's CEO. Speaking at an Asia Pacific economic summit in Shanghai in 2001, Fiorina asserted that corporate social responsibility is good for HP's business:

> I honestly believe that the winning companies of this century will be those who prove with their actions that they can be profitable and increase social value—companies that both do well and do good. In fact, business leaders will no longer view doing well and doing good as separate pursuits, but one unified pursuit. And, increasingly, shareowners, customers, partners and employees are going to vote with their feet—rewarding those companies that fuel social change through business. . . . This is simply the new reality of business—one that we should and must embrace.

This is the twenty-first-century legacy of Bill Hewlett and Dave Packard and their belief that a good company has to make a contribution to society.

HP's future won't be decided by Fiorina or by anyone else. Remember the question with which we began this chapter: "Can one person change a company?" The answer is no, whether the one person is a CEO like Fiorina or a middle manager like Barbara Waugh. But one person who can find ways to mobilize and energize others can make a significant difference, as Waugh's story has shown. Waugh remains an optimist, believing that Fiorina, working with the hierarchy and with the informal networks at HP, will find ways to renew and reinvent the HP Way.

"Just about any CEO you could point to would have canceled anything as far-out and speculative as eInclusion in times like these, or at least reduced it. But Carly gets it," Waugh said. "And she was the CEO who showed up at the world summit on sustainable development in Johannesburg. Why, with everything on her plate? Because she believes that the world will reward the companies that help solve the world's problems." After nearly two decades in the belly of corporate America, Waugh has more faith than ever that she is just where she belongs: "I think HP has a great shot at being best for the world."

10

THE BUCK STOPS
WHERE?

STAPLES AND PEPSICO

Mark Buckley has always felt passionately about the environment. If you visit his hometown of Essex, Massachusetts, on Cape Ann, about an hour's drive north of Boston, you'll understand why. Essex is known for clams—Buckley dug plenty as a kid, and he still likes to go clam digging with his family—and Cape Ann is home to a rugged coastline, hiking trails and whale-watching expeditions. After majoring in biology in college, Buckley spent a year working on an aquaculture project for the U.S. Department of the Interior. "We were growing fin fish and shellfish," he said. "Rainbow trout in salt water. Winter flounder. European oysters. It was a terrific experience." Buckley thought he had found his calling. "I was going to be the next Jacques Cousteau," he said. "That was my vision. It just wasn't where I ended up."

Where Buckley ended up was at Staples, the fast-growing chain of office supply stores based in Framingham, Massachusetts. But, as he explained to me when we met, he never stopped working for the environment. He spent several years at a supermarket chain, which, thanks to his efforts, became the first in New England to recycle plastic bags. After joining Staples as manager of facilities and purchasing in 1990, he got the company to recycle the thousands of corrugated cardboard boxes in which office supplies were delivered to the stores. Back home in Essex, he served on the town's first recycling committee and won election to the Board of Health. Then, in 2002, his career took a felicitous turn. Buckley was named to a new position, vice president for environmental affairs, which gives him responsibility for all of Staples' environmental initiatives: selling recycled paper and other eco-friendly products, promoting the recycling of cell phones and ink-jet cartridges, leading energy conservation efforts, buying "green" power and educating Staples employees and customers about the environment. "It's a dream job for me," he said.

He can thank environmental activists for his new assignment. Staples created the job after negotiating with protest groups that had mounted an aggressive campaign accusing the company of destroying timberland. This newspaper ad captures its tone:

> The ugly truth is that thousands of acres of forest are needlessly destroyed every day to supply Staples with cheap, disposable paper products. . . . Staples is dragging its feet in response to consumer concern at a time when over 400 companies have made commitments to our forests.
>
> Staples says that doing the right thing for the environment costs too much. But company financial concerns didn't stop the CEO, Tom Stemberg, from making over $63 million in 1999. It's all a matter of priorities.

Even Buckley thought that went too far. "My heritage is Irish, so I can tell you I had my Irish up," he said. "It bothered me."

But Buckley and the environmentalists share a common goal: they want to move Staples, as well as the timber companies who make paper, toward a business model that can be sustained over time—forever, actually. Since the protestors went on the attack, Staples has moved in that direction; more important, the company's leaders have become convinced that being environmentally responsible can be good for business.

Where does a company's responsibility begin, and where does it end? This is a big question, and one that has provoked spirited debate in corporate America. It's also a spiritual question—the world's religious traditions see all people as interconnected, and so they see our responsibility for others as almost boundless. ("Mind your own business" is not a sentiment you will find in spiritual books.) No company can afford to see its responsibilities as boundless, but Staples, after some resistance, agreed to assume some responsibility for the origins of the paper it sells—even though it does not own forests or cut down trees. The claim that a company should be held accountable for the actions of its suppliers is a relatively new one, with wide-ranging implications. Timberland, with its enlightened approach to overseas labor, and Starbucks, with its coffee-buying practices, define their obligations very broadly. In business terms, they have chosen to build sustainable relationships with their suppliers. More typically, companies take a narrower view of their obligations and say they cannot be expected to police their supply chain. Yum! Brands, which owns Taco Bell, has told critics that it can't be held accountable for the plight of migrant workers who pick tomatoes, even if the tomatoes they pick end up at a Taco Bell. Wal-Mart doesn't seem to care where its products come from, so long as they are cheap.

PepsiCo, as we'll see later in this chapter, faces a slightly different question: can the company be held accountable for the way its products are consumed? Soft drinks are the number one source of sugar in the diet of Americans, and the nation is burdened by an epidemic of obesity, at an enormous cost. PepsiCo has responded by diversifying its holdings to offer healthier choices, from Tropicana orange juice to Baked Lay's. But the company says it should not be blamed if people get fat or become ill from drinking too much soda or eating too much junk food.

The story behind the greening of Staples begins on Vancouver Island in British Columbia in 1993. About 850 activists were arrested after they engaged in one of the largest acts of mass civil disobedience in Canadian history, to protest the logging of the old-growth forests surrounding Clayoquot Sound. The protests helped preserve those forests, but the timber companies simply moved elsewhere. Place-based campaigns to save a forest, coastline or river are important and they can be effective, but they have limited impact, some of the activists decided. They formed a group called Forest Ethics to approach the problem from the demand side: they would identify a big company, ideally a market leader that cared about its brand and reputation, and then lobby that company to change the way it buys and sells forest products like lumber or paper. Other groups embraced that approach. The Dogwood Alliance, a coalition of seventy organizations in the southern United States, started out trying to change government policy to protect forests in the South but "quickly found that we can have a lot more impact in a lot less time by working in the marketplace," said Danna Smith, the group's campaign director. In the late 1990s, the Rainforest Action Network, working with Forest Ethics and the Dogwood Alliance, led the first major "markets campaign" against Home Depot, which, you may recall, agreed to stop buying wood from old-growth forests.

Staples made itself the next target. Forest Ethics had asked a group of companies, including Staples, to promote recycling and not to buy forest products from the Great Bear rainforest in British Columbia. "Staples became the squeaky wheel," said Todd Paglia, executive director of Forest Ethics. "Everybody kept shunting us off to someone else. They'd miss conference calls. They were disrespectful." In 2000, Paglia said, his group "needed a big campaign to brand ourselves in the United States." They analyzed several companies and industries—telephone books were considered briefly—

before settling upon Staples. Paglia then sent the company "one of the more fun letters I've ever written," he told me. And what did it say? "You've been ignoring us for eighteen months. You're the target of a national campaign. We'd love to chat," he said.

The letter found its way to the desk of Staples' vice chairman Joe Vassalluzzo, a veteran executive who took charge of the company's response. Vassalluzzo, a personable fifty-five-year-old Philadelphia native who resembles the character known as Big Pussy on *The Sopranos,* is a real estate guy at heart. He's visited just about all of Staples' fifteen hundred stores. (When I told him where I lived, he knew the locations of three nearby Staples, as well as which one has a crowded indoor parking lot.) Vassalluzzo was surprised and dismayed to learn that Forest Ethics and the Dogwood Alliance had set their sights on Staples. People at Staples had done a lot for the environment, he felt. They sold recycled products, they recycled their own waste, and they were aggressive about saving energy in their stores. Much of this was Mark Buckley's doing. It was true that Staples did not sell a lot of recycled paper. But recycled paper costs more than ordinary paper and suffers from a lingering reputation for poor quality. Was that Staples' fault? Vassalluzzo didn't think so. "Maybe we were a little bit defensive initially," he said. "Why were they targeting us?"

But Vassalluzzo knew he could not ignore what was being called the Paper Campaign. He and others from Staples—though not Buckley, who was still working in facilities—flew to Seattle to meet the activists. What struck Paglia at the time was how little thought the Staples people had given to the impact of the products they sold or to forestry issues. The Staples executives were unaware, for example, that the logging industry and nonprofits had developed competing certification standards for sustainable forestry practices. "They had no idea what we were talking about," Paglia said. This was nothing like dealing with the timber companies, where battle-hardened lawyers and public relations people have tangled with environmentalists for years. Paglia sensed that Staples' naiveté created an opening. He also warmed up to Vassalluzzo, who impressed him as a good listener and as someone who could be trusted. For his part, Vassalluzzo was eager to find ways to do more for the environment, so long as they were consistent with Staples' business needs. He grew to respect the activists. "They're very passionate," he said. "They're very knowledgeable. And they're very smart."

You can't blame Vassalluzzo for not being up to speed on forestry management practices. He'd been busy helping to run one of the fastest-growing retailers in history. Founded in 1986 by Tom Stemberg, who previously operated discount supermarkets, Staples had revolutionized the office-supply business. While corporate America knew where to buy cheap pencils before Staples came along, the rest of us had little choice but to shop at what used to be called stationery stores. These stores were usually mom-and-pop operations where the prices were high, the selection was limited and most of the stock was hidden away in a mysterious back room to which customers were rarely, if ever, permitted entry. "We applied supermarket principles to the office supply industry," Vassalluzzo explained. "Instead of one-thousand-square-foot stores, we built seventeen-thousand-square-foot stores where you can see, feel and touch all the products. They're bright and well lit. You can wheel your shopping cart down and serve yourself if you want. Plus, the prices were anywhere from 30 percent to 70 percent less." A typical Staples store carries about seventy-five hundred different items, and the company's catalogs and Web site offer many more. Despite competition from copycat retailers like Office Depot and Office Max, Staples has become an enormous success. The company generated $13.2 billion in revenues and net income of $490 million for the fiscal year that ended January 31, 2004.

Along the way, Staples had done its part for the environment. Buckley, as head of facilities and purchasing, had gotten the company to invest in balers to recycle corrugated cartons, to use skylights and motion detectors in its warehouses to save energy, and to invest in energy-efficient heating, cooling and lighting systems.

Early on, to promote recycling within Staples, Buckley promised to use the proceeds to finance the company Christmas party. "We were able to get a deejay and rent the VFW hall," he remembered. As the company grew, so did its recycling projects: in 2002, Staples recycled twenty-seven thousand tons of paper products and three hundred thousand fluorescent bulbs. This did more than help the environment. It saved the company money, too. "Anything we can do to save money," Vassalluzzo said, "the entire organization rallies around."

But Staples had not given much thought to its responsibility as a buyer and seller of paper. Paper matters to the environment more than you might think in this digital age: nearly half the trees cut in North America are used for papermaking, and U.S. consumption averages two pounds per person per day—hard to believe but true because the figure includes newspapers, magazines, books, catalogs, telephone directories, junk mail and the like. U.S. pulp mills consume more than twelve thousand square miles of forests around the world each year, according to Green Seal. Staples is responsible for only a fraction of that, but the retailer is big enough so that when it speaks, the timber companies—and the public—take notice.

The environmental groups asked Staples to immediately begin to phase out all paper products made from old-growth trees and trees on U.S. public lands, and to pledge that within two years an average of 50 percent of the paper it sold would come from recycled or alternative sources, among other things. They were joined in their efforts by the Calvert group of socially responsible mutual funds, whose director of research, Julie Fox-Gorte, a former U.S. forest service worker with a Ph.D. in resource management, has a passion for forestry issues. To see if the demands were even feasible, Vassalluzzo began talking to the timber companies that supply Staples and hired PriceWaterhouseCoopers, the big accounting firm, to analyze the issue. "The more we delved, the more we said, there's an opportunity here," Vassalluzzo said. "An opportunity to do good and to build the business."

The Paper Campaign kept the pressure on. Activists organized six hundred protests at Staples stores. (The company says most were very small.) Forest Ethics released a report called "The Credibility Gap at Staples: Destroying Old-Growth Forests, Misleading Consumers." The rock band REM taped a music video supporting the campaign, which aired on MTV and VH-1, and the *Wall Street Journal* and PBS's *NewsHour with Jim Lehrer* covered the story. At Staples' 2002 annual meeting, a minister named Pat Jobe, whose rural church in South Carolina stood near a mill owned by International Paper, read a letter from 127 Christian and Jewish leaders. Among other things, it said:

> We are called by God to serve as good stewards of creation. God's promises are not just for tomorrow, or the next quarterly earnings, but from generation to generation, forever and ever. We want to make sure that we give to our children's children a land that is at least as full of the wonder of creation as we know now.

Jobe concluded by asking the company to "join us in protecting God's creation."

In November 2002, Staples announced its new paper procurement policy. The company agreed to reduce its demand for virgin wood fiber, to phase out paper sourced from endangered forests with high conservation value and to increase to 30 percent the average of postconsumer waste and alternative-fiber products made available in its stores. (Currently, the average of recycled content in the paper Staples sells is less than 10 percent.) The company also promised to work with a timber certification system to ensure that its virgin paper products come from well-managed forests, and to strive to carry only certified paper products by 2006, market conditions permitting. While Staples did not agree to hard-and-fast timetables, it promised to report publicly, at least once a year, on its progress. Buckley was put in charge of all of the firm's environmental practices, including the paper-buying policy. And the company's new CEO, Ron Sargent, and Vassalluzzo flew over Cumberland Plateau in Tennessee, at the request of the Dogwood Alliance, to see firsthand the effect that paper consumption has on southern forests.

Although they didn't get everything they wanted, the environmentalists declared victory. Staples had become the first office supply company to accept responsibility for its supply chain and to identify a specific target for recycled content; this was a big step, they felt. More important, they sensed a genuine change of heart at the company. "They're making a good-faith effort," Danna Smith said. Said Todd Paglia: "Three years to get Staples is a long time, but we will be working with Staples for the next decade." On behalf of Staples, Buckley has even written to the federal government opposing logging of public land in Alaska, saying the supply was not needed.

Vassalluzzo feels good, too. He believes that Staples managed to turn a threat—the negative buzz generated by the Paper Campaign—into a competitive advantage by embracing environmentalism. (Its biggest rival, Office Depot, later followed suit.) A growing number of Fortune 500 companies who buy office supplies have begun to express a preference for sellers who are environmentally conscious; nonprofits and government agencies, too, want to buy more recycled goods. Hoping to build a reputation as a green supplier, Staples has thrown itself into a host of environmental initiatives. Bring in a used ink-jet or toner cartridge, and Staples will take it back and sell you a replacement, made from a remanufactured cartridge, for less than it costs to buy a new one. If you have an old cell phone, pager or PDA, Staples will take it off your hands and give it to a start-up called CollectiveGood, which recycles mobile electronics and sells phones at low cost to people in the developing world who couldn't otherwise afford them. Staples also has joined a small group of companies that are working with the World Resources Institute to buy and promote renewable energy, from water, wind, solar and other sources. "Our commitment is very broad-based," Buckley said. "It's not just about paper products. We think there's a huge opportunity to differentiate ourselves in this arena."

To promote recycled paper, Staples has literally given it away. For a time, anyone who brought in a cartridge for recycling got a free ream of Staples brand recycled paper. In 2003, it ran a promotional campaign during which 10 percent of all sales of Staples-brand recycled copy paper were donated to the Boys & Girls Clubs of America, up to $500,000. All of this suggests that Staples wants to be thought of as a good citizen and not just as a purveyor of low-cost office supplies.

No wonder Mark Buckley is excited about his new job. "The sun, the moon and the stars are all starting to line up," he said. "Businesses and consumers are starting to embrace this concept of sustainability."

As I left Joe Vassalluzzo's office, I noticed a poster on his wall. It was a full-page ad from *USA Today,* signed by Forest Ethics and the Dogwood Alliance, congratulating Staples for its environmentalism.

"We've been calling Staples names for years," said the headline, in big type. Below, it said: "Never thought tree hugger would be one of them."

WHEN I visited Brock Leach at PepsiCo's campus in Purchase, New York, we spent most of our time talking about how PepsiCo, one of the world's most successful food and beverage companies, is responding to the epidemic of obesity in America. The company is doing its part, he told me. Since the mid-1990s, PepsiCo has revamped its portfolio of brands, spinning off Pizza Hut and KFC, which serve mostly high-calorie foods, and acquiring Tropicana and Quaker Oats, whose products are associated with good health. PepsiCo also has steadily expanded the number of drinks and snacks that it sells that are lower in fat or calories. Its Frito-Lay unit has removed trans fats, which raise bad cholesterol and contribute to heart disease, from nearly all of its products. PepsiCo also invited Dr. Kenneth Cooper, the founder of aerobics, and Dr. Dean Ornish, the cardiologist and low-fat-diet guru, to consult with the company and help its food scientists develop healthful products. Keep an eye out for orange juice fortified with soy protein and potato crisps dotted with flecks of broccoli. "Wellness is a big opportunity for us," said Leach, a former marketer of potato chips who is now PepsiCo's corporate leader for health and wellness.

Near the end of our interview, Leach, who has a medium build and is forty-five years old, told me about his own weight loss plan. He lost twenty-three pounds, he said, by changing his diet and working out on an elliptical machine several times a week. For breakfast, Leach has a glass of Tropicana orange juice and a Quaker Oats breakfast square. "It's got all the nutrition of a bowl of instant oatmeal and 220 calories. I can go until noon on that," he said. "I didn't used to eat breakfast, and by time I got to lunch, I had to have something like a grilled cheese sandwich and fries." Lunch these days is a salad, accompanied by Baked Lay's potato chips and a Diet Pepsi. For dinner, he eats fish or lean meat and vegetables. Sometimes at night he'll snack on Baked Lay's. "I still have room for the fun stuff," Leach said.

After twenty-one years at PepsiCo, Leach's loyalty is unimpeachable. But he wants to make another point, too. Denying people foods they like is not an effective way to help them lose weight. Nor are gimmicky diets. Weight control programs that work, experts say, do so by helping people change their lifestyle so they expend more calories and take in less. They become more active. They eat healthier foods, curb portion sizes or switch to diet drinks or low-fat snacks. Usually, they try to better understand the emotions that swirl around food; many of us eat to reward ourselves or relieve stress. "I've become personally convinced that this isn't about depriving yourself," Leach said. "It's about figuring out how to get the balance right."

Getting the balance right is a good way to describe the challenge facing PepsiCo. PepsiCo says that it wants to act responsibly and to help Americans live healthier lives. People who know Steve Reinemund, PepsiCo's CEO since 2001, tell me that he cares deeply about fostering good values, and there's no bigger social issue for the company than its impact on its customers' health. Reinemund, a devout Presbyterian, has served on the board of directors of the Avodah Institute, a group that helps business executives integrate their faith and work, and he sends company executives to the Corporate Athlete, a training program that helps leaders tap into their values to become more passionate about what they do. His interests, in other words, go well beyond next quarter's sales figures.

But PepsiCo also wants to sell more of its most popular products, which include sugary sodas like Pepsi-Cola and Mountain Dew and high-fat snacks like Lay's and Ruffles potato chips, Doritos and Tostitos tortilla chips and Chee-tos. Pepsi-Cola alone generates more than $15 billion in annual retail sales. A twenty-ounce bottle, the most popular size in my supermarket, contains 67.5 grams, or about 14 teaspoons, of sugar. PepsiCo would like to have it both ways, offering what it calls "fun foods," or indulgences, while expanding its product line to include healthier choices. "The consumer wants a balance of indulgence, as well as [foods that are] better for you," Reinemund has said. "If we overreact . . . in either direction, we won't get the balanced growth we want."

But can values be "balanced"? Can a company like PepsiCo care about health, wellness and the obesity problem even as it markets junk food to children and teenagers? How should we react when the company says that "any PepsiCo product, consumed in moderation, can be part of a healthy, balanced diet"? That is literally true, but PepsiCo also needs people to consume vast quantities of soda and snacks to keep sales growing. Where does PepsiCo's responsibility end and the consumer's begin?

Like Staples, PepsiCo would like to find a way to turn a threat to its business into an opportunity. No one has picketed PepsiCo—not yet, anyway—but activist groups have taken the offensive. The Center for Science in the Public Interest calls soda pop "liquid candy" and says that obesity rates have doubled in children and tripled in teens over the past two decades. One government study found that teenage boys who drink soda consume an average of two and a half twelve-ounce cans a day. Commercial Alert, a nonprofit that tries to protect kids from marketing messages, has urged governments to ban the sale, marketing and distribution of junk food in schools. State legislators introduced more than 175 bills dealing with food and obesity in 2003, and California enacted a law banning the sale of soda and junk food from elementary schools. Some legislators want to tax junk food, and liability lawyers are circling the industry.

I asked Michael Jacobson, who runs the Center for Science in the Public Interest, whether he holds PepsiCo and other food and beverage companies responsible for the obesity epidemic. He said there's plenty of blame to go around—parents, in particular, need to be more vigilant about what their kids eat—but he said companies like PepsiCo, Coca-Cola and the fast-food chains have made matters worse by marketing to kids and "supersizing" portions. "Remember when Coke and Pepsi were sold in six-and-a-half-ounce bottles?" he asked. "Then it went to twelve-ounce cans. Now they sell twenty-ounce bottles." He paused to do a calculation. "If you offered someone fourteen or fifteen teaspoons of sugar in a pile, just sitting there, they would be sickened," he said. "But drinking a big bottle of soda is considered reasonable behavior."

Not even Jacobson—the unofficial chief of the food police—has asked PepsiCo to stop selling soda. Maybe, he suggested, the label on a can of Pepsi or Mountain Dew should advise people to drink no more than one a day. PepsiCo is highly unlikely to take such a step. Investors expect growth from the company, which generated $25.1 billion in sales and $3.3 billion in net income in 2002. Many of PepsiCo's 140,000 employees depend on soda and snack foods for their livelihood. What's more, sodas and snacks obviously fill a need; if they didn't satisfy people's thirst or hunger or desire for a treat, PepsiCo wouldn't be doing as well as it is. "We're in every household in America," said Leach. "We're about giving people a little pleasure." Sometimes a little too much pleasure.

Leach joined PepsiCo's Frito-Lay unit after business school, working mostly in sales and marketing, until he became CEO of Tropicana from 1999 to 2002. He has embraced his new job as the "wellness czar." He acknowledges that obesity is a serious problem—how could he not?—but he points out that PepsiCo has offered healthy alternatives to its traditional products since it introduced Diet Pepsi in 1964. Reduced-fat potato chips, fat-free pretzels and baked tortilla chips came along in the 1980s and 1990s, as did Aquafina, which became the nation's top-selling bottled water. PepsiCo bought Tropicana in 1998 and Quaker Oats, which owned Gatorade, in 2001.

With the help of Drs. Cooper and Ornish, PepsiCo recently divided all of its products into three categories. "Fun-for-you" treats such as Pepsi, Mountain Dew, Fritos, Chee-tos and Doritos contributed 62 percent of the company's North American sales in 2002. "Better-for-you" offerings, with fewer calories or less fat, such Diet Pepsi and the baked lines of Lay's, Tostitos and Doritos, represented 22 percent of sales. "Good-for-you" products like Tropicana orange juice and Quaker oatmeal account for 16 percent. Reinemund says he'd like the "good-for-you" and "better-for-you" categories to grow to 50 percent of North American sales. (He has not set any targets for global sales. Almost 50 percent of PepsiCo's sales come from outside North America, but changing the product mix is complicated, so the company is beginning in this country.) Meanwhile, Reinemund has already done something unusual for a CEO—he has advised people to use less of what he makes. "Overindulgence in any of our products is not something we encourage or recommend," Reinemund said in a videotape sent to food service managers in schools. Of course, that is not the same thing as putting that message on the labels of bottles and cans or in TV commercials, as, for example, the alcohol industry does.

Leach told me flat out that the company should not be held responsible for how its products are consumed. Many people, after all, stay slim even though they are exposed to the same products and marketing messages as those who develop weight problems. "There are no bad foods," Leach said. "There are only bad eating habits." This reminded me of the National Rifle Association slogan—"Guns don't kill people, people do"—but there's a significant difference between a machine gun and a bag of chips. A machine gun has no socially redeeming value. Tostitos do. In any case, as a practical matter, there's no way to limit the cornucopia of food choices that are available to Americans, for better or worse. "You can't go through the marketplace and take out all foods that could possibly be fattening," Leach said. Even if you could, American cheese and apple pie, not to mention Ben & Jerry's ice cream, would have to be prohibited along with Pepsi and Chee-tos.

Instead, PepsiCo would like to encourage people to exercise more and consume more of its healthier products. This is, to be sure, a self-serving strategy. Leach told me that the epidemic of obesity is so severe and so costly to society—obesity contributes to heart disease, high blood pressure and diabetes, among other illnesses—that it represents an opportunity that food and beverage companies can't afford to ignore. Already, some health insurance companies, alarmed by the cost of treating obesity-related diseases, offer their customers incentives, including lower rates, to exercise and maintain a normal weight. As more people become health-conscious and baby boomers choose to eat a more balanced diet as they age, PepsiCo wants to be ready to sell them orange juice, oatmeal and good-tasting, convenient low-fat snacks. "This is a big consumer opportunity, and we're particularly well positioned to capitalize on it," Leach said.

Eliminating trans fats from the Frito-Lay brands was a significant step. Doritos, Tostitos, Chee-tos, Lay's and Ruffles will all be made with trans-fat-free oils, instead of partially hydrogenated oils. Baked snacks, which have sold well, have lower fat and calorie content. PepsiCo is also pushing salsa—it's the number one company in the category—as a healthy alternative to cheese or sour cream dips. But even the "better-for-you" products have to be positioned as tasty and fun, Leach said. "You eat to feel good," Leach said. "Some portion of that is physical, and a lot is emotional."

The challenge for society—whether it's corporations, the government or nonprofits—is to find ways to tap into people's emotions and thereby get them to adopt a healthier lifestyle. Nagging doesn't work. Few companies are better equipped to sell good health than PepsiCo, with its well-oiled marketing machine. Already, sales of its "good-for-you" and "better-for-you" categories are growing much faster than sales of traditional products. Calcium-fortified Tropicana, for example, has driven that division's growth in recent years. "Two glasses of Pure Premium a day will lower your blood pressure in six weeks," Leach said. "We've done clinicals on it." Communicating that message isn't easy, but PepsiCo will try. The company also plans to add soy protein to Tropicana juice and to market a line of Quaker products that fit women's nutritional needs. But, again, the appeal to consumers has to be emotional as much as rational. "You're signing up for a lifestyle that is healthier, richer and fuller," Leach said.

When PepsiCo sells Gatorade, it sells the value of exercise as well as a sports drink. "Gatorade became a $2-billion-plus brand on the basis of marketing a healthy lifestyle," Leach said. "That's an example, to me, of how food companies can play a very aggressive positive role." PepsiCo supports numerous programs to promote physical activity among young people, and it is the national sponsor of America on the Move, an initiative designed to persuade Americans to eat more healthfully and to take simple steps—literally, by walking more each day—to improve their health.

As Leach explained all of this, he almost had me convinced that PepsiCo wants to be part of the solution, not part of the problem, when it comes to the obesity epidemic. Certainly the company will go all out to sell bottled water, orange juice, and oatmeal and to promote its "better-for-you" products. This is no small matter—when a company as big as PepsiCo makes even incremental changes, the impact is substantial. Removing trans fats from Frito-Lay snacks, for example will surely prevent heart attacks and save lives, especially if, as seems likely, other food companies follow PepsiCo's lead. In the arenas where the needs of the business and the needs of society are aligned, Reinemund and Leach deserve credit for what they've done.

But in other ways, PepsiCo seems to be bumping up against the limits of what a company beholden to its shareholders can do. Consider this: PepsiCo will not stop marketing the sodas and snacks in its "fun food" category to kids and teenagers. What's more, the company pays school systems for the exclusive marketing rights to sell PepsiCo drinks and snacks in vending machines in middle schools and high schools. (So does archrival Coca-Cola. Schools have the option of requesting only healthy choices, but few do so.) It would be relatively easy to fill vending machines with Aquafina, Tropicana, Diet Pepsi and Gatorade, but PepsiCo wants to sell Pepsi and Mountain Dew in schools, too. It also wants to offer its full line of snacks, not just the "better-for-you" ones. Why? "We want kids to learn how to make choices," said Leach. Really? It's more likely that PepsiCo wants to create brand loyalty among teens and tweens. Why else hire Britney Spears to do commercials?

PepsiCo also markets three brands—Gatorade, Chee-tos and Cap'n Crunch—to younger kids, on such TV networks as Nickelodeon. That troubles Gary Ruskin, who runs Commercial Alert, and I can't say that I blame him. "They have to stop marketing to kids, period," he said. "We have an epidemic of childhood obesity in the United States, and here's a company that wants to gin up kids to whine and throw tantrums and sow strife in the house. For a bag of Chee-tos." Leach sidesteps the question when I ask why PepsiCo advertises to kids. "I think the answer is, is there anything wrong with Chee-tos as a treat in a kid's life?" he said. "Would you say that kids shouldn't have chocolate chip cookies? No. To me, that's part of growing up." Fine—but sell Chee-tos to parents, then, not to kids.

I don't mean to be harsh on Leach or Reinemund. They have obligations to the company's employees and to its shareholders that they cannot ignore. What's more, competing food companies, including Coca-Cola and Kraft, continue to market to kids. No one wants to unilaterally disarm, an industry executive told me.

What the PepsiCo story suggests is that there are times when a company's interests and society's interests unavoidably diverge. There are also limits to what even well-intentioned executives can do, particularly if their company makes products that are subject to abuse. This is why socially responsible mutual funds don't invest in alcohol, tobacco and gambling companies; those companies have little choice but to drive sales as aggressively as they can. It is also why some of the Notre Dame business students we met questioned whether a good Catholic could market Pepsi or Coke.

Still, PepsiCo could do better. The company could try to persuade the food and beverage industry to adopt labels warning against the dangers of obesity, similar to the labels on cigarettes. It could seek an industry agreement to halt marketing to kids—again, just the way tobacco companies stopped advertising cigarettes on TV and radio. This isn't to suggest that junk food is the equivalent of tobacco or that individuals are not responsible for their own health. But if Reinemund wants PepsiCo to be admired for its values as well as its business savvy, the company will have to do more to discourage excessive consumption and stop marketing unhealthy products to kids and teenagers. That's asking a lot. But no one said marrying faith and fortune would be easy.

11

WHO'S THE BOSS?

AMY DOMINI AND SOCIAL INVESTING

A stock tip changed Amy Domini's life. It did not make her rich. What it did was make her think.

The year was 1978. Domini, just a few years out of college, was working for a brokerage firm called Tucker Anthony in Cambridge, Massachusetts, as one of its first female brokers. Most mornings, before the market opened, the firm's research analysts would deliver stock recommendations to retail brokers across the country, who gathered around a device called a "squawk box" to listen. The brokers were then expected to peddle the stocks to their clients.

On this particular morning, an analyst recommended shares of a military contractor that was about to sign a big contract with the U.S. Department of Defense. The contractor had the right lobbyists, it employed well-connected former government officials and there was no doubt that the deal would get done, the analyst reported. Dutifully, Domini wrote the information down and put together a list of clients to call.

"And suddenly I thought, 'Amy, how far have you fallen?'" she said, recalling the moment many years later. "How far had I fallen that I might consider calling people I was fond of and urging them to make an investment in a killing machine, a company that had essentially bought its way, or bribed its way, into a contract?" She did not—she could not—make the calls.

It was not the first time that Domini had thought about how to align her values with her work as a stockbroker. One of her clients, an avid bird-watcher, had asked her not to buy Scott Paper, whose forestry practices endangered birds. Another client wanted to avoid shares of tobacco companies. And the issue of what role, if any, U.S. companies should play in South Africa, with its racist system of apartheid, had begun to emerge.

These questions about business and values intrigued Domini. After getting the stock tip about the military contractor, she began to research companies and their social impact. "You'd find out from the Quakers who made weapons," Domini said. Her bird-watcher friend had heard about Scott Paper from the Audubon Society. Surely, Domini thought, there had to be a place that tracked corporate behavior in a comprehensive way—but there was not. She kept on researching the issue and thinking about how to invest ethically. Several years later, Domini decided to teach a class on what she called ethical investing at an adult education program in Cambridge. An editor at a Boston publishing company saw the course description and asked Domini if she wanted to write a book. *Ethical Investing,* by Domini and her then-husband, Peter Kinder, a lawyer and writer, was published by Addison-Wesley in 1984, and, to her surprise, Domini became known as an expert on investing with values. She was asked to work with the peace and justice office of the Episcopal Church on the South Africa issue, and she gave talks to church groups and led investing seminars. Investors with a conscience, she came to believe, just might be able to change the way that corporations behaved—and in so doing change the world. "It became an obsession for me," she said.

Let's be clear about this: Amy Domini did not invent social investing. In 1928, evangelical Protestants created a mutual fund called the Pioneer Fund that screened out alcohol and tobacco companies. The Pax World Fund, launched in 1971 by Methodists who opposed the Vietnam War, offered mutual fund investors a way to avoid war-related businesses. And in 1972, the mutual fund company Dreyfus began the Third Century Fund, which screened companies based on their environmental records. Not until 1982, though, when a money manager named Wayne Silby created the Calvert Social Investment Fund, did a fund use a range of social and environmental issues, including South Africa, to screen out companies while simultaneously seeking out responsible firms. For years, social investing was dismissed as a refuge for churchgoers or aging hippies who didn't understand business. "When I told people what I was doing," Silby recalled, "they thought I was on drugs."

It took Amy Domini, who was willing to go almost anywhere and do almost anything to promote the idea of social investing, to bring the industry into the mainstream. She created the first social investing index to identify and track "better companies," a concept that has since been copied by financial industry giants Dow Jones and the *Financial Times.* She started her own social investment fund, which has become one of the largest social equity funds, with about $1 billion in assets under management at the end of 2003. As a shareholder advocate, she helped convince the Securities and Exchange Commission (SEC) to require all mutual funds to disclose their votes on shareholder resolutions. "Amy and her people are representative of the best thinking in social investing," said Tim Smith, an industry veteran and former advisor to Domini who is now senior vice president at Walden Asset Management, a social investment firm in Boston. "They are screening, they are active as shareholders, they do lots of education and they are a voice in the public policy arena."

Social investing should matter—a lot—to anyone who cares about business and its impact on society. That is because social investors such as Domini, along with shareholder advocates such as Robert A. G. Monks and Nell Minow, have come up with a simple but profound answer to the question of why corporations should care about the common good: they should care because their owners do. Not all their owners, of course—day traders and speculators who are seeking quick gains don't care how a company treats its workers or the environment. But most public companies are owned, in large part, by pension funds established to provide retirement income for millions of workers and by mutual funds held by investors with long time horizons. Investors who are saving for their retirement, which may be ten or twenty or thirty years away, or those who are setting aside money to put their children through college want a good return, of course. But they want more. "They have a long-term viewpoint," Monks told me. "And they have a spacious viewpoint. They want to retire into a clean, civil and safe world." Or as Domini put it: "The message that we want top management at corporations to hear is that investors care. You can't just consider my wallet. You've got to consider me. I'm not better off if I can't breathe the air. I'm worse off. I'm not better off if my child is afraid to walk down the street. I'm worse off. My wallet is not me."

The beauty of this argument is that it lives within the boundaries of shareholder capitalism. Some critics of corporate America would like to change the paradigm by, for example, requiring companies to put stakeholders—workers, customers or community leaders—on boards of directors. This is unlikely to happen anytime soon, however, given the political climate in Washington. Stakeholders have no legal rights. More important, it is no simple matter to decide who the right stakeholders are, or to assemble them or their representatives into a room.

By contrast, we know exactly who the owners of public companies are. They are, in the aggregate, you and me. Public-employee pension funds like the California Public Employees' Retirement System, or CalPERS, and the California State Teachers Retirement System, or CalSTRS, which represent millions of employees, are often the single largest holders of stock in big companies. (CalPERS alone had about $150 billion in assets at the end of 2003.) Because they invest mostly through index funds, public pension funds are virtually permanent, universal owners, with an enormous stake in the overall health of the economy. About twelve hundred union pension funds manage $400 billion on behalf of their members. Besides that, half of all U.S. households owned equities either directly or through mutual funds in 2002, according to the Investment Company Institute, an industry group; the typical investor is married, employed, college-educated, middle-aged, earning in the low $60,000s, holding stocks for the long haul and saving for retirement, its survey found. So who's the boss? We are.

What's more, shareholders already have legal rights, which are limited but expanding. They include the right to elect a company's board of directors and to vote on matters of corporate policy in the proxy statements mailed to owners every year. In a significant reform, the SEC has proposed giving shareholders the right under some circumstances to nominate candidates for the board and get their nominees on the proxy ballot. As owners, in other words, we have ways to make own views known to corporate managers, and they are supposed to listen.

This is not to suggest that corporations are anything close to perfect democracies. Rich people own a lot more stock than others. Most directors are picked by CEOs and act accordingly. And, as we've learned from the corporate scandals, executives cannot be trusted to work for their shareholders, especially when ownership is widely dispersed and shareholders are passive. (Bob Monks once wrote: "A corporation with a million shareholders has no owners.") The good news is that owners, especially institutional investors, are paying more attention to how corporations are governed and run. And virtually all investors, rich or middle-class, want to live in a healthy, safe and stable world, as Domini and Monks both argue. How to get there is a matter of vigorous debate, as it should be— military contractors, for example, may or may not have a role to play in creating a safer world. But the challenge is to get the managers to run companies for the benefit of their long-term owners—and for the common good. That is what Amy Domini and social investing are all about.

AMY Domini never met Joseph Lee, but her great-grandfather would surely be proud of the work she is doing today. In the 1890s, Lee, a Harvard-educated lawyer from a prominent Boston family, read a newspaper story about two boys who had been arrested for playing in the street. He was outraged, and so at his own expense he built a children's playground, one of the first in the United States. Lee has been called the father of the American playground movement—the library of the National Recreation and Park Association in Ashburn, Virginia, is named after him—and he passed his ethic of public service on to his descendants. As World War II ended, Amy's mother, Margaret Cabot Colt, left her comfortable New York home to do volunteer work in Europe. "She found herself pulling orphans out of caves in the south of Italy, picking the lice of out of their hair, fattening them up and trying to find a nun or relative to take them in," Domini told me. There she fell in love with a fellow rescue worker named Vincenzo Vicedomini, the son of an Italian socialist party leader.

They married in Naples. Nine months and a day later, Amy Domini was born. She was raised in Newtown, Connecticut, where her mother taught elementary school and her father, who shortened his name to Enzo Domini, took the only job he could find, as a distributor of Italian food. Growing up, Amy moved between the privileged milieu of her mother's family, well-educated liberals with a sense of noblesse oblige, and the down-to-earth world of her father and his friends, who delivered Italian specialties in the working-class precincts of Bridgeport. She taught Sunday school, attended Northfield, a liberal New England boarding school for girls and volunteered at a state institution for the mentally retarded. Later, like others of the 1960s generation, she got involved in the antiwar movement.

Domini graduated from Boston University with a liberal arts degree and no particular career in mind. At a friend's suggestion, she took a Katharine Gibbs typing course and got hired as a clerk at Tucker Anthony. It was 1973, and the market was slumping. "People were losing money," she said, "and I saw all these guys who looked like they were very important men helping them to lose their money, and I thought, 'I could do that, too.'" She became a broker and then found herself drawn to the idea of ethical investing.

Domini, who is fifty-three, still lives in Boston, but she spends much of her time on the road or at the offices of Domini Social Investments in New York, where we met. (The mother of two grown sons, she and her husband separated several years ago.) The Domini company headquarters are located in a cozy, tastefully renovated space in Soho. It's a smaller operation than I'd expected—the company employs about fifteen full-time people, most in marketing and customer service—given Domini's high profile in the industry. *(Barron's* named her one of the twenty-five most important people in the mutual fund industry in the twentieth century.) A petite woman with short black hair, she spoke quietly, almost shyly, during our discussion, while displaying flashes of anger and passion.

Her thinking about social investing has evolved over the years. Initially, she had been attracted to the idea because of her clients' desires, and her own, to integrate their values and their portfolios by avoiding certain industries. Her mutual funds, like all social funds, still screen out companies in industries that are deemed undesirable—typically, tobacco, alcohol, gambling and weapons. (Religious investors used to call these "sin stocks.") But Domini quickly recognized the limits of this approach if the ultimate goal is promoting social change. "The sums most of us can afford to invest will not, if withheld, cripple an industry or even put a crimp in a company's stock price," she wrote in *Ethical Investing*. "Selling stock in a publicly traded corporation has no real effect on the company." This is why shareholder activists, who favor holding on to stocks and pushing company managers to change, tend to scorn the negative screens. "The screens are about feeling good," said activist Bob Monks. "Rather than sell stock in a bad corporation, we try to change the corporation because it is ours. It ought to do what we want it to do."

The South Africa divestment campaign of the 1980s went well beyond screens and demonstrated the power of social investing. It got started when the presiding bishop of the Episcopal Church traveled to a General Motors shareholders meeting to ask GM, then the largest American employer in South Africa, to leave the country to protest apartheid. GM refused, saying it was doing more good by staying, but the Rev. Leon Sullivan, an African American minister from Philadelphia who had just been elected to the GM board, seized on the issue. Sullivan got a committee of experts together to draft a code of conduct for companies doing business in South Africa. Social investors, working with civil rights groups, churches and college students, convinced dozens of big companies, including GM, Ford, General Electric and Mobil, to sign the code, which became known as the Sullivan Principles. As signatories, the companies agreed to report on their racial policies and practices in South Africa; other firms curbed investments there or pulled out entirely. Eventually, the apartheid government agreed under pressure to negotiate a peaceful transition of power. "Data led to social action," Domini said. "And corporations couldn't argue against the data." The South Africa campaign became a model for social investors who wanted to do more than feel good: It proved that social investing, in concert with solid research, shareholder activism and pressures from outside groups, could be a powerful force for change. Said Domini: "The goal of socially responsible investing had, for me, morphed into being a way to use finance to ensure human dignity."

Traditional finance, according to Domini, fails to account for the human costs of irresponsible corporate behavior. To the contrary—it creates incentives for companies to pay their workers less, externalize their costs and even to disregard basic human rights.

When, for example, California-based Unocal and its partners built a natural gas pipeline in Burma in the mid-1990s, the big energy company, its shareholders and the analysts who recommended its stock stood to gain, even though, to get the pipeline built, the Burmese government used forced labor, crushed dissent and terrorized villages in the path of the project, according to human rights groups. Wall Street was indifferent. "Nowhere in that system do the lives of the thousands of people who used to be free and are now in chains come into the thinking," Domini said. Even well-meaning investors rarely stop to contemplate the role they play in the system. "As the owner of a mutual fund in your 401(k) plan that happens to own Unocal, you think of yourself as a good steward of your family assets. You don't think of yourself as exploiting labor in Burma," she said. "But people have got to recognize that there's a difference between making money and stealing it." The Domini Social Index Fund screens out Unocal, in part because of its ties to the repressive Burmese government, but that's not enough. What Domini wants to do is use social investing to change corporate behavior.

For that to happen, the social investing industry has to get much bigger. So, for most of the last twenty years, Domini has focused on breaking down the barriers holding it back. The first was a lack of solid data on corporate behavior. No organization systematically collected social and environmental research on a broad array of public companies. Without such data, it was difficult to construct a portfolio of companies that acted more responsibly than others. Second, and more important, financial professionals believed that an investment portfolio shaped by social or political values would not perform as well as one designed solely to maximize financial return. Anything that limited the universe of investments, they argued, would limit returns. Most investors, when forced to choose between their values and their money, would go for the money, and social investing would remain a backwater. This, at least, was the thinking on Wall Street. "The big concern that people had," Domini said, "was that you can't make money this way."

Domini set out to upend the conventional wisdom. With her then-husband Peter Kinder and researcher Steven Lydenberg, she formed a company to construct an index for social investors. The index would attack both barriers at once: it would compile reliable data about corporate conduct, and it would create a benchmark to measure the performance of a broad portfolio of socially responsible companies. That meant Domini and her colleagues had to define standards for social responsibility—no easy task, as we'll see in a moment. They began by adopting the negative screens historically used by social investors, which eliminated companies in the alcohol, tobacco, gambling, nuclear power, adult entertainment, firearms and weapons industries. They then set out to identify companies that treat their workers, their customers, their communities and the environment better than their peers. "Trying to establish which companies operated with greater regard for the stakeholder was really at the heart of social investing," Domini said. No company is all good or all bad, she says, but the index is designed to consist of what she calls "better companies." About half of the stocks in the S&P 500 qualified for the index. Another 150 smaller firms were added, some because they are model corporate citizens and others to provide industry diversification. The public companies in this book—Southwest Airlines, UPS, Starbucks, Timberland, Herman Miller, Hewlett-Packard, Staples and PepsiCo—are all among the four hundred companies in the index.

The Domini 400 Social Index launched on May 1, 1990. KLD Research & Analytics, which still manages the index, operated out of the back of Domini's house. "It was a classic start-up, very much a labor of love," Lydenberg recalled. KLD had hoped to support itself by selling its research to social investors and by licensing the index to an established mutual fund company. But when Domini tried to license the index to Fidelity, Vanguard and Calvert, so they could use it to create a socially responsible fund, all but Vanguard turned her down. (Vanguard offered a token $5,000 a year.) Although she had no experience running a mutual fund, Domini decided to start one of her own. The Domini Social Equity Fund, which holds the four hundred stocks in the index, was launched in 1991 with a $600,000 investment from the retirement fund of a well-to-do colleague.

Amy Domini was the fund's first and only salesperson for years. "No audience was too small," she said. "Put four people in a church basement who want a speaker? I'm there. It was all word of mouth." Assets grew slowly—the company could not afford to advertise— but money began to pour in when the returns of the Domini Social Equity Fund surged ahead of the S&P 500 Index. From 1995 through 1999, the Domini Fund's share price grew by an average of nearly 30 percent annually. It earned a five-star rating from Morningstar and won praise from *Consumer Reports*. By early 2000, at the peak of the boom, the fund managed assets of more than $1.5 billion.

The stellar performance was partly luck, as Domini admits. The technology companies that thrived during the 1990s were overweighted in the Domini index; most are green—software doesn't pollute—and most treat their workers well because they compete aggressively for talent. By contrast, so-called smokestack industries, which trailed the market during the 1990s, were underrepresented in the social index. The Big Three auto companies failed the screens because of their defense work; major utilities operate nuclear power plants, so they are screened out; and big oil and chemical companies have environmental issues. As a result, when the Internet bubble burst and technology and telecom valuations collapsed, the Domini index fell sharply—by 15 percent in 2000, 13 percent in 2001 and 21 percent in 2002.

Still, over the fourteen-year life of the index, Amy Domini has made a strong case that social investors can make a difference and make money, too. Since its inception, the Domini 400 Index has closely tracked the S&P 500 Index, growing by 10.52 percent a year, compared to 10.92 percent for the S&P 500. The Domini Social Equity Fund has bested other funds in its class, too, albeit by a hair. (This is partly because its fees are higher than average. All that social research costs money.) For the period from June 1991 through July 2003, the Domini fund outperformed the average large capitalization blend fund by 74 basis points on an annualized basis, or 0.7 percent a year, according to Morningstar.

Actively managed social funds have generally done well, too. A total of 42 percent of the socially screened funds tracked by the Social Investment Forum, an industry group, received a four- or five-star ranking from Morningstar; by comparison, about 32.5 percent of all mutual funds get the four- and five-star rankings. At minimum, Amy Domini and her peers have proven that there's no penalty for investing with your values. At best, their experiences suggest that companies that practice social responsibility outperform their peers in the long run, albeit by the slimmest of margins. The question of whether good values and responsible conduct pay off over time is so important that I'll return to it in the final chapter.

Deciding which companies qualify for the Domini 400 Social Index is as much art as science. The avoidance screens, for example, reflect both the religious roots of social investing and its beginnings during the antiwar era of the 1960s. If General Motors announced tomorrow that it would sell only low-polluting, hybrid electric cars, the company would remain ineligible for the Domini 400 Index because it generates more than $1 billion in revenues from military contracts. This is fine for those investors who do not want to profit from military spending, but after September 11, I wonder how many people believe that every company in the defense industry is somehow tainted. The point is, the negative screens employed by social investors inevitably reflect religious or political beliefs: social funds designed for Catholics screen out drug companies that support abortion, while Islamic funds will not invest in conventional banks because the Koran prohibits the collection of interest.

When I asked Domini about the screens, she replied that her investors might not oppose national defense or alcohol per se. "I drink," she confessed, "and my friends drink." But most social investors, she said, do not want to make alcohol, gambling, weaponry and the rest more easily available. The job of a company, after all, is to expand its customer base and sell as much as possible of whatever it makes. "Are you willing to state that it is in society's best interest to deliver alcohol, tobacco, gambling or weapons as cheaply and broadly as possible?" Domini asked. The negative screens are applied in a straightforward way: benchmarks are established—a company cannot generate more than 2 percent of its revenues from defense contracts, for example—and companies either pass through the screens or do not.

It's a much trickier business for Domini to decide which companies that have passed the screens merit a place in the index. KLD employs twenty-five people who analyze data about workplace practices, diversity, charitable giving and environmental conduct, all of which are factored into the decision-making process. "The human judgment that comes into play is based on data—information that is ascertainable, quantifiable and significant," Domini said. But there are no formulas to determine who's responsible and who's not. Does a company that plays hardball with its competitors belong in the index? Microsoft, which was convicted of violating federal antitrust laws, was the biggest holding in the Domini Social Equity Fund for years. (This is partly because the index is market-weighted, meaning companies with bigger market capitalizations make up a bigger share of the index.) What about companies that shift manufacturing overseas? "We can talk all day about sweatshops, but I can't define a sweatshop," Domini said, although the company does its best to try. PepsiCo and Coca-Cola are major holdings of the Domini fund, despite the controversy over their role in the obesity epidemic. So were Enron and WorldCom before they collapsed under the weight of accounting scandals.

Turnover in the index is infrequent. In 2001, KLD took the unusual step of removing Wal-Mart after concluding that the giant retailer had not done enough to ensure that its vendors operate factories that meet human rights and labor standards. In a detailed report, KLD said that Wal-Mart bought products made in repressive conditions in factories in Burma and in China, refused to allow independent monitoring of its vendors and did not respond adequately to shareholders who raised the issue. "By most reports, they're the worst," Domini said. "And they would not come to dialogue on it." Wal-Mart has special responsibilities as a market leader, she argued, because a change in its standards would improve the lives of millions of people and have a major influence on industry practices.

McDonald's is the most controversial holding in the index. Because I've spent time at McDonald's, I know people there who take their social and environmental responsibilities seriously. McDonald's has used its clout as a buyer to get farmers to stop giving antibiotics to chickens, to treat animals better and to promote sustainable agricultural practices. But McDonald's also sells lots of fatty food and sugary soda, markets to children and opposes unions. In a spirited debate in a magazine called *GreenMoney Journal,* Paul Hawken, the environmentalist, author and businessman, took Domini to task for owning shares in McDonald's. "What does socially responsible investing mean?" he asked. "Is it a way for upper-class people to launder their money?" Their exchange is worth reading because it illuminates the complexity of social investing. First Hawken:

> McDonald's business model is to entice and lure children with clowns, toys and advertisements into a lifetime of junk food consisting of burgers, fries, Coke and food additives. This diet causes obesity, heart disease and type 2 diabetes, a debilitating disease. Fast food is the number one cause of childhood obesity and diabetes. . . .
>
> How can a company whose mission harms children and its workers be called socially responsible? The work at McDonald's is numbing, stupefying and demeaning by every account. The vast majority of workers at McDonald's lack full-time employment, do not have any benefits, have no or little control over their workplace and quit after a few months.
>
> I see a socially responsible investing movement that has gotten

lazy about standards and meaning. The question I have to ask you is when is McDonald's big enough for Domini? Is it enough for you that one in five meals in the U.S. is a fast food meal? Would you think your investment successful when 30% of the world is obese just like Americans are? Do you think that every third global meal should be comprised of greasy meat, fries and caramelized sugar? I hope you do because that's McDonald's mission.

Here's part of Domini's reply:

Why do we own McDonald's? First, understand that we do not look for the best; we look for the better. . . .

Despite the health concerns that Mr. Hawken highlights . . . mainstream social investors have not yet decided that they will refuse to invest in companies that sell fast food or that make use of factory farming. For instance, although Ben & Jerry's (now owned by Unilever) has been criticized for selling a high-fat food product, it has still been considered a forward-looking company by most social investors.

As a restaurateur and as a major seller of beef, the company has done a number of very positive things. . . . The company responded to environmental concerns by entering into a partnership with Environmental Defense to reduce solid wastes at the company. . . . Our diversity profile shows that McDonald's has created more successful African-American entrepreneurs than any other U.S. corporation. It has promoted minorities and women to middle and upper management positions in percentages matched by few U.S. companies. . . . McDonald's has an impressive record of responsiveness to our concerns. They responded on the beef sourcing issue . . . on the chicken sourcing issue . . . on the sweatshop issue [regarding toys].

Accusing me of being inconsistent or misleading because I own McDonald's is naive and hurtful. Mr. Hawken would place socially responsible investors into the same camp as fundamentalists: all about personal purity and throwing stones . . . We are not applying eco-fundamentalism to investments, we are entering the belly of the beast of the financial/corporate juggernaut and we are shaping it.

When I asked Domini about McDonald's, she acknowledged some discomfort in defending the fast-food giant. "I don't eat beef myself," she said, "and I think beef industry practices are very unpleasant." But McDonald's is "ahead of the curve," she said, when it comes to accepting and reporting on its social obligations. The company is also open to dialogue with activists and shareholders.

Domini and her funds are very active shareholders. Shareholder advocacy, she said, has become the funds' most effective weapon: By using their access and clout as shareholders, often in coalition with activist groups, social investors have changed the behavior of dozens of companies. Since 1994, Domini has filed more than eighty shareholder resolutions on issues ranging from CEO pay and the expensing of stock options to Fair Trade coffee, workplace diversity and climate change. While such resolutions are the most visible form of shareholder advocacy, sometimes the mere threat of a resolution can induce a company to change, or at least sit down with critics. A coalition of shareholders, including Domini, helped convince PepsiCo and Coca-Cola to include recycled content in their plastic bottles. Another group helped convince Home Depot to stop using old-growth timber, and yet another persuaded Procter & Gamble to begin selling Fair Trade coffee. Not long ago, Domini brought pressure on Merrill Lynch that helped get the investment bank to meet with the National Wildlife Federation about the financing of a controversial dam on China's Yangtze River; before she stepped in, Merrill had refused to meet with the environmental group, the group said. Domini and her people have also talked with McDonald's, Nordstrom and Disney about global labor practices, urging the firms to strengthen their monitoring of vendors.

Amy Domini believes so strongly in the power of shareholder

activism that she has dragged the entire mutual fund industry into the fray. In 1999, Domini became the first mutual fund company to publish its votes on shareholder resolutions and its voting guidelines, posting them on its Internet site. (Shareholders cast proxy votes once a year on corporate policy.) Other social funds followed suit. Two years later, Domini asked the SEC to require all funds to publish their proxy votes. "A mutual fund is by its nature and founding a populist vehicle," she said. "The idea that fund are not telling investors how they vote on shareholder resolutions is absolutely outrageous." Similar proposals for disclosure had failed before because "the mutual fund industry totally dominated the regulators," said Bob Monks. If mutual funds could be convinced to become more vigilant shareholders, they could make a big difference—funds own about 22 percent of all U.S. equities. As Warren Buffett wrote in a letter to his shareholders: "Twenty, or even fewer, of the largest institutions, acting together, could effectively reform corporate governance at a given company, simply by withholding their votes for directors who were tolerating odious behavior. In my view, this kind of concerted action is the only way that corporate stewardship can be meaningfully improved."

The mutual fund industry hated the idea of disclosure. In an op-ed column in the *Wall Street Journal,* Vanguard chair John J. Brennan and Fidelity CEO Edward C. Johnson III warned: "We believe that requiring mutual-fund managers to disclose their votes on corporate proxies would politicize proxy voting. In case after case, it would open mutual-fund voting decisions to thinly veiled intimidation from activist groups whose agendas may have nothing to do with maximizing our clients' returns." They were right about the pressures that openness will bring but wrong to say that it's a bad thing or that it has nothing to do with shareholder return. Responsible corporate conduct, as we've seen, can help drive long-term corporate performance. In any case, shouldn't mutual fund investors know how their shares are being voted, and why?

What Brennan and Johnson did not say was that Vanguard and

Fidelity already face "intimidation"—their word, not mine—from CEOs who want to preserve their pay, their perks and their do-nothing boards without answering to shareholders. These same CEOs also decide which fund company manages the 401(k) plans they offer to their employees, a lucrative business for firms like Fidelity and Vanguard. In other words, fund managers are conflicted—do they answer to the CEOs whose business they covet, or do they vote the interests, as best as they can discern them, of their own investors? The SEC enacted the disclosure requirement in 2003. It won't eliminate the conflicts, but at least fund managers now have to disclose their votes. Investors can then decide whether to applaud, object or move their money out of the fund. Getting that reform through over the industry's objections was "an incredible accomplishment," Monks told me, and Domini deserves a lot of the credit.

Domini's funds also support community investing, which provides loans to people and businesses with limited access to capital. In 2000, Domini started the Domini Social Bond Fund, which has accumulated about $50 million in assets. While most of its portfolio is invested in government bonds and mortgage-backed securities, about 7 percent flows to inner-city banks and credit unions to promote economic development in poor neighborhoods. Domini's company also offers an insured money-market account to investors who wish to deposit money with ShoreBank, the nation's oldest and largest community development bank. This account has funneled about $56 million in deposits to ShoreBank, making the Domini fund ShoreBank's largest depositor.

This is a far cry from touting stock in a defense contractor to brokerage clients. And while Amy Domini has come a long way since then, so has social investing. An industry that offered a handful of social funds in the early 1980s now offers dozens—seventy-seven, according to Morningstar; more, say others who define the category more broadly. The Domini 400 Index has inspired formidable competitors. Dow Jones and a Zurich-based consultancy called Sustainable Asset Management launched the Dow Jones Sustainability Indexes (DJSI); Vanguard licensed a social index created by Calvert and offered its first social fund; and the London-based FTSE Group created a set of global indexes known as the FTSE4Good (which is pronounced "footsie for good"). Each social index takes its own approach, but together they have driven the growth of social investing. About $2 billion, for instance, has been invested in financial products offered by DJSI licensees. As the industry grows, pressures will mount on corporations around the world to report on, and then improve, their social and environmental conduct.

But social investing has not made enough of a difference to satisfy Amy Domini. "Sometimes it feels like climbing a mudslide," she said. "You look around the world and the challenges are so daunting." Social investing is no longer a backwater, to be sure, but most investors either remain unaware of social investing or choose not to trust their money to social funds. The Social Investment Forum, an industry group, claimed in 2001 that nearly one out of every eight dollars under professional management in the United States is shaped by social criteria, but this estimate seems generous. More telling is the fact that the assets under management by social funds amounted to $162 billion in 2003. By comparison, Fidelity alone manages $500 billion—without a single socially responsible fund. "This is still a niche industry, although you have to acknowledge that it has matured and grown," said Shannon Zimmerman, a mutual funds analyst with Morningstar. Social funds are still not enough of a force to command the attention of Fortune 500 CEOs.

Why the industry has not grown bigger is unclear. Many investors don't know that social funds have performed as well as or better than conventional mutual funds. Others are unaware of the impact social investing has on corporate conduct. Because the social funds remain relatively small, they cannot market themselves as aggressively as the big fund groups do. The industry has a chicken-and-egg problem: social investing will make a bigger impact only if the industry grows, and it will grow only if Domini and others can demonstrate that it is making an impact. The expense ratios of social funds also tend to be high, although that's not the case for the Domini Social Equity Fund.

The problem could go deeper than any of that, Domini suggests. Generally, people don't feel empowered to change society. So it is not easy for investors to absorb the idea that switching their money from one mutual fund to another can help change the world. "The barrier that exists, in my opinion, is the question of whether social investing can make a difference," Domini said. All she can do, for now, is try to sell one investor at a time and change one corporation at a time. "If I can get someone to try social investing, they may feel better next time they read about a sweatshop because they know they are not part of the problem," Domini said. "It will help them redefine themselves from being one of the helpless to one of the empowered."

12

WHAT IS A SPIRITUAL LEADER?

RICARDO LEVY

Consider the celebrity CEO, that titan of American industry who graces the covers of business magazine and attracts a crowd to CNBC. He—and yes, the CEO is almost always a man—is often, although not always, a commanding presence, a charismatic figure who enjoys being the center of attention. His authority is unquestioned. His energy and ambition appear boundless. This man literally soars above the rest of us—did you know that corporate jets fly at higher altitudes than commercial planes?—and he is rarely plagued with self-doubt. You know the type. Jack Welch. Sandy Weill. Bill Gates and his successor, Steve Ballmer. In his heyday, Lee Iacocca. Ross Perot before he ran for president, and Michael Eisner before Disney stumbled—and, for that matter, after.

This isn't the only model of a chief executive, of course. Intel's Andrew Grove, a Hungarian refugee with a Ph.D. in engineering, comes across as a scholarly man of science, and Warren Buffett projects a folksy, midwestern charm along with his piercing intellect. But because the media relies on personalities to tell stories, television and the business press tend to portray business leaders as heroic, larger-than-life figures, giving them more credit than they deserve for a company's success—and more blame than they merit for its failure. One result is that we tend to be underwhelmed, at least initially, when we come across a CEO who does not fit the mold.

I felt that way when I met Ricardo Levy. His physical presence is unremarkable; he is balding, with brown curly hair, and he usually dresses casually in clothes that seem like an afterthought. He speaks slowly and quietly, with a slight accent of his native Ecuador; my tape recorder barely captured his words when we first talked. Levy does not seek out the spotlight, and he is generous with his praise for others. Nor is he afraid to display uncertainty; indeed, he tries to be cognizant of his limits and seeks to practice humility, seeing that as a strength, not a weakness.

Yet there is no arguing with Levy's track record in business. In 1974, he and a partner started a tiny consulting firm that they called Catalytica in the basement of Levy's home in suburban New Providence, New Jersey. Twenty-five years later, Catalytica had grown into a publicly traded, high-tech research firm and manufacturer with headquarters in Silicon Valley, a factory in Greenville, North Carolina, that produced lifesaving drugs, eighteen hundred employees and a market capitalization that peaked at $1 billion. In August 2000, after considerable agonizing, Levy agreed to sell the bulk of the company to a Dutch pharmaceutical giant called DSM for about $800 million. Today, he remains chairman of the board of Catalytica Energy, a small research-and-development firm that has developed a fuel-burning technology to reduce smog; essentially, it's what is left of the old Catalytica after the rest was sold. A wealthy man, he sits on the boards of several high-tech companies.

Levy would never describe himself as a model of a spiritual business leader—he's too self-effacing for that, and besides, no one person can embody that idea—but he is worth getting to know because, as much as any chief executive I've met, he has thought systematically about the interplay between spirituality and leadership. Fact is, he formally studied the topic. In 1997, Levy was one of a small group of CEOs and graduate students who took a course called Spirituality for Business Leaders that was taught by Professor André Delbecq at the business school of the University of Santa Clara, in the heart of Silicon Valley. I came across Delbecq on the Internet when I plugged the words *spirituality* and *business* into a search engine and turned up the syllabus for his course. After we talked, he suggested that I get in touch with Levy, who was his star pupil and a friend. I visited Levy early in 2001, soon after the deal to sell Catalytica's pharmaceutical operations to DSM had closed. We've met several times since then and stay in touch occasionally by e-mail.

We met that first time in a small conference room at Catalytica's headquarters, which occupy a nondescript, single-story building in Mountain View, California. Levy ordered sandwiches and began to tell me about himself.

Like many baby boomers, Levy has fashioned a personal brand of spirituality that draws from a number of religious traditions. He was born and raised Jewish, but he has not practiced conventional Judaism for many years. With his Asian American wife, Noella, he enjoys practicing tai chi, a physical discipline rooted in Taoism. And while studying with Delbecq, he was exposed to such Christian thinkers as Thomas Merton and Thomas Keating, who made a strong impression on him.

"For me, spirituality is a very individual issue," Levy explained. "Although I consider myself fully Jewish, I'm not a member of a synagogue. Those of us who are less affiliated have to uncover our own path, and that's hard. Especially when, at the same time, we are CEOs of fast-growing companies. I didn't have a road map, although I felt I had the need."

Spirituality and business are intertwined in Levy's family history. His father, Leopold Levy, was an entrepreneur who fled

Nazi Germany and settled in Ecuador in 1941; he started several businesses, including an insecticide company that Ricardo's older brother, Werner, still runs. Although Leopold Levy attended synagogue and the family socialized with other German Jewish immigrants, his mother was less observant and the Levys did not give their sons a rigorous Jewish education. "The best way to express it is to say that there was a spiritual undertone in the family," Ricardo said. Born just after the end of World War II, Ricardo spoke German at home, Spanish at school and enough Hebrew to become a bar mitzvah in 1958. He subsequently learned English well enough to attend college in the United States, where he earned advanced degrees from Princeton and Stanford. By then, he had drifted away from Judaism but not from spirituality. "My own mind-set led me to be very interested in spiritual matters, so I would read a lot," he said. He and Noella were married by a Reform rabbi; twenty-five years later, they invited him to preside over a ceremony where they renewed their vows, with their two grown children looking on.

After graduate school and a brief stint as a researcher at Exxon, Levy joined with two colleagues to start Catalytica. They didn't have a clear plan, other than to use their intellect and their ability to innovate to build a business; they began as consultants to the energy and petrochemical industry, focusing on technologies built around catalysts, or accelerators of chemical change. Many of their ideas failed, but they did come up with a couple of promising processes— a combustion system that reduces pollution by using catalysis to convert natural gas to energy, which is now at the heart of Catalytica Energy, and highly efficient ways to manufacture complex molecules for the drug industry, which became their big business. They raised venture capital in the 1980s, took the company public in 1993 and then transformed Catalytica into a full-fledged operating company by buying a small California drug manufacturing plant.

In 1997, Levy and his partners took a big gamble by acquiring a much larger, state-of-the-art factory in Greenville, North Carolina, from pharmaceutical giant Glaxo Wellcome for about $240 million. With that, Catalytica became one of the pharmaceutical industry's biggest contract manufacturers; its products included the cold medicine Sudafed and the anti-AIDS drug AZT. Levy loved his work and relished the idea that Catalytica's technologies were helping to make the world a better place. Speaking of AZT, he said, "These are lifesaving drugs, and we produced the form that was then injected into a patient. Wonderful." But he also felt busier and more pressured than ever. "It meant moving into a completely different domain," he said. "We had been a notable company, in a small way, as a R&D company. Now we were running a company with well over a thousand employees."

Gradually, Levy's world became more hectic and complex. Instead of managing a small, private company whose progress was measured by its technical accomplishments, he was leading a publicly traded company with significant capital requirements, sophisticated investors such as Morgan Stanley Capital Partners, coverage from stock market research analysts and quarterly earnings targets. He faced a constant pull-and-tug between Wall Street's insistence that Catalytica make its numbers each quarter and the longer-term rewards that come from investing in research, plant and equipment, and people. "The pressures of quarterly earnings are very intense," Levy told me. "They are like a hungry monster. How to keep that balance between the long term and the near term is a fascinating and extremely difficult task for the CEO." The time pressures on Levy also intensified; his daily to-do list had never been longer. "One of the challenges," he said, "became how to make a transition like that and maintain your equilibrium and balance."

It was at this juncture, with his business expanding rapidly and the Silicon Valley economy exploding, that Levy took André Delbecq's course. The two men had known each other as members of the local chapter of a global business organization called the Executive Committee, where Delbecq, an expert on innovation, had talked about his burgeoning interest in spirituality. At age sixty, Delbecq had taken a sabbatical from the Leavey School of Business at Santa Clara to explore the connections between spirituality and business leadership. He read widely outside of his own Catholic tradition, visited with such spiritual leaders as Rabbi Zalman Schachter-Shalomi, the Jewish mystic, and Chung Liang Huang, of the Living Dao Foundation, and then spent a semester at the Graduate Theological Union at Berkeley developing his course.

Although Santa Clara is a Jesuit institution, the curriculum did not reflect a Catholic or even a broader Judeo-Christian perspective. To the contrary—one goal of the course, Delbecq told me, was to help businesspeople of different faiths discover ways to talk about spirituality without either tripping over religious differences or resorting to watered-down generalities. So while Delbecq spoke from his own Catholic perspective, he encouraged his students to talk about their own beliefs and experiences. "The focus is on spirituality rather than dogma," Delbecq explained. "Spirituality is each person's lived experience. It's informed by the dogma or the scriptures or the tradition. But it's their personal journey."

His reading list included such books as Huston Smith's *The World's Religions,* Thich Nhat Hanh's *Living Buddha, Living Christ,* and Rodger Kamenetz's *The Jew in the Lotus,* all of which explore the connections between faiths. "It's one God speaking in an infinite variety of languages" is the way Delbecq put it. This interreligious approach, he says, is essential if the gap between spirituality and business is to be bridged on a broad scale because individuals from many different religions merge in the workplace. Delbecq also had a practical concern as he began the class: the nine CEOs and nine MBAs who signed up came from different spiritual traditions—Buddhist, Catholic, Hindu, Jewish, evangelical and mainstream Protestant, and Unitarian. He didn't want class discussions to deteriorate into sectarian arguments.

Levy dove into the course with gusto. He felt overwhelmed by his expanding responsibilities as CEO. He wasn't even sure whether he still wanted the job. "Do I even belong here?" he asked. "Is this my calling? I was struggling with a lot of questions." The idea of being "called" by God to do a particular kind of work, which comes out of the Judeo-Christian tradition, was much discussed by Delbecq and the class. Everyone agreed that clergymen, teachers, social workers, medical professionals and the like could feel called to lives of service. But could business be a calling?

Delbecq was sure that it could be. Business plays such a central role in America, as the primary creator of jobs, wealth, goods and services, that without a robust economy fueled by business, there could be no helping professions or nonprofit institutions. What's more, because business has enormous potential to do both great good and great harm, Delbecq argued that business leadership can be seen as an invitation from God to service. Running a company, in this context, is not primarily a route to material well-being or even self-fulfillment, but a way to serve the common good, provided the company operates with that purpose in mind. As the writer and theologian Michael Novak puts it in his book *Business as a Calling,* which was part of the curriculum, business is "not only a morally serious vocation but a morally noble one." Levy had never thought about his work as a calling, although he had tried to behave ethically and he took pride in Catalytica's contributions to health care and pollution control. He found that the notion of business leadership as a calling helped him connect his work to a grander purpose.

For much of the course, Delbecq encouraged Levy and the other executives to read and think about spiritual leadership. This was worthwhile but insufficient; he wanted to touch their hearts as well as their minds and to persuade them to look inside themselves. So he urged them to try meditation, exposing the class to several approaches: Buddhist and Hindu practices, the Christian centering prayer developed by Thomas Keating, and an ancient Benedictine contemplative practice known as Lectio Divina that includes reading, meditation, prayer and contemplative silence. Then Delbecq issued a challenge. He asked the executives to set aside twenty minutes a day to meditate for the next thirty days, and only then to decide whether to stay with it. He also organized a weekend retreat at a nunnery in the Santa Cruz foothills, where the businesspeople tried meditation, storytelling and prayer.

Finally, near the end of the term, Delbecq asked each of the CEOs and MBAs to take a field trip that would expose them to suffering in an unmediated way—that is, they were to spend time with poor people, AIDS patients, battered women or the elderly. They were to do so not in their usual role as a volunteer or potential benefactor or provider of business know-how, but simply as a fellow human being. "The focus is on being with, rather than doing for," Delbecq told the class. "This is an 'I-thou' encounter with each person, not with a category of people. Listen to the individual voice, the life story, the sources of desolation and consolation." He urged the students to try to reach outside of their comfort zone, to travel to a place where they would rather not go. This, he hoped, would help the class to feel gratitude for their own good fortune, as well as connect them to the needy in a personal way.

Levy visited a homeless shelter in San Jose. He chose to spend time with homeless people because seeing them on the streets made him uncomfortable, and that bothered him. "I'd go to New York on a business trip, and I'd avoid these people," he said. "And then say to myself, 'Look, what are you doing? They're not animals. They're not going to attack you.' And yet I felt it." He visited the shelter twice, arriving in the late afternoon, helping to serve dinner, and then talking with people until they were ready to go to sleep. "It wasn't easy," he said. "I felt like I didn't belong. It was a little strange because I had the luxury of being able to go home." But he was able to shed his prejudices and see the homeless as other people, not as a threat. "Some of them were a little bit gone in terms of their mental framework, and you have to be compassionate in that regard," he said. "Some of them were just plain stuck. They'd lost their jobs and couldn't afford a place to live. They were no less worthy than I was." The experience was unsettling because it reminded him that he had not always been as compassionate as he would like to be. When he returned to work, Levy could not help but wonder about how receptive he was to the needs of his employees at Catalytica and how clearly he was able to see them as who they are.

In the aftermath of the course, Levy's spiritual practice deepened—and it began to reshape him as CEO. In our interviews, he described three distinct but interconnected ways in which his spirituality had changed him as a leader. "One is the capability to center, the ability to quiet the mind through meditation. The second one is the ability to discern. The word *discernment*—I never really thought about it until I took the course—is a key to these issues. The third idea is recognizing the need to remind ourselves of our humility." Like Levy, I had tried meditation, so I had no trouble grasping the idea that a harried executive would benefit from a few minutes of quiet reflection every day. But I knew nothing about discernment, which is an ancient Christian practice intended to divine the will of God. As for humility, well, that was a word I hadn't had much occasion to use in my years of writing about CEOs.

Humility was especially scarce in Silicon Valley during the 1990s tech boom that transformed legions of engineers, entrepreneurs and venture capitalists into swaggering millionaires. Levy, who had lived in the valley since 1974, had seen some of his neighbors change as they got rich. He'd felt the effects, too. "People lose perspective as they gain wealth and power," he said. "It is horribly seductive. Suddenly you feel, 'Man, I made money, I must be good.' You may not say it consciously, but the temptation is to suddenly feel a step above. As we went from a hundred employees to a thousand, I had to be careful not to get too giddy. I've felt the temptation, it's there, and it's treacherous." Treacherous, indeed—more than one promising executive's career has been destroyed by arrogance.

But if arrogance can derail a career, does it follow that humility can strengthen a business leader? Certainly the major religions speak of the importance of humility, often in similar terms. "Humility is the foundation of all the other virtues," wrote St. Augustine.

Lao Tzu said, "Humility is the root from which greatness springs." In a business setting, as Levy explained it, humility is predominantly about knowing your limits, appreciating the contributions of others, learning to listen and striving to see things as they are, as opposed to seeing them through the distortions of ego. "It is not meekness. It is not passivity and neutrality," Levy said. "It is perspective. It is a recognition of what things are truly valuable. That means recognizing the fact that you have made a million dollars means squat."

More than a state of mind, humility should guide the behavior of a spiritual leader. "It can be as little a thing as walking into an office and smiling at a receptionist, even if you are not having a good morning. Or how a CEO walks down the hall. He sets a tone," Levy said. "A CEO is really the ultimate source of comfort and concern in a company, but most people are afraid to talk to the CEO. How can you be an effective leader if no one wants to talk to you? The effectiveness of an open-door policy is strictly a function of how open people feel you are, not how open you say you are. You can't just put up a sign." When coupled with a willingness to listen, humility opens up channels of communication between an executive and others in a company, as well as business colleagues, customers and suppliers. Its opposite, hubris, all but ensures that an executive will operate in the dark.

Levy's argument—that humility translates into effectiveness for a business leader—appealed to my own softer side, but when I first heard him articulate it I wondered if it was a little naive. Most of the media moguls I'd written about were anything but humble. Viacom's Sumner Redstone could be stunningly self-absorbed. Michael Eisner of Disney blamed others for the company's troubles. Gerry Levin, the former CEO of AOL Time Warner, reacted to critics with a stubborn defensiveness. Nor are the business heroes celebrated by the press—Bill Gates, Jack Welch, Sandy Weill, Steve Jobs of Apple, Amazon's Jeff Bezos—reputed to be self-effacing. Occasionally, I had come across executives who seemed humble. Thomas Murphy and Dan Burke, the leaders of Capital Cities/ABC in the

1980s and early 1990s, were reluctant to claim credit for themselves when their company did well, and the late Frank Wells, Eisner's second in command at Disney during the company's glory years, was a modest man. But my experience as a reporter suggested that an outsized ego and success in corporate America often went hand in hand.

Then I read *Good to Great,* the best-selling book by Jim Collins published in 2001. Collins is a brilliant business researcher, consultant and writer who has spent years trying to understand corporate success; his first book, *Built to Last,* argued, among other things, that great companies are born out of a powerful vision that goes beyond making money. As an analyst, Collins has always been skeptical about the popular conceit that business success is all about leadership; the point of his extensive research projects, which take years to complete, is to dig deeper, analyze lots of data and uncover other forces at work. For *Good to Great,* he began by identifying eleven ordinary companies that made themselves great, using as his primary benchmark long-term stock market return relative to the firm's industry. All the companies, in other words, had been terrific investments. What else, he then asked, did they have in common? Collins discovered that one key to greatness is what he terms a Level 5 leader, which he defines as "an individual who blends extreme personal humility with intense professional will." There was that word again—*humility.*

When I went to see him in Boulder, Colorado, Collins told me that he was as surprised as anyone by the link between humility and leadership. "I have no religious background," he said, although several of his superstar CEOs turned out to be men of faith. "The research was purely secular, purely clinical, purely data-driven." And how humble were the CEOs he celebrates? Well, I'm a business writer, and I'd never heard of any of them. (Their names and companies, if you're curious, are Fred Allen of Pitney Bowes, George Cain of Abbott Laboratories, Joe Cullman of Philip Morris, Lyle Everingham and Jim Herring of Kroger, Ken Iverson of Nucor, David

Maxwell of Fannie Mae, Colman Mockler of Gillette, Carl Reichardt of Wells Fargo, Darwin Smith of Kimberly-Clark, Cork Walgreen of Walgreen's and Alan Wurtzel of Circuit City.) All of these men, Collins found, were fiercely committed to building their companies, but they all shared a reluctance to claim credit for themselves and an eagerness to praise others. "It's not that Level 5 leaders have no ego or self-interest," Collins writes. "Indeed, they are incredibly ambitious—*but their ambition is first and foremost for their institution, not for themselves.*"

The more I thought about Collins' findings, the more they made sense: leaders who are humble are likely to be good listeners, they are likely to develop healthy and collegial relationships with others and they are likely to surround themselves with talented people. Most people would much rather work for a humble and bighearted executive than they would for a boss who hogs credit. Out of curiosity, I went back and checked Capital Cities/ABC's stock market performance; as I'd thought, the company had done far better when it was run by Murphy and Burke than it did after they sold it to Disney and Eisner took over.

"On one level, it's so simple," Collins said. "If we have any faith in what we know in our guts about the best in people, it's got to work." But, he found, the makeup of Level 5 leaders is actually quite complex. During his research, he asked the widow of one Level 5 CEO whether her husband had been a happy man; she seemed puzzled by the question and said her husband didn't look at life that way. He could never be truly happy, she said, because he was almost "physically revolted by the idea of unrealized potential left on the table." That was why he was determined to bring out the best in others. Collins has come to think of Level 5 leaders as almost artistic in temperament. He said: "The drive is creative. The drive is compulsive. The canvas they were painting on was the company." Put another way, the spiritual leader has a burning desire to help others to flourish and build an enterprise with lasting value.

There's another bottom-line value to humility. It engenders

curiosity, a healthy quality in any executive. After all, if you are aware of what you don't know, you are likely to seek out answers from others. This, at least, is one explanation that Sir John Templeton, the renowned money manager, gives for his success as an investor and, in particular, for his single greatest insight about investing—the idea that to diversify as well as to maximize returns, investors should seek opportunities outside of the United States. Nothing in Templeton's background led him to be a global investor—he grew up in a small town in Tennessee—but he came to believe that it was egotistical of other money managers to believe that all good companies and investment ideas were to be found in the United States. Even today, Templeton, a man of faith whose foundation awards a $1 million prize each year for innovation in religion, says that he continues to "work at being a humble person." (This can't be easy when you're known as Sir John.) Recently, he wrote: "Humility about how little I know has encouraged me to listen more carefully and more wisely." When I read this, I was struck by how few of the top executives I'd met had ever asked me a question and listened to the answer. They were accustomed to doing all the talking.

But can one, as Sir John Templeton says, "work at being a humble person"? Or is humility mostly a matter of character and upbringing? I put the question to Levy, who said that he believes that because pride and arrogance are learned traits, they can be unlearned as well. "Some people are hardened by life experiences," he said. "They become harsh." But they can then be softened by new experiences—by service to others, by reflection, by prayer, even by the inevitable daily setbacks of business life, so long as they are open to acknowledging them. I asked Delbecq the same question and got a blunter answer. "You learn humility by being humiliated," he said. "To be a leader is to be a magnet for criticism." The key, he said, is to listen to critics and to learn from them.

Levy found that keeping his ego in check became easier after he began his daily meditation practice. This was the second way in which the course changed him. Before studying with Delbecq, he'd been intrigued by meditation but felt he couldn't take the time to sit every day; after Delbecq issued his thirty-day challenge, Levy figured he would try it for a month. "Sure enough, it became habitual," he said. "Now, no matter what happens or where I am, early in the morning, the first thing I do is twenty minutes of quiet meditation." Even on busy days? "Especially on the busy days. It's on days when there's a lot of stress, a lot of tension that you really need it." Typically, Levy reads a short, inspiring passage from a spiritual book. Then he tries to let his mind settle into total quietness. When, inevitably, his thoughts intrude and he's about to get caught up in whatever's on his mind that day, he tries, as he puts it, to "gently let the thought leave again, and invoke a spiritual word that reminds me of my intent to connect with the divine inside me."

On the simplest level, meditation and centering are about stopping and being quiet. "It has been very rare in my hustle and bustle of twenty-five years that I have paused," Levy said. "Until people attempt to do it, I don't think they realize how noisy our lives are. People kind of know, 'I'm getting too many phone calls' or 'Too many people want to see me' or 'My schedule is too crowded.' Those are the surface manifestations. Beneath that, our mind is just trained to spin its wheels, to create little scenarios, to look at alternatives. Even if we don't do it consciously, it's happening all the time." One goal of meditation is to stop, or at least slow down, all these mental gymnastics, which some Buddhists call the monkey mind. Levy said: "If I had not started to develop the ability—or, let's say, the intent, or at least the habit of taking time to quiet myself and reach in—I would have been a much less capable executive," particularly during the months leading up to the Catalytica sale. "So if we talk about what does spirituality do, a very real part is how it helps to quiet the innumerable noises that an executive hears. It's a very salutary thing just to get into that mode." Once in a rare while, he told me, he'll figure out the answer to a thorny business problem during or after a meditation session, although that is not the purpose of the practice. More often, he finds that the quieting of the mind is a "rejuvenating tonic" that helps him be more present and more open during the rest of his day. These qualities—being present, open, calm and receptive to others—are all elements of spiritual leadership.

Having talked about humility and meditation, we turned to the topic of discernment—one that was foreign to me at first and not a little off-putting. When Levy first described this ancient Christian practice, which is aimed at divining the will of God, I could not see its relevance to business. Would God really have an opinion about whether an entrepreneur like Levy should sell his business? If so, could a business executive try to discern whether to open a new plant or develop a new product? For that matter, could an investor discern whether to buy or sell or a stock? I couldn't see how a religious practice that is inherently rooted in mystery could be of help in making pragmatic business decisions.

But Levy and Delbecq gradually persuaded me that my initial reaction reflected the conventional wisdom that the sacred should be kept apart from the secular. People who bring their faith to work say instead that the sacred-secular divide is a false one that must be bridged. As David Miller of the Avodah Institute had told me when I was just beginning to think about faith and work: "The mystery that some call God lives in all of creation, not just in the heavens, but in the skyscraper, the suburban office park and on the factory floor." So, for example, a CEO who contracts with suppliers in Asia might want to ask, as Jeff Swartz does, what do we owe the workers there? Or an investor trying to pick a stock might want to ponder a few spiritual questions, as Amy Domini does: how does the company treat its workers, or the environment, or consumers? This doesn't mean that God, however defined, has a point of view about free trade or stock picking. But it does mean that even so-called pragmatic business decisions have spiritual dimensions.

In practical terms, this meant that Levy did not rely solely on logic or analysis to make the most difficult decision of his career—

whether to sell Catalytica's biggest, most profitable division and, in effect, dismantle the company that had been his life's work. "I had never considered selling," Levy said. "An entrepreneur wants to keep the baby and take it all the way." To complicate matters, Levy had taken a strong dislike to the point man for DSM, the potential buyer. Their discussions became "very cantankerous, and it was almost a matter of animosity between the parties," he recalled. So many factors had to be weighed—the selling price and his obligations to Catalytica shareholders, the business judgments about how the company would fare under new owners, the loyalties he felt toward his employees, his own feelings about starting anew. "I have a bunch of constituencies," he said. "The investors and Wall Street are only a piece." His employees had to be considered; many had come to Catalytica because they wanted to work in a start-up, not a big corporation like DSM. They had joined for the long term, in some instances accepting smaller salaries in exchange for stock options. Could they commit themselves to the new owners? He talked the situation through at length with some of his key people. Then there were his customers, the drug companies, and particularly his biggest customer, Glaxo Wellcome. Would they be supportive of the new owners? Levy also had to consider the future of Catalytica's smaller fuel-combustion division, now called Catalytica Energy Systems, which DSM did not want to acquire. Its technology had not yet proven itself in the marketplace. Could it survive on its own?

With so much at stake, Levy felt like he was bumping up against the limits of rational decision making. "These are subtle issues that don't fit into an Excel spreadsheet. It's not writing a list on the left and a list on the right," he said. "It's really more than anything a matter of feeling. The question is, feeling what? Really, it's your compass. How your total psyche, how your intellectual and spiritual being interfaces with the issue." The idea is to let go of logic, if only momentarily, to admit what you don't know—which is where humility comes into play, again—and try to dig deep inside. "My whole environment is control, my whole environment is reaction, my whole environment is action," Levy said. "Discernment is allowing yourself to say, 'I don't know, and let me dwell in it.' To learn to rest in the unknown." This may simply be a way of describing what other executives call a gut decision, except that a good deal of patience and discipline is brought into play. Levy sat with himself for months, trying to rest in the unknown and to overcome the aversion to uncertainty that had been drilled into him as a problem-solving engineer.

As Levy gradually made up his mind to sell, he faced one last obstacle: he just plain didn't like the DSM executive who had been sent by the Dutch firm to do the deal. They were getting along so badly that it would not have taken much to scuttle the talks. Once again, Levy turned to his meditation practice, this time to try to overcome the hostility he was feeling. He sat quietly and tried to find a way to empathize with his adversary. "At the times of greatest stress, I would reach out, internally, in a humanistic, in a loving way, if you can imagine that word, reach out in the recognition that each person is following his or her own calling. Much as they may be so far off that they are idiots or obnoxious, they are trying. This act of reaching out changed my mind-set," he said. "And it's marvelous to see what happens when you then deal with the other person in a more empathetic way. It's miraculous. Because somehow—I don't know how—they feel it or you influence them. One's own demeanor can make a difference." This ability to empathize in a deep way is yet another key to spiritual leadership. Of course, it's also a valuable business skill.

In August 2000, Catalytica agreed to sell its drug business to DSM; its combustion division now operates as Catalytica Energy Systems, a stand-alone public company that Levy serves as a part-time, unpaid chairman of the board. "I go to the office when I think I can be of help, but my schedule is my own, and I'm enjoying that," he told me recently. He serves on the boards of several other high-tech companies, including one called Stem Cells Inc., so he is trying to learn more about molecular biology. And he continues to read widely about spirituality and business leadership so that he can discern his next steps. "One day a week, I spend several hours really studying," he says.

Religious traditionalists probably won't be much impressed by Levy's personalized brand of spirituality. He is, after all, a Jew who doesn't go to synagogue, meditates like a Buddhist and relies on an ancient Christian practice to make up his mind. The whole deal, admittedly, sounds mushy. Why, then, should we pay attention to him at all? One reason is that he's more typical than you might think. Millions of Americans, like Levy, proudly exercise their right to pick and choose the values and rituals that suit them from the extravagant buffet of American religious practices. A recent survey of business executives found that more than 60 percent had positive feelings about spirituality and a negative view of religion. Their religious practices, it's safe to assume, are neither conventional nor orthodox.

The bigger reason to listen to Levy is that he's enjoyed a great deal of success in business, building a company that he sold for $800 million and spinning off another enterprise with great promise. He's done a lot of good, too, by helping companies make drugs more efficiently and developing emission control processes for utilities. He's also one of the most thoughtful executives I know. Sometimes when he talks about humility and centering and discernment, I have to remind myself that the words are coming from a Stanford-educated scientist and a battle-tested CEO who's at home both in the laboratory and the boardroom. By their nature, scientists don't just accept a theory when it comes along; they test it to see if it works. Levy's done just that with his spiritual practices. His approach, at heart, is a disciplined way of trying to stay close to the values that matter to him and to the people who are crucial to the success of any business enterprise. "People are the most intangible, the most complex element of any business equation," Levy said. "The only way to reach people is to start by reaching into yourself—by understanding yourself." He does not claim his approach will work for everyone, or that there is any road map to becoming a spiritual leader. "This subject matter, by definition, is not a matter of ten steps," he says. "It's a matter of awakening to what's inside."

13

WHERE DO WE GO
FROM HERE?

It was time for a reality check. I had enjoyed visiting Southwest Airlines, Starbucks and Timberland, meeting the good people of Greyston, UPS and Herman Miller, and feeling the passion of Tom Chappell, Amy Domini and Barb Waugh. When you spend all your time with humane and generous businesspeople, it's easy to forget about the dark side of corporate America.

So I left my office at *Fortune* in Rockefeller Center, took the subway downtown to Franklin Street, walked four blocks east to 111 Centre Street, and rode up to the thirteenth floor in a grimy, slow-moving elevator. A big plastic tile was missing from the ceiling, and the walls looked as if they hadn't been painted in years. Clearly, no one pays much attention to the aesthetics of the building that houses the New York State Supreme Court, least of all the accused criminals who go there to stand trial. I'd come to see one of them—Dennis Kozlowski, the former CEO of Tyco International.

Tyco is an industrial conglomerate that makes fire and security systems, medical devices, valves, pipes, electrical components, plastics and engineered materials. People used to compare Tyco to General Electric. In 2001, *Business Week* put Kozlowski on its cover, calling him "The Most Aggressive CEO." Little did they know.

Until 1995, Tyco was headquartered in Exeter, New Hampshire, in the same corporate park as Timberland. (Jeff Swartz told me he never met Kozlowski.) But Kozlowski's ambitions were too grand for small-town New England. He shifted Tyco's legal headquarters to Bermuda, to shelter earnings from U.S. taxes, and relocated its executive offices to midtown Manhattan. He spent $30 million to buy and furnish an apartment on Fifth Avenue, and another $30 million to build a mansion in Boca Raton. He bought a $15,000 umbrella stand, a $6,300 sewing basket, a $6,000 shower curtain and a $2,200 trash basket.

Spending money, even lavishly, isn't against the law, and Kozlowski had plenty to spend. In 1999 alone, he was paid $170 million. The trouble is, that wasn't enough for him. So Tyco paid for the homes in New York and Boca Raton and the furnishings with money that belonged to shareholders, the prosecutors say. According to Tyco, Kozlowski also used $43 million in corporate funds to make charitable donations in his own name; he gave $5 million to his alma mater, Seton Hall, which named its business school building Kozlowski Hall. The company also paid half of the $2 million cost of his wife Karen's fortieth-birthday party in Sardinia. Altogether, the prosecutors allege, Kozlowski and Mark Swartz, Tyco's former chief financial officer (who is not related to Jeff Swartz) looted the company of $170 million and misappropriated another $430 million through tainted sales of stock. Both defendants pleaded not guilty to all of the charges. In a separate legal proceeding, Kozlowski has been accused of scheming to evade sales taxes on expensive art, a charge he also denies.

Not much was happening when I got to the courtroom. Kozlowski and Mark Swartz watched as their lawyers screened potential jurors, a process that would drag on for days. The trial itself brought out more allegations of malfeasance. Kozlowski, it turned out, had

had romantic relationships with two women while at Tyco, both of whom were rewarded with big salaries and perks. His board of directors had exercised little oversight. Other senior executives got what appeared to be unauthorized payments from the company. (The trial of Kozlowski and Swartz ended in a mistrial in April 2004.) No further reminder was needed that there are plenty of businesspeople who are driven by selfishness and greed when they go to work each day. More than a few, it turns out, are religious men. Marrying faith and fortune, as we've said, is not easy.

The new millennium's business scandals provided vivid evidence of the Sunday-Monday gap that allows people to separate their religious faith from their work. Mark Belnick, a respected New York lawyer who became Tyco's general counsel and earned an astonishing $200 million in 2000, misappropriated another $10 million to buy and renovate a vacation home in Park City, Utah, according to the company. Raised as an observant Jew, Belnick had been president of a Westchester County synagogue before he converted to Catholicism; he used some of his newfound wealth to make generous donations to charities associated with Opus Dei, a conservative Catholic organization. Belnick has denied wrongdoing and pleaded not guilty to the charge of falsifying business records. Enron's CEO, Kenneth Lay, meanwhile, was a trustee of one of the biggest Methodist churches in Houston; while he has not been charged with a crime, he is guilty, at the least, of fostering a culture of criminality, arrogance and greed. Another fallen CEO, Bernard Ebbers, who presided over WorldCom's $11 billion accounting scandal and the biggest bankruptcy in history, defended himself from the pulpit of a Baptist church in Brookhaven, Mississippi, which he serves as a deacon and Sunday school teacher. "No one will find me to have knowingly committed fraud," Ebbers told his fellow parishioners—a statement that, with its qualifiers, sounded like his lawyers had written it.

There seemed to be no end to the scandals. Mutual funds were charged with favoring insiders and big investors at the expense of everyone else. Big accounting firms were accused of overcharging their clients for travel expenses. In the industry I cover, media and entertainment, accounting scandals tainted AOL Time Warner, Vivendi, Cablevision and Gemstar–TV Guide. My own theory was that executives at traditional companies grew envious of people in the technology and Internet businesses who made overnight fortunes in the late 1990s, and a get-rich-quick mentality took hold.

The scandals were disheartening. But they did spur reforms. The worst of the business rogues were fired. Some went to jail. Government regulators woke up. And, arguably, the scandals created an incentive for many companies to rethink their roles in society and take steps to show their workers, their shareholders and their customers that they care about more than making money.

More troubling, in some ways, for anyone who cares about business, values and social responsibility, was the everyday, perfectly acceptable behavior of solid, well-established and respected corporations. By far, the biggest and most important of these is Wal-Mart.

In 2003, Wal-Mart topped two *Fortune* lists. It was voted the most admired company in America, and it ranked number one in the Fortune 500, a perch it was unlikely to relinquish for years. How big is Wal-Mart? Gigantic. The company generated $259 billion in revenues in 2003, making it easily the world's largest company. With 1.3 million people in uniform, more than the U.S. Army, Wal-Mart is the biggest employer in the nation. About 82 percent of Americans shop there at least once a year, and about seventy million stop by a Wal-Mart each week. Wal-Mart is the most important customer for such big companies as Procter & Gamble, Disney, Kraft, Revlon, Gillette and Campbell. It is the nation's biggest seller of "groceries, toys, guns, diamonds, CDs, apparel, dog food, detergent, jewelry, sporting goods, videogames, socks, bedding and toothpaste—not to mention its biggest film developer, optician, private truck-fleet operator, energy consumer and real estate developer," my colleague Jerry Useem wrote in *Fortune.* Wal-Mart is the most powerful company in America, and it is relentlessly driven by a single goal—to drive down the price of everything it sells and thereby capture an increasing share of the money spent by consumers everywhere.

Wal-Mart's impact on corporate America—its impact on all of America, for that matter—is difficult to overstate. We know that its scale and efficiencies have crushed local rivals and emptied some downtowns. We know that many thousands of supermarkets have closed since Wal-Mart entered the grocery business. We know that Wal-Mart has enabled millions of poor and working-class people to buy things that they otherwise could not afford. But much of Wal-Mart's influence is not as well understood. The company, for example, plays an enormous role in setting wages and working conditions around the world.

The U.S. Census Bureau, for example, recently reported that the number of full-time workers without health insurance rose by nearly 900,000 in 2002, to 19.9 million; even in businesses with more than a thousand employees, the percentage of those without employer-sponsored coverage grew, to almost 32 percent. Wal-Mart leads the way: fewer than half of its employees are covered by health insurance, in part because turnover is high and hourly workers must wait six months to sign up for benefits. It spent about $3,500 on benefits for each employee, compared to an average of about $4,800 for other retailers and $5,600 for all employers, according to Mercer Consulting. While Wal-Mart provides generous benefits for catastrophic illnesses, it won't pay for flu shots, eye exams, child vaccinations, chiropractic services and other treatments that are commonly covered by insurance. When General Motors was the nation's biggest employer, the contracts it negotiated with the autoworkers' union raised the bar on wages and benefits for all workers. Wal-Mart will drive competitors to provide less. And it competes with most retailers in America.

Wal-Mart will not say what it pays its employees, but it's not much. The company is implacably opposed to unions. Documents filed in a lawsuit against the company say that, on average, Wal-Mart salesclerks earned $8.23 an hour, or $13,861 a year, in 2001. That is just below the federal poverty level for a family of three. (Costco, a competitor, pays $10 an hour to start.) In 2000, Wal-Mart paid $50 million to settle a class action lawsuit charging that sixty-nine thousand of its workers in Colorado had been forced to work unpaid overtime. It has been accused of employing illegal immigrants through third parties.

The Wal-Mart effect extends into the developing world, too. If you wonder why Wal-Mart no longer boasts that its products are "made in America," as its founder Sam Walton did in the 1980s, consider this: Wal-Mart imported $12 billion worth of Chinese goods in 2002, which represented about 10 percent of all U.S. imports from China. Unlike, say, Timberland or Gap or Nike, Wal-Mart has not done much to protect the human rights of people who make the products it sells.

Then again, Wal-Mart's goal is to help people better afford the things they want. Most of the savings that Wal-Mart squeezes out of its workers and suppliers are passed on to shoppers. Customers appreciate those "everyday low prices," which is why the chain keeps growing. Investor Warren Buffett, who knows something about value, told *Fortune:* "You add it all up, and they have contributed to the financial well-being of the American public more than any institution I can think of." This may well be true—I'm not going to argue with Warren Buffett—but Wal-Mart does business very differently from Starbucks, UPS, Southwest and the other companies I've written about in this book. It doesn't seem to feel much responsibility for its workers here or overseas, for the environment, for local communities (aside from its charitable giving) or for *anything* other than those everyday low prices. This is the most admired company in America?

The question for this final chapter is, is Wal-Mart the future of American business? It is certainly a Wall Street darling, and there are no signs that its growth is slowing. Or does the future belong to companies like the ones I've profiled, which try to serve all of their stakeholders—not just customers and shareholders, but workers, suppliers, communities and the natural world? Will business as usual triumph? Or will more companies be persuaded, or prodded, to serve the common good? Will corporate America be transformed by spiritual values? Or are the companies we've visited destined to remain on the margins?

S ITTING on my desk are several books that argue the business case for values, ethics, sustainability or corporate social responsibility. *Walking the Talk: The Business Case for Sustainable Development,* by three global business leaders. *The Sustainability Advantage: Seven Business Case Benefits of a Triple Bottom Line,* by a former IBM executive. *The SRI Advantage: Why Socially Responsible Investing Has Outperformed Financially,* by advocates of social investing. I would like to be able to tell you that these books, academic research on the topic or my own reporting provide irrefutable evidence that practicing corporate social responsibility builds shareholder value. None does. What I can say is that there is a growing body of evidence that links companies that are great places to work, or have good reputations, or take their pursuit of social and environmental goals seriously—firms guided by spiritual values, if you will—with superior stock market performance. The companies on *Fortune*'s 100 Best Places to Work list, for example, as a group have generally outperformed the broader market.

That doesn't prove much, unfortunately. It may well be that great workplaces drive shareholder value. Or it could just as easily be that companies with good business models whose stocks have done well—think of Southwest or Starbucks—are able to pay people generously and create great workplaces. Correlations are not causes. The truth is, no study has proven convincingly that social responsibility is good for business, and it may be that none ever will. The definitions are fluid and fuzzy, and the interplay between values and profitability may be too complex to be reduced to numbers.

No one knows more about research in this field than Lloyd

Kurtz, a senior vice president and research analyst with Harris, Bretall, Sullivan and Smith, a San Francisco money management firm. Kurtz is a devoted student of research on values and business and a judge for the Moskowitz Prize, which is awarded annually by the Social Investment Forum for outstanding research in the field of socially responsible investing. He has read hundreds of studies and written several of his own. And although he has a rooting interest in social investing—he worked with Amy Domini in the early 1990s— he says the research is inconclusive. "Despite all the talk, it's really hard to find a study, using tools that a sophisticated investor would accept, that shows a concrete return to social responsibility," Kurtz told me. "The problem is complicated enormously by the many different definitions of socially responsible."

Comparing social investment funds to the broader market is a very crude way to approach the issue, he explained, because many factors account for the performance of social funds. People called Kurtz at the height of the tech bubble, excited to see the Domini and Calvert fund families doing so well. What they did not see was that those funds were overweighted in technology and finance stocks, which were soaring, and underweighted in so-called old-economy businesses, which investors scorned during the 1990s. "You had people who were outperforming because they owned Microsoft, Intel, Dell and Cisco, and they thought they were doing well because they were investing in companies that didn't pollute and gave away lots of money to charity," Kurtz said. "People who take the view that social investing should outperform—that's a simplistic view. There are lots of companies that have done well over a long period of time that have been pretty bad, pretty unlikable. Obviously, the tobacco industry." Oil companies, too, are scorned by social funds, but they have made money for other investors. "Exxon's a very well run company from a financial perspective," said Kurtz, who focuses on energy, materials and health care stocks for Harris Bretall.

Indexes of socially responsible companies provide no more evidence that values pay off. The Dow Jones Sustainability Index, a global index of about 250 companies, was created in 1999 by dividing the twenty-five hundred largest-capitalized companies in the Dow Jones World Index into industry groups and then selecting the best 10 percent from each industry based on environmental criteria. Although about $2.3 billion has been invested in funds tied to the sustainability index, it has trailed the broader market by a slim margin since its inception. In 2001, the *Financial Times* and the London Stock Exchange launched the FTSE4Good Index Series, which consists of four socially responsible indexes, one each for stocks in the United Kingdom, United States, Europe and the world. They, too, have closely tracked their benchmarks, suggesting that there's no penalty for investing in companies with good values but also no advantage to doing so. Still, the indexes have done some good: some companies change their practices because they want to be included.

Of all the attempts to track the relationship between social and environmental responsibility and shareholder value, the most intriguing is the work of Innovest Strategic Value Investors, a research firm with offices in Toronto, New York and London whose clients include such money managers as T. Rowe Price, Neuberger Berman and Wellington Management. Matthew Kiernan, a former senior partner at KPMG Peat Marwick and the first director of the World Business Council on Sustainable Development, founded Innovest in 1998. Traditional financial reporting, he believed, captured only a fraction of the value of a company, and it especially gave short shrift to the risks and opportunities related to the environment. Innovest developed a sophisticated methodology to assess the environmental performance of about sixteen hundred global corporations, which it rates on a scale from AAA to CCC. Depending on the industry sector, companies with above-average Innovest EcoValue '21 ratings have consistently outperformed lower-rated companies by 300 to 1,500 basis points, or 3 percent to 15 percent, per year, the company says.

That shouldn't be surprising, Kiernan told me. A company's environmental practices have direct implications for the business in many industries. For utility companies and automakers, today's carbon dioxide emissions become tomorrow's liability if governments regulate carbon to curb global warming. In the computer industry, companies that design their hardware with environmental issues in mind will find it easier to comply with tightening legislative requirements and meet the needs of energy-conscious users. Moreover, these environmental issues are a useful proxy for management quality and corporate agility, Kiernan argues. "If you go to the top twenty petroleum companies and visit their finance, marketing or treasury departments while blindfolded, I guarantee you wouldn't be able to tell the difference between them," he said. "But if you go to their environmental or corporate social responsibility departments, that's where you can really start differentiating between them."

Not everyone agrees. Wall Street investors have been slow to embrace the Innovest model. "The logic for what Innovest does is blatantly obvious to a ten-year-old child," Kiernan said. "Unfortunately, we don't have a ten-year-old child in the J. P. Morgan boardroom." If he sounds frustrated, that's because he is. "The U.S. institutional market has been resistant since day one," Kiernan said. He recalled one head of a New York investment bank telling him: "You're totally full of shit. All the evidence goes in the other direction." This is clearly not so, but old canards die hard.

Still, Innovest has been growing, adding clients and staff; it employs forty professional analysts. Besides selling its research to money managers, Innovest has been hired as a subadvisor on portfolios whose clients want social and environmental factors taken into account. It is currently applying its research to about $1.1 billion of investments. Contra Costa County in California used Innovest to develop an "eco-enhanced" version of the S&P 500 Index, which, according to Kiernan, has outperformed the index itself.

Because Innovest sells its research and considers its methods proprietary, its claims have not been independently verified. "They have never published a study in a refereed journal," said Lloyd

Kurtz. But if Innovest produces consistent results for its clients, it should be able to win over skeptics. The company got a significant vote of confidence in 2002 when the Dutch pension fund giant ABP took a substantial stake in Innovest.

While finance professors continue to analyze the question of whether social and environmental responsibility pays off, business-people need not wait around for answers. There are several reasons why. First, companies embrace ideas and strategies all the time before they are proven to have value. Think about all the money they invested in the Internet. While the arguments for going green or try-ing to find ways to serve the world's four billion poor are anecdotal and analytical, not quantifiable, no opportunity comes without risk. Ultimately, like most business decisions, the question of whether a company should embrace spiritual values will come down to judg-ments made by business leaders.

Second, just to ask the question of whether ethics and values pay is to miss the point, in a sense. I've looked at the research in an effort to get a sense of where business may be headed. But the case for cor-porate social responsibility should not have to rest on a financial foundation. By making the argument only in terms of money and math, we are undermining the kind of moral reasoning that busi-nesspeople need to learn to practice. As Lloyd Kurtz put it: "If you're only to act ethically when it's profitable, the concept of ethics goes out the window. It's a pretty corrupting way to think." Some-times cutting ethical corners pays, especially in the short term. Slav-ery was good business for plantation owners for a long time. That didn't make it right.

Finally, the world has changed dramatically in the last half cen-tury, and even more so in the last decade. (Think about it: What year did you first get connected to the Internet? Start recycling? Meet a gay couple with kids?) Business is nothing if not sensitive to the cli-mate within which it operates. Until very recently, no one in corpo-rate America gave much thought to saving Canadian forests by selling recycled paper, or to the impact of coffee-buying practices on

Latin American farmers, or to the potential market for information technology among the poor of South Africa or India. Few companies paid attention to organics—or obesity. Campaigns by activist groups, the threat of government regulation, shareholder advocacy, the values of employees, shifts in consumer behavior, new models of leadership—all of these, as we've seen, affect markets and change corporate behavior.

It's easy to forget that corporations are made up of people—not just their CEOs, but also the people who work in them. They are responsive, too, to the people who do business with them, buy from them and invest in them. People do not always recognize it, but they have enormous power, especially when they act together. They can, and do, change the world. Some are hard at work, right now, building the better businesses of tomorrow.

N OT long after starting work at Microsoft in 1989, John Sage was summoned by e-mail to a pep rally by the lake, known as Lake Bill, on Microsoft's campus in Redmond, Washington. Hundreds of people stood around a shrouded object, about ten feet tall, as company executives exhorted them to crush a new product from rival software firm Novell. When the shroud was removed, it revealed a guillotine with a box of Novell software beneath the blade. Sage, a marketing executive in Microsoft's consumer division, had barely heard of Novell, but he found himself swept up in the emotion of the moment.

"I remember feeling kind of bemused, and a little surprised at how excited I got, not even knowing who Novell was," Sage recalled. "When the blade came down and cut the box in half, we were going crazy. It was intoxicating."

Sage spent five years at Microsoft. The company did not lack excitement or vision—Bill Gates wanted to get a computer powered by its software onto every desk in America—and Sage, who had just graduated from Harvard Business School, worked eighty-hour weeks, made good friends and learned a lot. By the time he left, as the director of marketing for Microsoft Office, he was a wealthy man. But Sage wanted more—not more money, but more meaning. "Making people more productive only takes you so far," he said. "It wasn't enough for me."

So Sage and a friend from business school started a very different kind of company. Pura Vida Coffee is a gourmet coffee company owned and operated by a charity set up to benefit at-risk children and their families in coffee-growing countries. The company sells only Fair Trade–certified coffee, which helps raise the living standards for farmers, and it donates 100 percent of its profits to its charitable parent. This company will not make anybody rich, at least not in monetary terms. "Our only reason for starting this company was to create a sustainable funding source for at-risk kids in Central America," Sage said. We met in his sparsely furnished office in a low-rent industrial district of Seattle, just two blocks down the street from Starbucks. As much as I had admired the people and the values at Starbucks, I could see right away that Sage was animated by a higher purpose. "I want to prove that there's a replicable model melding capitalism, business and faith," he said. Pura Vida's motto is "Great coffee . . . great cause."

Sage, who is forty-two, met Chris Dearnley, his partner in Pura Vida, through a campus Christian group called Intervarsity when they started business school in 1987. Sage went on to Microsoft and Starwave, an Internet start-up, while Dearnley felt called to the ministry in San Jose, Costa Rica. There he started a church and several social service projects, including a soup kitchen and a program to help children living in a drug-riddled neighborhood. The friends, who stayed in close touch, started Pura Vida in 1997. Dearnley needed financial support to sustain his work in Costa Rica. Sage, a devout Presbyterian, wanted to integrate his faith with his business.

Originally envisioned as an Internet company, Pura Vida maintains an attractive Web site where you can order coffee and read about its work in Central America. But most of the company's $2 million in annual revenues come from sales to colleges, churches, businesses and nonprofits. More than fifty colleges serve Pura Vida in their dining halls or student centers. College is where people form their coffee-drinking habits. "The Fair Trade movement has really caught on with colleges," Sage said. One campus food service manager told him: "You keep students from protesting outside my cafeteria." While Pura Vida is no threat to Starbucks, its success adds to the pressure on the entire coffee industry to demonstrate that growers are dealt with fairly.

Pura Vida is one of dozens of emerging companies that have married faith and fortune in new ways that are having an impact on the rest of business. These companies, most of them founded in 1990s, are explicitly about using the power of business to serve the common good. They are enriching the practice of business as well as the debate about how to integrate spiritual values and capitalist enterprise.

Unlike the hippie entrepreneurs who launched the first generation of socially responsible companies—Ben & Jerry's, the Body Shop, Smith & Hawken or Patagonia—the people leading these new companies actually like business. (Ben Cohen hated calling himself a businessman.) They take business seriously and respect the skills required to do it well. Many are MBAs, and those who are not have hired people with business experience.

But, unlike most big companies, even those that take their social responsibility seriously, these emerging firms put their mission at the center of what they do. In that, they are closer in spirit to Greyston or Domini Social Investments than they are to Starbucks, UPS or Hewlett-Packard. The people who started these companies might have gone into politics, government or advocacy twenty or thirty years ago. These days, they are going into business because they think they can make more of a difference that way. They are trying to let their values guide all their operations, from the way they deal with their workers (lots of collaboration and teamwork) to their dealings with suppliers (no sweatshops allowed) to the impact on the natural world (sustainability is the watchword). They make products that, for the most part, are designed to enhance health and well-being. No Chunky Monkey, thanks.

Here are three examples of these emerging mission-driven businesses:

- "A generation ago, rebels staged sit-ins and set their bras aflame. Today, rebels create startups and light their companies on fire." So writes Chip Conley, the CEO of Joie de Vivre Hospitality, a San Francisco hotel, restaurant and spa business whose mission is, quite simply, to create opportunities for people to experience the joy of life. A Stanford MBA, Conley started the company in 1987 by buying a bankrupt, pay-by-the-hour motel in the Tenderloin neighborhood of San Francisco. Today, Joie de Vivre operates thirty hospitality-related businesses, employs about a thousand people and generates annual revenues of about $55 million.

  Conley, an ebullient forty-three-year-old, takes his commitment to joy seriously. "We want to do work that brings smiles to people's faces," he said. He urges his employees to make a difference in the lives of hotel guests, for example. "These are people who are far from home, vulnerable, and our job is to make them feel good," he said. Just as important are his efforts to share joy with his employees, who get good pay and benefits, including a month's sabbatical every three years. (One reason Joie de Vivre bought and renovated the Kabuki Springs and Spa, San Francisco's biggest day spa, was to offer complimentary and discounted benefits to its workers.) Workers also get kudos and rewards on a regular basis. "We try to catch people doing something right," Conley said. His primary role as a leader, he said, is to show people that the business has a purpose that goes beyond the bottom line. "In good times and bad, what keeps people together? It's having a sense of meaning," he said.

- If tea, not coffee, is your beverage of choice, you should know about Seth Goldman. Goldman, thirty-six, is "Tea-EO" of Honest

Tea of Bethesda, Maryland, a maker of bottled teas and tea bags. (Seth is an acquaintance and a fellow congregant at Adat Shalom.) Despite his whimsical sense of humor—investors in the privately held firm get "equitea"—Goldman is serious about selling socially responsible tea. Honest Tea is brewed with organic tea leaves and, because it is only barely sweetened, it is better for you than the sugary drinks sold by Lipton, Nestea and Snapple. (A sixteen-ounce bottle of Honest Tea has between eighteen and thirty-four calories, depending on the flavor; a similar-sized bottle of Snapple's best-selling lemon tea has two hundred calories, the equivalent of thirteen teaspoons of sugar.) The company uses recycled packaging and buys teas from subsistence farmers in South Africa and Crow Indians in Montana. Goldman started Honest Tea in 1998 with Barry Nalebuff, his former professor at the Yale School of Organization and Management. Before that, he taught in China, helped start an inner-city nonprofit, worked as a Capitol Hill press secretary and marketed social investment funds for the Calvert Group. "My resume's eclectic," he said, "but I feel like every part of my past experience applies here." Revenues for Honest Tea were about $5 million in 2003.

• Besides their values, Herman Miller, Hewlett-Packard, Starbucks, Timberland and Tom's of Maine have another thing in common: they are customers of New Leaf Paper, a San Francisco company whose goal is to drive, through its success, a fundamental shift toward environmental responsibility in the paper industry. Founded in 1998, New Leaf designs, sells and distributes recycled paper; it finds manufacturers to produce the paper and connects them to environmentally conscious customers. Jeff Mendelsohn, New Leaf's cofounder and CEO, said his goal is to stimulate enough demand for recycled paper so that the conventional paper industry will build or retrofit mills to make high-quality recycled paper at a low cost. "There's nothing inherent about environmentally responsible paper that makes it more expensive," said the thirty-seven-year-old Mendelsohn. "It has everything to do with the infrastructure of the industry, and the demand."

Utne, Mother Jones, and *Ms.* magazines all use New Leaf, and authors Alice Walker, Barbara Kingsolver, Nell Newman and Paul Hawken convinced their publishers to have their books printed on New Leaf. Even Harry Potter has gone green: In 2003, Raincoast Books, which publishes all of the Harry Potter books in Canada, decided to print all of them on New Leaf paper made from 100 percent postconsumer waste. Company revenues were about $17 million in 2003.

I could cite many other new companies that embrace spiritual values. San Francisco–based Wild Planet Toys sells nonviolent, non-sexist toys at such major outlets as Wal-Mart and Toys R Us. Under the Canopy, an Internet and catalog company in Boca Raton, Florida, pioneered EcoFashion, a line of stylish and high-quality clothes made from organic and natural fabrics and dyes. Clif Bar of Berkeley, California, makes energy bars with all-natural ingredients, shares profits with its employees and gives them trainer-led work-outs and paid time to exercise each week.

These companies and others like them are having an impact on business. They attract exceptionally bright, committed, well-educated young businesspeople, MBAs from Harvard, Stanford and Yale. They are winning the loyalty and commitment of their employees. They are building brands. Not all will succeed, and they may not, in the end, represent the future of business. But they already represent a better way of doing business.

WHEN I started work on this book, I began with the premise that corporate America has enormous power to change the world, for better or worse. By living our values at work, I thought, we can harness the power of business so that it serves the common good.

I still believe that. But in the course of my reporting, I have come to understand that corporate power has its limits, too. Think about the power of William Clay Ford Jr. He is not merely the chairman and CEO of Ford Motor. He represents the family that remains the company's biggest shareholder. His name is on the door. By all accounts, Ford, who considers himself an environmentalist, would like the company to make cars that use less gas and pollute less. But Ford Motor keeps churning out SUVs. This is not because Bill Ford is ineffectual or a hypocrite but because American consumers continue to buy SUVs. Yes, as we've seen, companies can shake up and reshape markets. But they can't ignore them.

Mark Buckley at Staples made a similar point. The company has sold recycled paper since the late 1980s—just not very much of it. If customers don't want to pay 25 or 50 cents more for a ream of recycled paper, what can Staples do about that? As it turns out, the company can do more—and it is doing more—to promote recycled paper, displaying it more prominently and even pushing suppliers to bring down the costs. But Staples can't give it away. Nor can Timberland's Jeff Swartz compel consumers to reward his company for its social and environmental practices. He can barely get them to listen. "Consumers and kids in that regard aren't all that different," Swartz said. "They've got a short attention span. They don't want to hear a long speech about values."

The point hit close to home when I went to see Amy Domini. I make an effort to support good companies. I wear Timberland boots, fly Southwest and brush my teeth with Tom's of Maine. I drink Starbucks coffee, sit in a Herman Miller chair and use a Hewlett-Packard printer. But even as a business writer, I never took the time to investigate the performance of social investment funds. Without paying much attention, I had my money in conventional index funds. So I was lending my unconditional support to all of business—to Dennis Kozlowski, Wal-Mart, Exxon Mobil and the tobacco companies. I pondered this, and realized that I also buy all my gasoline at a Mobil station. It's a convenient place, and so what if the company has done more than any other to undermine efforts to curb global warming? Nor, until recently, did I buy recycled paper or compact fluorescent light bulbs, which cost more than ordinary bulbs but pollute less and generate significant energy savings.

"We have met the enemy and he is us," Pogo said.

I don't mean to take corporations off the hook. They have a lot of power, and the way they use it matters. But so do we.

Most of this book has been about the power of businesspeople to change things for the better. If I have done nothing else, I hope that I have persuaded you to think about how you might live your own values in your business life. You need not live with a Sunday-Monday gap. If you aren't already doing so, try to bring your beliefs, your passion and your commitment to work. It will be good for you, good for your company and good for the world.

But we probably should think a little more about another gap, too—the gap between our values and our consumption. (The Sunday morning at church–Sunday afternoon at the mall gap?) As Rabbi Fred Dobb reminded me, the way we travel to work, the homes we live in, and the piles of stuff we surround ourselves with are all expressions of our values. "People must take the time to understand the implications of what they do," he said. "What kind of car we drive, what kind of coffee we drink—these are issues of faith, and many congregants, even in the best-educated communities like this one, haven't stopped to think about it."

This is not a new idea. In the late 1980s and early 1990s, Alice Tepper Marlin, one of the pioneers of corporate social responsibility, wrote several editions of a book called *Shopping for a Better World: A Quick and Easy Guide to Socially Responsible Supermarket Shopping.* It sold a million copies and generated lots of debate. Since then, scores of people have embraced an idea known as voluntary simplicity, in an effort to become more conscious about how they consume, for both personal and political reasons. In 1995, a woman named Betsy Taylor, the executive director of the Merck Family Fund, convened a meeting of about a hundred people, most of them environmentalists, to talk about sustainable consumption. Two years later, Taylor helped start a nonprofit group called the Center for a New American Dream.

As I wrapped up work on this book, I stopped by the center's offices in Takoma Park, Maryland, not far from my home. The center is a small organization—fewer than two dozen staff people, a budget of less than $2 million—with a big dream. It aims to "help Americans consume responsibly to protect the environment, enhance quality of life and promote social justice." Its motto is "More fun, less stuff." I like that.

Rather than preach to people or depress them with gloomy prognostications about the state of the earth, the people at the center—Taylor, who remains president, and its executive director, Diane Wood—encourage people to slow down, enjoy life more, be grateful for what they have and live their lives fully in service of a better world. "Most people want to do the right thing," Wood said. "With the right information and opportunity, they will do the right thing. That becomes contagious."

For such a small group, the center has a lot going on. It publishes books and newsletters, trains public officials to buy green and encourages consumers to join together to take small steps to help the planet, like stopping their junk mail, skipping a car trip or shopping at "alternative gift fairs" that promote fair trade and social justice. It produces a Web site called "The Conscious Consumer," which encourages people to buy environmentally and socially responsible products, and another, called ibuydifferent.org, that encourages teenagers to be more purposeful consumers.

The young people I met at the center were impressive. Tracy Fisher, thirty-two, who runs the Web site for teens, is a former Peace Corps volunteer in Guatemala. "We're trying to tell kids that there's a story behind the product sitting on the shelf, to help them see the connections between their purchases and the environment and the rest of the world," she said. "The message we're trying to send out is that every little thing you do makes a difference."

Kathryn Delonga, twenty-three, who taught English in Vietnam after graduating from Princeton, came to work at the center because she was disillusioned with American consumerism. "By living consciously and making choices, you can step off the work-and-spend treadmill," she said. "It's not about sacrifice. It's about feeling good. That's where the change is going to happen."

I think she's right. One challenge, for all of us, is to understand that we can make a difference. Another is to understand that making a difference feels good. Most of us have the ability to make our workplaces more caring and humane. All of us can become more conscious consumers, so that socially responsible companies are rewarded in the marketplace. But these ideas are not easily sold in twenty-first-century America. One of the consequences of living in a culture of individualism and competition is that we feel isolated from one another and powerless to do much about our problems, let alone the global challenges that confront us and await our children.

But those of us in business know from our own experience that when we work together, there is virtually nothing that we cannot accomplish. Corporate power has transformed America more than once—it built the railroads and gave us the telephone, the automobile, air travel, fast food, skyscrapers, suburbia, television and the Internet. I believe that it has begun to transform America again, to give us a way of life that is humane and sustainable. This is what the quiet revolution is all about. What it will take to drive it forward are people—workers, consumers and investors—who are determined to act collectively to get corporations to embrace spiritual values and serve the common good. Let's try it. It's good business—in every way.

A NOTE ON SOURCES

Nearly all of this book is based on my own reporting. In a few instances, I used information and quotations from the sources cited below. My reporting and thinking were also guided by the works of others who I would like to acknowledge here.

1: A QUIET REVOLUTION

Brenner, Joel Glenn. *The Emperors of Chocolate.* Random House, 1999.
Chandler, Alfred D. Jr. *The Visible Hand.* Harvard University Press, 1977.
Curry, Mary Elizabeth. *Creating an American Institution: The Merchandising Genius of J.C. Penney.* University of Maine Press, 1993.
Drucker, Peter F. *The Essential Drucker.* Harper Business, 2001.
Nash, Laura, and Scotty McLellan. *Church on Sunday, Work on Monday.* Jossey-Bass, 2001.
Paine, Lynn Sharp. *Value Shift.* McGraw-Hill, 2003.
Useem, Jerry. "Tyrants, Statements and Destroyers (A Brief History of the CEO)." *Fortune,* November 11, 2002.

2: WHAT IS A SPIRITUAL BUSINESS?

Chappell, Tom. *Managing Upside Down.* William Morrow & Co., 1999.
Chappell, Tom. *The Soul of a Business.* Bantam, 1993.
Glassman, Bernard, and Rick Fields. *Instructions to the Cook.* Crown, 1996.

3: CAN A BIG COMPANY HAVE A HEART?

Dallas Morning News and *Dallas Times Herald.* News stories about Southwest.
Freiberg, Kevin, and Jackie Freiberg. *NUTS!* Broadway Books, 1998.
Labich, Kenneth. "Is Herb Kelleher America's Best CEO?" *Fortune,* May 2, 1994.
Brooker, Katrina. "The Chairman of the Board Looks Back." *Fortune,* May 14, 2001.

4: What Does a Company Owe Its Workers?

Hamburger, Philip. "Ah Packages!" in *Mayor Watching and Other Pleasures.* Rinehart & Co., 1958.

Putnam, Robert D., and Lewis M. Feldstein. *Better Together.* Simon & Schuster, 2003.

5: Can a Company Fight the Marketplace?

Schultz, Howard, and Dori Jones Yang. *Pour Your Heart into It.* Hyperion 1997.

Gulati, Ranjay, et al. "The Barista Principle." *Strategy & Business,* August 2002.

6: A Priest, a Minister and a Rabbi

Salkin, Jeffrey K. *Being God's Partner.* Jewish Lights Publishing, 1994.

Stackhouse, Max L., et al. *On Moral Business.* Wm. B. Eerdmanns Publishing, 1995.

8: When Bad Things Happen to Good Companies

DePree, Max. *Leadership Is an Art.* Dell, 1989.

DePree, Hugh. *Business as Unusual.* Herman Miller, 1986.

9: Can One Person Change a Company?

Anders, George. *Perfect Enough.* Penguin Putnam, 2003.

Packard, David. *The HP Way.* Harper Business, 1995.

Waugh, Barbara. *The Soul in the Computer.* Inner Ocean, 2001.

10: The Buck Stops Where?

Klingbeil, Abigail. "Battling Obesity Is Part of Growth Strategy." *Journal News* (White Plains, NY), July 28, 2003.

McKay, Betsy. "PepsiCo Challenges Itself to Concoct Healthier Snacks." *Wall Street Journal,* September 23, 2002.

Stemberg, Tom, and David Whitford. "Putting a Stop to Mom and Pop." *Fortune Small Business,* October 2002.

11: Who's the Boss?

Domini, Amy. *Socially Responsible Investing.* Dearborn Trade, 2001.

Domini, Amy L., and Peter D. Kinder. *Ethical Investing.* Addison-Wesley, 1984.

ACKNOWLEDGMENTS

I am deeply grateful, first of all, to my editors and colleagues at *Fortune*. They are a talented and big-hearted crew, and without their support, encouragement and collaboration, I could never have written this book. I owe special thanks to Rik Kirkland and John Huey, who hired me and made me feel comfortable from day one, even though I was a newcomer to business writing. Tim Smith has been the best editor any reporter could want. Thanks, too, to Peter Petre, Brian Dumaine, Hank Gilman, Rick Tetzeli, Vera Titunik, Henry Goldblatt, David Whitford, David Kirkpatrick, Jerry Useem and Pattie Sellers. You are the best.

Some experienced travelers helped guide me through the worlds of spirituality and corporate social responsibility. Thanks to David Miller of Avodah, the indefatigable Mark Albion, Kenny Moore, André Delbecq, Martin Rutte, Greg Pierce of BEEJ, Bob Dunn of Business for Social Responsibility, Ben Klasky of Net Impact, shareholder advocates extraordinaire Bob Monks and Nell Minow, Pam Chalout of Social Venture Network and Richard Carlson, who taught me not to sweat the small stuff. I've learned more about business from reading and talking to Jim Collins than I have from anyone else.

Every company in this book generously opened its doors to me and responded to my many questions. Thanks to Kathleen Taggersell at Tom's of Maine, Norman Black of UPS, Megan Behrbaum of Starbucks, Robin Giampa of Timberland, Mark Schurman and Bruce Buursma of Herman Miller, Dave Berman of HP, Owen Davis of Staples, Dick Detwiler of PepsiCo and Kimberly Gladman of Domini Social Investments.

In the publishing world, I'm grateful to my editor at Crown, Annik La Farge, who was constructively critical and reliably enthusiastic—an ideal combination. My agent, Esther Newberg, was steadfast in her support, even when we struggled initially to find a publisher.

Many other friends and colleagues provided ideas, encouragement and support. They include Bill Child, Tom Crisman, Keith Ferazzi, Julie Fox-Gorte, Michael Lichtenstein, Ed Maibach, Bill Osborne, Donna Schaper, Tony Schwartz, Roy Spence, Judy Trabulsi and David Wittenstein.

My oldest and closest friend, Warren Goldstein, read every word of this manuscript and provided wise counsel. I relied on my family—my wife, Karen Schneider, my brothers, Noel and Andy Gunther, my father, Edgar Gunther, and my mother, Irene Weinstock—not only for love and support but also for editorial commentary. When the book took over my life, they never complained. Karen has been loving, patient, understanding and helpful in countless ways. Her activism inspires me.

Finally, I want to thank my daughters, Sarah and Rebecca. They, too, inspire and energize me. *Faith and Fortune* is dedicated to them. They are the great joys of my life, and their love blesses me every day. It is my hope and prayer that this book will help its readers to make the world a better place for them and for all of our children.

INDEX

ABOUT THE AUTHOR

MARC GUNTHER is a senior writer at *Fortune* magazine. He has written about corporate social responsibility, corporate governance and spirituality in the workplace, notably in a July 2001 cover story, "God and Business."

Mr. Gunther joined *Fortune* in 1996 after working as a newspaper reporter for twenty years, mostly at the *Hartford Courant* and the *Detroit Free Press.* He is the author of *The House That Roone Built* and coauthor of *Monday Night Mayhem,* a book about ABC's Monday Night Football that became a television movie. A graduate of Yale, he lives in Bethesda, Maryland, with his wife, Karen Schneider, and their daughters, Sarah and Rebecca. He can be reached at www.marcgunther.com.